W9-CPF-766

MODERN JEWISH MASTERS SERIES
General Editor: Steven T. Katz

SHMUEL YOSEF AGNON
A REVOLUTIONARY TRADITIONALIST

Gershon Shaked

TRANSLATED BY
Jeffrey M. Green

NEW YORK UNIVERSITY PRESS
New York *and* London
1989

Library of Congress Cataloging-in-Publication Data
Shaked, Gershon.
Shmuel Yosef Agnon: a revolutionary traditionalist.
(Modern Jewish masters series; 3)
Bibliography: p.
Includes index.
1. Agnon, Shmuel Yosef, 1888-1970. 2. Authors,
Israeli—Biography. I. Title. II. Series.
PJ5053.A4Z88 1989   892.4′35   89–12119
ISBN 0–8147–7894–1 (alk. paper)

In memory of the victims and survivors
of my ancestors' Galician shtetl—*Belcz.*

CONTENTS

CONTENTS

CONTENTS

ix

CONTENTS

PREFACE

THIS BOOK is an introduction to the work of the greatest artist of Hebrew fiction. Shmuel Yosef Agnon is one of the few Hebrew writers besides those of scripture to gain international recognition, which was granted him especially after receiving the Nobel Prize for literature in 1966.

I have tried to capture the author's artistic character both factually and interpretively. On the one hand, this book presents Agnon's biography and the history of his social environment and the literary tradition to which he belongs. It is also an effort to present the author's principal artistic characteristics and to interpret a selection of his works from the perspective elaborated in the body of this book. In a general sense, I regard Agnon as a "revolutionary traditionalist" in regard to the themes of his work and within literary conventions.

This book could not have been written without the pioneering works of the first Agnon scholars—Eliezer Meir Lipschuetz, Dov Sadan, Meshulam Tochner, and Baruch Kurz-weil—and the later studies of such researchers as Gavriel Moked, Adi Tsemach, Hillel Barzel, Arnold Band, Baruch Hochman, and Robert Alter. Each has contributed in his own way to expanding our insight into the works of Agnon.

Where translated versions of Agnon's writings were available I have used them, such as the translations of *The Bridal Canopy* by Israel Meir Lask (1937), *A Guest for the Night* by Misha Louvish (1968), "Agunot: A Tale" by Baruch Hochman (1966), and *A Simple Story* by Hillel Halkin (1985). The English translations were published by Schocken Books of New York City, and the Hebrew works were published by Schocken Books of Jerusalem and Tel Aviv.

I have been quite pluralistic in my literary approach. Although I have not referred directly to most of my theoretical sources, anyone familiar with current literary theory will find traces of disciplines established by various theoreticians of literature and the history of literature.

I began writing articles about Agnon as early as 1954. My first book about him, *The Narrative Art of Shmuel Yosef Agnon*, was published in Hebrew by Siphriat Poalim in 1973. A chapter on Agnon was included in the second volume of my *History of Hebrew Narrative Fiction: 1880–1980*, which was published in Hebrew by Keter and Hakibbutz Hameuchad in 1983. Some of the ideas elaborated in my books in Hebrew reappear here, although this study has an altogether different point of departure and general outlook. I also have included portions of two articles published in English: "Midrash and Narrative: Agnon's 'Agunot,'" from *Midrash and Literature* (1986), and "Portrait of the Immigrant as a Young

Neurotic," which appeared in *Prooftexts* (1987). I am grateful to the Hebrew publishing houses, to Yale University Press, and to *Prooftexts* for allowing me to reprint some of the material I published there. I am especially grateful to Schocken Books (Pantheon) for granting permission to quote from Agnon's works. Passages of works that have not yet been translated in toto were translated for the purposes of this book by its translator, Jeffrey M. Green.

I would like to take this opportunity to thank my translator, Jeffrey M. Green, and the editor of this series, Steven T. Katz, who guided me in adapting this book for an American audience. I also would like to thank my friends, Shlomit Rimon-Keinan and Ann Hoffman, who read various chapters of this book and suggested changes and improvements. I am grateful to all of them and also to the editor of this manuscript, Renee Shur, and Despina Papazoglou Gimbel, the managing editor of the New York University Press, who labored tirelessly over the smallest details.

CHAPTER I

ROOTS: TRADITION AND REVOLUTION

Reality, Tradition, and Revolution

THE SAGES OF THE gentiles were astonished that no one arose to recount the glory of the great events which happened to their nations. Stendhal was surprised that after all the heroism displayed by the French under Napoleon in the Polish war, nothing changed in French literature. Scholars of German literature were also amazed that, after all the battles and heroism of the 1870s, their hopes for a new poetry proved illusory. In the footsteps of the gentile sages some of our critics also cry out that great deeds have been done in the Land of Israel, but where is the author to tell of them?

I have gone slightly beyond my home ground and discussed a subject in which I am not well versed. Nevertheless the truth must be told: the greater the deed, the less the author has the power to write of it. Only the history of the Jewish people from the creation till they were exiled from their land had the merit of being written down. But who wrote it? Moses, as dictated by the Almighty, the prophets, and others inspired by the divine spirit.[1]

Agnon's remarks concerning the relationship between literature and reality, with all their irony, merit our attention. Did the Hebrew literature written in the Land of Israel from the days of the Second Aliya* until the 1970s (Agnon's literary life span) in fact do justice to its materials? Or, as one of Agnon's forerunners termed it, was Hebrew literature in Agnon's time merely "fertilizer for a great writer of the future" who would recollect in tranquillity the passions of the moment?

Agnon argued that the character of the times exceeded the power of literature to express the times fully. Yet Agnon was himself the great writer for whom literature was hoping. All that had preceded him was filtered through him. He took the fictional conventions of Hebrew and of the European languages—as imparted by Mendele Mokher Seforim (1835–1917) and Micha Yosef Berdyczewski (1865–1921) and as renewed in the works of Yosef Hayim Brenner (1881–1921) and Gershon Shofman (1880–1972)—and overturned them.

The Mishnah says: "Turn it and turn it again, for everything is in it."[2] Agnon applied that dictum to traditional Jewish sources as well as to European literature. He jarred the

---

Aliya (literally, ascent) is the Hebrew word for immigration to the Land of Israel. The Second Aliya was comprised of secular immigrants, mainly from Russia, who arrived in Ottoman Palestine in the years between the turn of the century and the First World War. These immigrants were the founders of socialist Zionism.

2

conventions of literature and marked out a new aesthetic distance between the reader's expectations and his own innovations. He alone had the tools needed to grapple with the revolution in Jewish history and to meet the demands of critics who cried out for such an author. At the time, the critics did not *appear* to realize that Agnon had struggled with the entire period and had mastered it; but, in fact, they knew it full well.

Biography and Symbolic Biography

Shmuel Yosef Czaczkes, better known by his pen name, Shmuel Yosef Agnon, was born on the ninth of *av* 5648 (July 17, 1888) in Buczacz, Galicia. Agnon's father was a fur dealer and was a follower of the Hassidic rebbe of Chortkov. Traditional Hassidic lore permeated the Czaczkes' home, but the family also was receptive to European culture. Thus, Shmuel learned *Aggadah,* the rabbinical legends, from his father, while his mother told him stories from German literature. On his own he read the secular Hebrew and Yiddish writings of the Galician *maskilim.* Agnon was provided with private tutors in Talmud and in German, while he gleaned knowledge of Hassidic literature in his father's synagogue.

Agnon was a precocious writer, starting at the age of eight to write in both Hebrew and Yiddish. His first published works were a Yiddish poem about Joseph Della Reina and a rhymed preface in Hebrew to a work by Zevi Judah Gelbard —both in 1903. In 1904 Simeon Menakhem Laser, the editor of the Cracow publication *Hamitspeh,* began to encourage

Agnon and regularly began publishing his Hebrew work. Agnon also contributed poems and stories in Yiddish to *Der Juedischer Wecker,* a hometown publication. By the time Agnon left Buczacz, he had published approximately seventy pieces in Hebrew and Yiddish, some under his own name but most under pseudonyms.

His most ambitious early work, the Yiddish "Toytentants" (1911), shows both a well-developed literary talent and the influence of German neoromanticism. Interestingly, Agnon never again wrote in Yiddish after leaving Buczacz.

Agnon arrived in Eretz Yisrael in 1908. To support himself he gave private lessons and occasionally received fees for his writing. He also accepted various clerical jobs. For a time he was the secretary of Arthur Ruppin, one of the major Zionist leaders. Agnon lived in both Jaffa and Jerusalem. Although he had abandoned religious practices for some time, he never thoroughly identified with the ideological modernism of the new settlers.

The name Agnon, which he adopted officially in 1924, was taken from the pseudonym he used for the first story he published in Palestine while he was living in Jaffa. That story, "Agunot: A Tale" ("Abandoned Wives"), was printed in *Ha-Omer* in the fall 1908 issue and was the first of many stories. Yosef Hayim Brenner published one of Agnon's stories, "And the Crooked Shall Be Made Straight" ("Ve-Hayah he-Akov le-Mishor"), as a separate edition in 1912. This became Agnon's first book.

In October 1912 Agnon left Palestine for Germany. There, he had a strong influence on the Zionist youth, among whom was the young Gershom Scholem. After the war he courted

Esther Marx, and they were married in 1920 on *Lag Ba'Omer* (May 6).* The Marx family was highly respected and was active both in the Zionist movement and in Jewish scholarship. The young couple occupied an apartment in Homburg from 1921 to 1924, when the apartment was destroyed by fire. There, Esther gave birth to their children, Emuna (born in 1921) and Shalom Mordekhai (later called Hemdat, born in 1922).

At first Agnon supported himself in Germany by giving lessons and by editing for the *Juedischer Verlag.* Later, however, the wealthy businessman Salman Schocken took Agnon under his wing, supporting him and publishing his works. While in Berlin and Leipzig, Agnon led a varied and worldly life, associating with Jewish scholars and Zionist officials, increasing his knowledge of Judaica, and also reading widely in German and French (which he read in German translation) literature. He also acquired a valuable collection of rare Hebrew books.

Max Strauss's translations of Agnon's stories were published in Martin Buber's *Der Jude,* making Agnon well known among German Jews. Despite the inflation plaguing Germany, Agnon lived comfortably, being supported—like other Hebrew writers—first by the publisher Abraham Yosef Stybel and then later by Schocken. Agnon became a member of a circle of Hebrew writers in Homburg and worked with Martin Buber on a collection of Hassidic stories. Unfortunately, in 1924 most of Agnon's books and manuscripts were destroyed in the fire that destroyed his home—including a long novel,

* *Lag Ba'Omer* is a festive day during a seven-week period of semimourning between Passover and *Shavuot.* The day commemorates Bar Kokhba's rebellion.

Bi-Zeror ha-Hayyim (In the bond of life), the publication of which had already been announced by Stybel.

In his novel *A Guest for the Night,* Agnon frequently gives his biography a symbolic interpretation.[3] His home, like the Temple, was destroyed twice (first in Homburg in 1924 and later in Talpiyyot, Jerusalem, in 1929); and he regarded the times he left the Land of Israel as symbolic of Jewish exile. As previously noted, Agnon took his pen name from the title of the first story he published in the Land of Israel—"Agunot: A Tale." "Agunot" is a story of the eternal separation between a lover and his beloved, between a man and his soul, between the Land of Israel and the Diaspora, and between religion and secular life. Agnon named his son Hemdat after the secular protagonist in "The Hill of Sand" who is an expatriate artist and a member of the Second Aliya, who, unlike the pioneers, seeks to be built but not necessarily to build. Agnon's daughter's name, Emuna (meaning faith), stands for the faith for which Agnon struggled all his life—with and without success. The mythic element in his autobiography grew deeper as he began to use prose acrostics in his stories, giving his heroes names that, like his own, begin with the Hebrew letter *'ayin.* Agnon received the Israel Prize in 1954 and 1958 and the Novel Prize for literature. He died in Jerusalem in 1970.

All of the journeys of his life—starting with Buczacz, through the Second Aliya, and including his departure for Germany and his return to the Land of Israel—found symbolic expression in his work. Agnon asked tentative questions of imagined critics concerning the interaction between his literary texts and their historical contexts. His implied answer probably would have been that historical events are internalized, intensified, and transformed in his work. Events with enormous historical impact become personal biographical material. History becomes an integral part of the individuality of his characters and transforms the characters to become reflectors of major historical events—without losing the intensity of their unique and specific being.

The Second Aliya

The greatest upheaval in Agnon's life was his *aliya*—his immigration to the Land of Israel. That move was an expression of the secular change he underwent in his life. It was not only an upheaval in his beliefs but was also an upheaval in his personal and social life. Like those members of the Second Aliya who were the pioneers of the Labor Zionist movement, the young man from Buczacz came to Palestine alone, without his family. He plunged into the stormy social life of a social elite that to a great extent created the social and cultural institutions of the new *yishuv,* that is, the Jewish settlement in the Land of Israel.

It should be recalled that most of the leaders of the *yishuv* and, later, of the State of Israel came to Palestine as part of the Second Aliya. David Ben Gurion, the first prime minister of the State of Israel, Yitzhak Ben Zvi, the second president of the State of Israel, and Berl Katzenelson, the spiritual leader of the Labor Zionist movement, were all leaders of groups of pioneer immigrants. One cannot comprehend the enormous effect this experience had upon Agnon as a young man unless one bears in mind that although the people sur-

rounding him were few in number, they viewed themselves
—and actually might have been—the elite of the Jewish
people of their generation.

Although Agnon was not exactly an exemplary pioneer and
worked as Arthur Ruppin's secretary and at other nonpioneer-
ing jobs, his confrontation with the world of the Second Aliya
had an outstanding significance in his life. What was the
Second Aliya, and who were its major figures?

Between 1904 and the beginning of the First World War,
an estimated forty thousand Jewish settlers arrived in Palestine—then still under Turkish rule. Although many soon
left, by 1914 the Jewish population of Palestine had increased
to eighty-five thousand, roughly 12 percent of the total population. The new settlers came mostly from Czarist Russia;
they were a part of the huge number of Jews fleeing the
pogroms and poverty. Some were traditional Jews who built
new religious settlements, while others were middle-class,
secular young people motivated by Zionist ideology. They
were among the founders of Tel Aviv (in 1909), and they
brought the beginnings of industry to the country.

The secular Zionist settlers brought with them an ideology
that called for the regeneration of the Jewish people through
a return to productive labor—especially agricultural labor.
Forty Jewish agricultural settlements, with a population of
twelve thousand, had been established by the end of the
Second Aliya. However, the pioneers confronted two major
obstacles: the competition of cheap, experienced Arab labor
and the danger of attack from marauding Bedouins. In response to the first challenge, they formed two Hebrew socialist parties, Po'alei Zion and Ha-Po'el ha-Tsair; in response to

the second challenge, in 1909 they formed a self-defense group called Ha-Shomer, which began guarding the Jewish settlements in the Galilee and Judea. These organizations are the direct ancestors of the Labor Zionist movement and the Hagana, which ultimately became the Israeli Defense Forces.

The Second Aliya changed the character of the Jewish population of Palestine, bringing a dynamic, secular, and modern element that constituted one-third of the *yishuv* by 1914. It also brought the ascendancy of the Hebrew language and the culture of the *yishuv,* including daily newspapers and magazines published by the workers' parties. These publications were influential both in Palestine and in the Diaspora. Hebrew began to be used in modern educational institutions, such as the teachers' seminary founded by the German-Jewish Hilfsverein in Jerusalem in 1904 and the Herzlia Hebrew Gymnasium founded in Jaffa in 1905 (which would become the model for Hebrew secondary schools worldwide). In 1906 the Bezalal Art Academy was founded in Jerusalem, and in 1912 the cornerstone of the Technion in Haifa was laid.

Major Hebrew writers and thinkers immigrated to Palestine, such as Brenner, Aharon David Gordon, Jacob Fichman, David Shimoni, Aharon Reuveni, and Levi Aryeh Arieli-Orlof. Most of the writers who came with the Second Aliya had begun writing abroad. They came as more or less fully developed authors, adding to their opus in the Land of Israel. Brenner (1881–1921) is considered the central writer of the Second Aliya. He arrived in Jaffa after wandering from Russia to England and from England to Galicia. In each of those places, he was active as an editor and writer. In the Land of Israel, he continued in the same fashion, although he changed the material about which he wrote, adapting it to the local situation. In contrast to Brenner and to Devora Baron (1887–1956), whose formative years were passed in the Diaspora but whose work took shape in the Land of Israel, Agnon's immigration was a turning point in his literary life.

The critical date was 1908, the year of the publication in *Ha-Omer* of his first story written in the Land of Israel: "Agunot: A Tale." "Like our other brethren, who share in our redemption" (to paraphrase the famous opening lines of *Only Yesterday*), the young Czaczkes arrived in the Land of Israel in 1908. He joined the small colony of writers in Jaffa, which was led by Brenner and Simha Ben-Tsion (1870–1932). Like them, he also published in *Ha-Omer* and in the other publications of the Second Aliya: *Ha-Po'el ha-Tsair* (1908–70), *Beynatayim* (1913), and *Yezreel* (1913). Ben-Tsion published Agnon's first writings in the Land of Israel. Brenner singled him out for the highest of praise:"Through him [*Ha-Omer*] had the privilege of publishing something superior to anything else normally printed among us."[4] Agnon's relationship to the Second Aliya and its literary figures is expressed primarily in his deep respect for Brenner: "I am amazed that that great writer treated me as a friend and supported me all the time I was living in the Land of Israel. He lent me money and he printed my story ["And the Crooked Shall Be Made Straight"] at his own expense, giving me all the income from the book. Were it not for Brenner, most of my stories would have remained in obscurity."[5]

Brenner was not simply a writer but also was considered a kind of secular saint. He was the spiritual leader of a group of pioneers for whom asceticism and physical labor were basic values. Agnon described his relationship with Brenner in his wonderful essay "Yosef Hayim Brenner, in Life and in Death."[6] One can also trace Agnon's admiration for Brenner in the letters he sent to him from Jaffa to Jerusalem and later from Germany to the Land of Israel. Agnon and Brenner came from different literary traditions—Knut Hamsun (1859–1952) versus Fyodor Mikhailovich Dostoyevsky (1812–81). Nevertheless, like his colleagues, Agnon regarded Brenner as setting the standard for his work. Thus, he wrote to Brenner from Jaffa in 1909:

A few days ago I sent you a manuscript. Please tell me whether you have received it? Perhaps I might already learn the "verdict." To satisfy the demands of courtesy I'll ask you: How have you been recently?

I have been in the Galilee. Oh, the Galilee, the Galilee![7]

Agnon's high regard for Brenner was not based merely on literary matters. His correspondence frequently indicates an intimate friendship. A postcard to Brenner dated 8 May 1912 (sent from Jaffa to Jerusalem to the editorial board of *Ha-Ahdut*) ends with the salutation "From him who blesses you and wishes to cut his hair so that you might spread it out on your hard sofa beneath your suffering, tortured body."[8] And in a letter from Munich dated 16 February 1920, Agnon writes:

To Brenner, the darling of my soul. Perhaps some time my words will reach you and you shall know that all the time I have been separated from you I have been thinking about you. Several times I saw you in my dreams at night, and once when I was awake, in the middle of the day. You were sitting in a wagon like a Russian prisoner. Truly the full, loving acceptance of the burden of life was visible in you.

How much I wish to know what has been happening to you and to tell you what has been happening to me. I have met many people in my days of wandering, but none like you have I found.[9]

Those words indicate not only a deep spiritual bond but also a deep insight, for the "loving acceptance of the burden of life" was perhaps Brenner's deepest and most hidden aspiration. It could be that Agnon's deep reverence for Brenner expressed the reciprocal relationship between the young Galician immigrants from the Hapsburg Empire and the weighty Russian tradition that formed the new Hebrew culture in the Land of Israel.

The deep crisis of the Jews of eastern Europe had a different effect upon each of these Jewish communities, and its influence was reflected in their writers. Brenner was heavy, serious, and sarcastic. Agnon was light and ironic. Agnon respected the serious consistency, the gravity, and the constant self-accusation of Brenner's Dostoyevskian, Russian school; but just as he could not accept fully the feeling of sinfulness, he could not rebel fully and unequivocally against Jewish tradition. Agnon admired Brenner's single-mindedness, but he himself took a consistently ambivalent attitude toward the phenomena of his generation.

Brenner's direct influence, which I will discuss later, is evident in Agnon's works. Agnon did not accept the world-view of the naive writers of local color, such as Meir Wilkansky (1882–1949); instead, maintaining an aesthetic distance he described situations of "breakdown and bereavement" (the title of Brenner's major novel).

Agnon felt an affinity for the spiritual foundation of the

Second Aliya and its major figures. On various occasions he discussed this affinity, as during the speech he gave at the president's residence and especially in his eulogy for Berl Katzenelson (1887–1944), the spiritual leader of the Labor Zionist movement. In it, he linked Katzenelson's personality with the Second Aliya's philosophy of life, naming the four teachers who made their mark upon the *aliya* and upon himself: Brenner, the writer; Rabbi Avraham Yitzhak Kook (1865–1935), the first Ashkenazi chief rabbi of Mandate Palestine and an original theological thinker; Arthur Ruppin (1876–1943), the first Zionist representative in Palestine (as noted, Agnon served as Ruppin's personal secretary for a time); and Katzenelson.

Agnon stated that philosophy as follows:

Now I shall make my comments more explicit. Brenner taught me that young Jews have no place in the world except the Land of Israel. Though he spoke accusingly of the land and complained about its inhabitants, warning several of his friends not to come to "Palestina," in life he kept the commandment of dwelling in the land, and he died for the land. He also taught us to behave with modesty and humility and not to make the heavens ring with our small deeds. And if we look upon our comrades of the Second Aliya we see that the better part of them learned from him. And those few, who departed somewhat from his system, did not stray far afield.

Ruppin taught us not to expect great things but to do whatever was in our power. Our great Rabbi of blessed memory taught us the truth about the Land of Israel, that working the land was holy service. And Berl Katzenelson taught us all of those things.[10]

Here is a practical philosophy of life anchored in Zionist ethics.[11] The sanctification of the profane and the modest and daily labor became the criteria Agnon used to judge his characters, praising or condemning them.

Agnon's affinity to some of the authors of the Second Aliya is apparent only at the start of his career, in the stories printed during that time. [12] Like Levi Aryeh Arieli-Orlof (1886–1943), in *Broken Voices from Across the Valley;* Aharon Reuveni (1886–1971), in *The Last Ships;* and Dov Kimchi (1889–1961), in *The Book of Yearnings,* Agnon portrayed the immigrant as a young artist—as early as 1909 in "Miryam's Well." Hemdat, the hero of the story, wishes to emigrate to the Land of Israel, for so long as the artist is in exile, the Divine Presence is in exile. In other words, a barrier keeps the artist from his muse, and only in the Land of the Fathers is there the possibility of redeeming her: "Alas, the oppression of exile! So long as he is in exile, that barrier will never move. Only there in the beloved land will he set his heart free." [13]

In the Land of Israel—the source of the vision—the young artist will find his lost muse. A romantic form of determinism identifies the beloved land with the young artist's dreamland. However, this romantic determinism is somewhat ironic, especially since additional romantic factors are also introduced. In any case, Agnon's Hemdat is not a flat character like the figures in Wilkansky's *In the Days of the Ascent* (1918), a naive novel of local color. Wilkansky's heroes immigrate to the Land of Israel "to build and be built," hoping that "in the land beloved of our fathers all our hopes will be fulfilled." [14]

Wilkansky's novel is an example of the naive literature of some of the writers of that time who did not perceive the integration of the settlers as it actually was, but rather attempted to make their descriptions fit the Zionist ideal. These writers believed their accounts to be realistic; in fact, they merely made use of realistic effects and documentary materials in order to paint a utopian world. They made reality fit the dream. In contrast, Agnon tempered his romantic heroes through irony; thus, his heroes did not become saints of the Zionist ideal. Agnon's characters are quotidian heroes. Even when they immigrate as idealists, they are first of all human beings. Characters such as Na'aman and Hemdat end up in the Land of Israel and become involved in romantic entanglements that have nothing to do with the place and time in which the stories are set. (See "Tishrei," which later became "The Hill of Sand" and "Night.")

Along with the positive explanations for his characters' immigration, Agnon presented many negative ones (such as flight from military service). These counterbalance the visions of peace and tranquillity in "Hemdat" (1947), those of Yitzhak in "Yitzhak's Beginnings" (1934), and of Yitzhak Kumer in *Only Yesterday* (1945). Ironic explanations dull the glamour of the romantic ones, show them to be flawed, and bring them as close as possible to the actual reality. The tone of Agnon's description of immigration is typical of the anti-naive, ironic literature of the Second Aliya, which rejected the charms of local color. Brenner's Yehezkel Hefets, in *Breakdown and Bereavement*,[15] and Reuveni's Brenchok, in *The Last Ships*,[16] are similar characters to Agnon's Hemdat. The so-called immigration literature, as opposed to the idealistic, naive literature of local color, did not beautify its heroes. It is not a sentimental, romantic motivation that brings such characters to the Holy Land (as with the heroes in Moshe Smilanski's [1874–1953] *Hadassa*[17] and the characters of Wilkansky and Yosef Luidor), but rather a bitter and quite ironic reality.

Agnon's young immigrants are innocent and lack self-awareness; in that respect, the early Hemdat of "Miryam's Well" is like Yakov Rechnitz of "Betrothed" and Yitzhak Kumer of *Only Yesterday*. They are unaware of what causes them to act; and, like heroes of naive literature, they see only idealistic motivations. The author casts an ironic light upon such a romantic explanation. Agnon is the "Balak" (the canine protagonist of *Only Yesterday*) who lurks in readiness to ambush their innocence. In that sense, the opening of *Only Yesterday* is a gem: "Yitzhak used to imagine things, feeding his imagination on the place his heart desired." [18]

Agnon's revolutionary approach to the traditions of his generation is expressed in his mixture of elements from the Zionist naive school with the more critical and ironic elements of the antinaive reaction to it. In their visions, Agnon's heroes behave like regular heroes (they dig wells and journey to the Galilee); but in their actions, they behave like the frustrated protagonists of Brenner and Reuveni (Agnon's contemporaries). Agnon's heroes dream as though infused with the divine aura of pioneering, but they fail in their little romances and Zionist efforts. Agnon was more aware than were his colleagues that the heroes of the Second Aliya were largely failed dreamers; they were victims who had taken more upon themselves than they could handle. They were not heroes of despair, cynicism, or of an awareness of their own failure. Agnon's ambivalent attitude toward the Second Aliya emerges very clearly (and therefore somewhat less significantly than in other stories) in his posthumously published "To the Galilee," [19] especially if compared to Wilkansky's naive story of the same title.

Agnon's heart was divided. On the one hand, we have his

positive heroes (Reb Hayim Dov in Zikhron Yakov and Shma-
riya Bengis in Haifa); on the other, we have the characters
who show the *aliya* and the inhabitants of the fictional Palestine in an ambiguous light (such as the landlady in Haifa and
Velvil the corrupted cantor). The latter prefer life in the
Diaspora to life in the Land of Israel, and their criticisms
sound rather well taken. In any event, the following sentences
are very much in the spirit of Brenner and express the despair
of Agnon's generation: "Ships come and ships go. Some bring
Jews to the land, and others bear Jews away from the land. If
one percent of the Jews who came actually remained the entire
land would be full of Jews already." [20]

Velvil tries to cheat, and Bengis is cheated. Swindlers in
the Land of Israel take Bengis's money, preventing him from
"building and being built." Here, the narrator as protagonist
consciously reveals what had been implied only indirectly in
Agnon's other stories (which is perhaps the reason why the
story was not published in the author's lifetime).

The criteria of the Second Aliya at its best continued to
guide Agnon, even in a sarcastic story such as "To the Galilee"
and in his epic novel about the Second Aliya, *Only Yesterday,*
as well as in *Shira,* his novel about the 1920s and 1930s in
Mandate Palestine. In both novels, Agnon remained faithful
to a world that was entirely good in his eyes—that is, kibbutz
society.

In *Only Yesterday,* kibbutz society is idealized in the person
of Menachem Haomed, a literary portrayal in the utopian
setting of Ain-Ganim of an individual resembling Berl Katzenelson. *Only Yesterday* ends with a promise for the future, a
promise to return to "our brothers and sisters, the children of

17

the living God, who work the Land of Israel for its name, its praise, and its glory."[21] Although the promise is not kept, in *Shira* the author returns to the *kevutsa* (literally group, an agricultural collective) in Kfar Ahinoam. There lives Zohara, the daughter of Herbst and Henrietta; there Zohara marries Abraham-and-a-Half; and there her son, Dan, is born. The Herbsts' trip to Kfar Ahinoam, a kind of return to a utopian country, renews their existence. The hero of that country, Abraham-and-a-Half, is admired by the author for his own qualities and also for the qualities of the group he represents:

Now I shall mention his simple virtues. Nor shall I mention them all, just one of them, the love of the soil, a virtue which encompasses all other virtues. He clings to the ground and its plants. And you know that there is no virtue greater than that, since the entire Jewish settlement depends on working the soil, and were it not for the temptations of the age, they would acknowledge and know that there can be no redemption for the Jews except from the Lord above and the soil below.[22]

Such an idealization sounds ingenuous, but it remains unchanged throughout Agnon's opus. The *kevutsa* continues to be the ideal "meadow." True, Agnon's heroes — Yitzhak and Herbst — do not live there; but both of them, and their creator as well, view it as the place where human fulfillment is preserved. In both novels, the human relationships of the *kevutsa* are on a different level from those in the Jerusalem of Professor Weltfremd, in *Shira,* or in the Jaffa of Sonya Zwierling, in *Only Yesterday.* In the "meadow," the values of Brenner, Ruppin, Rabbi Kook, and Katzenelson are put into practice. Agnon went beyond the literature of the Second

Aliya but remained faithful to its basic values. He did not place those values at the center of his work nor is his work the embodiment of those values. Nevertheless, they provide a regulative idea against which Agnon measured deviants and those who left the Land of Israel—the failures and stumblers who are the majority of the characters populating his works.

Buczacz

Agnon's roots were not in the Jaffa or Jerusalem of the early part of the century but were rather in Buczacz, a town in Galicia on the western bank of the Strypa River between Ternopol and Lwow.[23] A man is patterned on the landscape of his birthplace, and Agnon's character stems chiefly from the town of Buczacz.

Agnon's birthplace lies on the banks of the Strypa and was founded at the end of the sixteenth century. It is 55 kilometers from Ternopol and 130 kilometers from Lwow, the capital of Galicia under the Austrian Empire. Most of the non-Jewish inhabitants of the area were Ukrainians. The city was originally a village belonging to the estates of the Buczaczki family, who were members of the Polish nobility.

From as early as 1500 there had been a Jewish community in Buczacz. While Agnon lived there, the town was a part of the Hapsburg Empire. In 1870 it numbered 8,959 inhabitants, of whom 6,077 (67.9 percent) were Jews. In 1900 there were 11,755 inhabitants, of whom 6,730 (57.3 percent) were Jews. Agnon was born there while the Holy Roman Emperor Franz Josef still sat on his throne; the Hassidim and

Mitnagdim were still locked in bitter controversy with each other; and the Zionists were gradually organizing themselves. In 1893 the Zion Society was founded in Buczacz.

Buczacz was for Agnon a vivid memory, and it became the prototype of the *shtetl* in his works. His relationship with his birthplace came both from actual recollections and from the image that he formed of the town after leaving. The conflict between his memories and that image is what gives his works their depth.

Agnon left Buczacz as a young man of around twenty, but the town stayed with him all his life. Early in his career he published the chronicle of "The City of the Dead" (1907) in *Haet*. He signed the authorship as "someone from the city." He wrote: "Not because wherever one digs, one finds human skeletons, . . . it is the 'city of the dead' because of the lack of life in it."[24] He went on to describe the city's tombstones, the great synagogue, and the legends in circulation about a Polish nobleman's castle.

The world of Buczacz followed Agnon everywhere he went. The most important novella written by him in the Land of Israel before he left the first time was "And the Crooked Shall Be Made Straight."[25] It is "a story about a man named Menashe Hayim, a resident of the holy congregation of Buczacz, may it prosper, who lost all his property, and poverty, God preserve us, made him lose cognizance of his Creator."[26] Henceforth, Buczacz never disappears from Agnon's works— both those written in chronicle form, such as the opening chapters of *A City and the Fullness Thereof,* and those written as novels, including the one which is entirely concerned with the decline of Buczacz, *A Guest for the Night.*[27] The inspiration for that work came from a short visit to the city in the 1930s. According to Moshe Kanpfer, Agnon chose to visit his hometown rather than travel to Scandinavia where he had been invited. His love for his native city was unbounded, even though he saw it in its shame and decline:

Every place was changed—even the spaces between the houses. Nothing was as I had seen it when I was little, nor as it had been shown to me in a dream shortly before my return. But the odor of Szibucz had not yet evaporated—the odor of millet boiled in honey, which never leaves the town from the day after Passover until the end of November, when the snow falls, covering all.[28]

Buczacz is often called Szibucz (pronounced *shibush*) in Agnon's works, a wordplay that illustrates the author's ambivalence toward the town where he was born. (The Hebrew word *sh-b-sh* means to spoil.) The town is described extensively in *A City and the Fullness Thereof*. In *In Mr. Lublin's Store,* Buczacz is juxtaposed with Leipzig. Buczacz appears as both a realistic background and as a symbol in *The Book of Deeds* and in many other works. In depicting the town Agnon used all his literary tools, from nostalgic pathos—in *Stories of Poland* and *The Bridal Canopy*—to satire—in "Two Great Scholars Who Where in Our City" and "Of Our Young People and Our Elders"—and from burlesque to the bitterly grotesque—in "The Frogs" and "Pisces."

Agnon's *shtetl* is different from the *shtetl*s of Mendele Mokher Seforim, Berdyczewski, Isaac Leib Peretz, or Shalom Aleichem—although in some of his works Agnon carried on the existing tradition. Like Berdyczewski, Agnon described the disintegration brought about by the forces of instinct, in *A*

Simply Story and in "Pisces"; like Mendele Mokher Seforim, he satirized self-important community functionaries and leaders; and like Peretz, he lost himself in reverie about the *shtetl*—both awake and in dreams.

In one respect Agnon is actually closest to Shalom Aleichem. Both writers described the *shtetl* as a living corpse, as a "city of the dead." Both felt that a "guest from the night" was incapable of bringing the *shtetl* back to life. Shalom Aleichem accepted that disintegration with forgiving, humorous insight (see Shalom Aleichem's Tevie the milkman and Menakhem Mendl), while Agnon described the final agonies of the *shtetl* with macabre grotesqueness. Agnon's vision of disintegration was a presentiment of the utter physical destruction of the Holocaust. His work is an apocalyptic dialectic in stages: an inner collapse that began with the war between the Hassidim and the Mitnagdim ("The Rejected"); its continuation in the generation gap that shook the *shtetl* to its foundations (*A Simple Story*); and the *shtetl*'s destruction with a description of the death blows falling upon the city after the First World War (*A Guest for the Night*). All of these processes culminated in the experience of the Holocaust, which for Agnon was not merely decreed from on high but was also a process determined from within ("The Covering of Blood"). Agnon took a familiar subject and brought it to its extreme expression in a distant and ironic and grotesque and distorted manner, in contrast to Shalom Aleichem, who described the same subject with humorous empathy.

The Jewish Tradition

In the geographical sense of culture, Buczacz and the Second Aliya left their mark on Agnon's works; but in the literary sense of culture, Agnon is a product of the mixture of the Jewish and European cultures. The dialectic tension between these two cultures has been extremely fruitful for modern Hebrew literature. In 1916 Martin Buber voiced extravagant praise for Agnon's affinity with the Jewish world. In fact, it was Buber who made Agnon known to the Zionist Jewish youth of Germany.[29]

The foundations of Agnon's Jewish world lie in Buczacz, but Agnon saw himself as the heir not only of the *shtetl* tradition but also of the Jewish tradition over its many generations. Although he ceased to observe all of the 613 commandments when he emigrated to Palestine, his bond with tradition remained a major factor in his life. In one of his stories Agnon expressed his principled relation to the tradition, writing:

From love of our language and adoration of holiness I abase myself before the words of the Torah, and starve myself by abstaining from the words of the Sages, keeping these words within me so that they may be fitted altogether upon my lips. If the Temple still stood, I should take my place on the dais with my fellow poets and daily repeat the song which the Levites used to chant in the Holy Temple. Now, when the Temple is still in ruins, and we have neither priests at their holy work nor Levites chanting and singing, I occupy myself with the Torah, the Prophets, and the Writings, the Mishnah, the Halakhah and the Haggadot, Toseftot, Dikdukei Torah, and Dikdukei Soferim. When I look into their words and see that from all our goodly treasures which we had in ancient days nothing is left us but a scanty record, I am filled with sorrow, and this same sorrow causes my heart to tremble. Out of this same trembling I write my fables, like a man who has been exiled from his father's palace, who makes himself a little booth and sits there telling of the glory of his forefather's house.[30]

This is a poetic expression of Agnon's fundamental attitude toward the relationship between modern literature and the tradition. For Agnon, intertextuality was neither a mere literary device nor an unconscious phenomenon. Rather, it was the very source of his creativity, perhaps even its main subject. Modern Hebrew literature, according to Agnon, is nothing less than a substitute for the sacred texts. The absence of sacred literature was the source of his inspiration. Moreover, the author saw himself as the heir of the holy scribes whose words were a communal creation and whose anonymity, which foregrounded the texts and hid the identity of the individual authors, was an integral part of their work.

Therefore, as a modern author, Agnon continued the ancient tradition in his work because it had become a part of his cultural heritage. But also as a modern author who could only imitate the language of the canon and could not enact its content as part of a living ritual, he could not be the true bearer of that canon.

Agnon did not, therefore, see himself as a transmitter of a great cultural lineage—the tradition that was built layer upon layer, beginning with the Bible and continuing through the Mishnah, the Talmud, and all of the works that stem from them. Instead, he viewed himself as belonging to a different culture altogether, one that inherited a multitextual tradition that could no longer be carried on. This culture relates to these earlier texts, but, because of the new social context, the texts can be made real only through invented fables—that is, fables that are not the sacred ones that the righteous of each generation were accustomed to telling but fables that are secular chambers, in which only echoes of the canon are heard. The work of the modern writer, claimed Agnon, serves as a secular substitute—a "booth"—for sacred tradition—the "palace." In order to understand Agnon's works, this connection between holy origins and secular expression must be kept in mind.

To a greater degree than the works of any other writer in modern Hebrew literature, Agnon's work is based upon inter-textual connections. Indeed, Agnon conceived of an ideal addressee for whom the traditions of sacred literature are totally native, one who can discern the relationship between the fable and the holy canon. Agnon's implied addressee, however, is not simply the reader who is close to these tradi-tions and is able to recognize them. The addressee is one who is able, like the author himself, to distinguish between the fable and the holy canon and even to create appositions be-tween them.

In order to understand Agnon's work, one must read his text not only as a link in the chain of sacred tradition but also as an "antitext" to the traditional literature. The text will not be understood by the addressee who is completely unfamiliar with the textual tradition to which the author is referring. Similarly, the text will be misunderstood by the addressee who credulously reads the text as a link in a chain of sacred texts, or "quasisanctified" texts (or even as a kind of Apocrypha), or as stories in which the author—by various devices—hints that his text is a link in the chain of sacred texts.

"Agunot: A Tale" ("Abandoned Wives") and "And the Crooked Shall Be Made Straight" are two such works. The first is prefaced by a pseudo-midrash. In the second, each chapter opens with quotations from the traditional literature, and the structure of the narrative as a whole—through the use of the introduction, the style, and the inserted tales—is based on the organization of the so-called tales of believers. (This was the name given to traditional religious and moral stories dealing with awe of heavenly power and deep religious faith.)

The same literary approach can be found in many later stories as well. But whether Agnon's works contain only hints pointing toward sacred texts or are actually written as if they are themselves quasisanctified, it is clear that the tales' creative power arises from the constant tension between the texts and the sanctified or semisanctified literary tradition (if we take into account the later literature of the religious community).

The intertextual allusions, which are frequently or even mostly parodic, make the secular modern text of the present an antimodel of the traditional "holy" text of the past. The permanent tension between the traditional model and the new antimodel becomes a source of stylistic and thematic ambiguity. The sanctified model is secularized, while, conversely, the secular antimodel sometimes seems to be sanctified. This is one reason why these texts are open to "writerly" interpretation (to use Roland Barthes's term). They lend themselves to

26

diverse and sometimes contradictory readings, for the contradictions are woven into the intertextual matrix of a variety of Agnon's texts.

To examine the tensions in Agnon's works, let us turn to his first story, "Agunot: A Tale," which in many ways determined Agnon's subsequent literary development—thematically, structurally, and stylistically. "Agunot" is built on a parallel between the fate of Dina, abandoned by Ben-Uri because his soul is drawn to his art and not to love, and Rabbi Yehezkel, who left his loved one, Fredela, to earn the crown of Torah in the Holy Land. Ben-Uri's aesthetic desires and Rabbi Yehezkel's nostalgic yearnings ("his feet are planted in the gates of Jerusalem, and stand on her soil, but his eyes and his heart are pledged to houses of study and worship abroad")[31] are related to each other. The parallel explains why both are willing to give up love for their creations and for inner wholeness, just as it explains the double rift in their hearts— between their inner worlds and their social status. Moreover, the parallel also exists between the fate of the two women, Dina and Fredela, who are deprived of husbands because fate is a cruel force that toys with people and destroys any possibility of harmony in the world—so much so that the rabbi who marries Dina to Yehezkel and also divorces them sees himself as being tragically fated to wander around the world in an attempt to set right what is awry.

Agnon's bond with his Jewish foundation is visible in the mythic parallel between the two heroes, Ben-Uri the artist and Yehezkel the prophet of exile. The characters express not only their own stories but also the struggle between the aesthetic and intellectual urges of the nation and the world.

The descriptions of the bond between Ben-Uri and the land and between Rabbi Yehezkel and exile seem to imply that the aesthetic element belongs to the Land of Israel, whereas the spiritual, learned element belongs to the Diaspora.[32]

The Jewish mystical stratum — restoration, the exile of the Divine Presence, and abandonment — appears in every part of the story, but it is emphasized mainly in the relationship between the midrash at the beginning and the rest of the story. According to Baruch Hochman's translation, "Agunot: A Tale" begins like this:

It is said: A thread of grace is spun and drawn out of the deeds of Israel, and the Holy One, blessed be He, Himself, in His glory, sits and weaves — strand on strand — a prayer shawl all grace and all mercy, for the Congregation of Israel to deck herself in. Radiant in the light of her beauty she glows, even in these, the lands of her exile, as she did in her youth in her Father's house, in the Temple of her Sovereign and city of Sovereignty, Jerusalem. And when He, of ineffable name, sees her, that she has neither been sullied nor stained even here, in the realm of her oppressors, He — as it were — leans toward her and says, "Behold thou art fair, my beloved, behold thou art fair." And this is the secret of the power and the glory and the exaltation and the tenderness in love which fills the heart of every man in Israel.[33]

The phenomenon of text as commentary, mediating between the tradition and a new context, is repeated in a number of ways in "Agunot." The most important of these is the relationship established between the introduction to the story (quoted above) and what the "author" (as he refers to himself) calls "the fable" — "a great tale and terrible, from the Holy Land."[34] The opening section is built along the same lines as many Hassidic tales, which open with a quotation from the writings that point generally to the works of the Holy Ari, Rabbi Isaac Luria (1534–72), the head of the kabbalistic community in Safed. The Ari's works were left unpublished. But "quotations" from the Hassidic books attributed to him were cited with a show of great authority, even though it was widely acknowledged that their authenticity was often doubtful.

Agnon revived the form of the quotation from the writings —which I call the *pseudoquotation*—supporting his fable with words that seem to have a sanctified status, almost an ordination. Furthermore, the sacred authority of these citations extends itself into the fable, with the fable becoming an exemplum of the imaginary quotation. However, the quotation is not reducible to the purely imaginary—that is, imaginary *in fact* and yet constructed of similarly "authentic" passages of sacred literature (that are themselves of dubious authority). We may say that a quotation is a genuine pseudoquotation because the well-informed reader can grasp not only the authenticity of the unfolding of its elements but also the spirit in which it is invoked. The pseudoquotation is a text derived from sacred texts—with many of the characteristics of those texts—but it is a text that is itself outside of the sacred context.

The opening of "Agunot" continues the midrashic form of writing signalized by Agnon's choice of name and title. As he or she reads, the addressee is half willing to suspend disbelief and to imagine that "Agunot" is not a secular work by a secular author but a religious work, in which the implied author carries on the midrashic activity of former generations.

The pseudosacred opening imitates the tradition in which the relationship between a secular story and the sacred canon having been revealed, the story itself takes on a sacred and sanctified significance. The fictionality is self-fulfilling. The secular and sacred are interwoven, and the reader does not know if the sacred sanctifies the secular or if the secular sanctifies the sacred. Indeed, the relationship between secular and sacred, and the fictive or real status of each, are perhaps the central themes of the tale.

Specifically, the opening follows the tradition of midrashic writing that depended upon the Song of Songs and the Midrash on the Song of Songs. The opening also renews the relationship between a metaphorical—or symbolic—character who represents the Jewish people and an anthropomorphic image of God. At the same time, the opening recapitulates a particular stage in the midrashic exegesis of that text, where, in the Song of Songs Rabbah, this connection is made suggestively to express the intimate and even reciprocal relationship between the people and their God. This relationship is made explicit later in the exegetical tradition; for example, in the Lurianic Kabbalah we find a detailed reciprocity between the deeds of the people and the deeds of God.

Agnon's midrash is simultaneously an interpretation of the Song of Songs and of the Midrash on the Song of Songs. In the opening of Agnon's midrash, the following phrases from the Song of Songs appear: "Behold, thou art fair, my love; behold, thou art fair"; "They smote me, they wounded me; they took away my veil"; "My beloved withdrew and was gone"; "I am love-sick." [35] Citations from the Song of Songs appear not only in the opening but also in the body of the story, where they take on increasingly complex significance. On the one hand, their application—like the fable as a whole —moves from the abstract, or conceptual, level of interpretation to a more literal, or reified, one. On the other hand, the citations bring to the body of the story the conceptual significance they possess in the opening. (I am referring to such verses as "my beloved descended into the garden"; "the time of the singing birds is come"; and "I sleep but my heart waketh.")[36]

These verses and similar phrases are the central elements of the intertextual connection. By appearing first in the opening and then returning in the body of the tale, they suggest that the story as a whole aims in two directions. On the one hand, the verses refer to the context of their secular or fictional elements; on the other, they point toward the more remote context of the pseudosacred opening. The more remote context establishes the relationship between the events of the more-immediate context and the traditional literature of past generations. The interaction between past text and present contexts accumulates the interpretive meanings of the generations and causes them to reverberate in new events and interpretations.

Of course, the introduction does not remain on the literal level of the love story of the Song of Songs. Instead, it quickly proceeds to evoke the Midrash on the Song of Songs, which compares the people of Israel to the "fair one," God to the "beloved," and interprets other elements of the love story in light of this comparison. In this way, "Behold, thou art fair" elicits the following midrash: "Behold, thou art fair with precepts, behold thou art fair with deeds of kindness, behold thou art fair in positive precepts, behold thou art fair in negative precepts; behold thou art fair in the religious duties of the house, with the *hallah, terumah,* and tithes; behold thou art fair in religious duties of the field, with the gleanings, the forgotten sheaf, the corner."[37] Or another example: "I adjure you, O daughters of Jerusalem . . . what will ye tell him? That I am love-sick. As a sick person yearns for healing, so the generation of Egypt yearned for deliverance."[38]

These midrashim do not appear in their original form in Agnon's text. They are, however, painstakingly implied in a discourse of authorial asides that compounds new expressions out of the interpretative echoes of various sacred texts. This process begins in the opening of the story, where, for example, the pseudo-midrash being created substitutes the expression "a thread of grace" (which, so far as I have been able to determine, is not found in the traditional texts) for the phrase "a thread of mercy," which is indeed repeated in various well-known midrashic contexts. See, for example, *Hagigah* 12b:*

Look down from heaven, and see, even from the holy and glorious habitation. Ma'on is that in which there are companies of Ministering Angels, who utter [divine] song by night, and are silent by day for the sake of Israel's glory, for it is said: *By day the Lord doth command His loving-kindness, and in the night his song is with me.*

Resh Lakish said: Whoever occupies himself with [the study of] the Torah by night, the Holy One, blessed be He, draws over him a chord of loving-kindness ["a thread of mercy"] by day, for it is said: *"By day the Lord doth command His loving-kindness."* Because

*Cf. also Bab. Tal. *Megillah* 13a and Bab. Tal. *Tamid* 29a.

"by night His song is with me." And there are some who say: Resh
Lakish said: Whoever occupies himself with the study of the Torah
in this world, which is like the night, the Holy One, blessed be
He, draws over him a chord of loving-kindness in the world to
come, which is like the day, for it is said: *"By day the Lord doth
command His loving-kindness, for by night His son is with me."*

The motifs of the prayer shawl, the hangings, and the
weaving, which appear in the concrete image of the prayer
shawl that is woven by God himself from the good deeds of
the people of Israel for the congregation of the people of Israel,
are found similarly in various forms in midrashic sources. For
example, the motif of the apparel of the *Shekhinah* appears in
Zohar 3, *Shelach Lecha* 163b: "When the *Shekhinah* is in the
pale blue she prepares for herself an outer covering of the same
pale blue which was found in the Sanctuary." The same motif
appears in earlier and later versions. For example, it appears
in *Hibbur Yafe Meyeshua* by the tenth-century writer Rabbi
Nissim of Kairouan and in the kabbalistic book of morals,
Shevet Musar, by Reb Elijah, son of Solomon Ha-Kohen from
Izmir, where good deeds are compared to a garment awarded
to the naked soul for its fulfillment of the commandments and
for other praiseworthy deeds:

Precious is the light and the upper [heavenly] garment created by
the light of the Torah and the performance of its commandments,
for through the commandments a precious, spiritual garment is
woven, lighting the body of heaven in its clearness; the soul, leaving this world naked of bodily cover, hovering, ashamed, seeing
itself naked, immediately puts on this clear, light-giving garment,
a garment it had made for itself in the world of flesh through

Torah and the commandments, and is overjoyed, seeing itself in the garment of Kingdom.[39]

One could present a long list of sources that would demonstrate clearly that Agnon's pseudo-midrash is assembled from authentic materials, which themselves provide varying contexts and interpetations. Concepts such as "grace and mercy"; "the Congregation of Israel"; "in her youth in her Father's house"; "the Temple of her Sovereign and the city of Sovereignty"; "neither been sullied nor stained"; "the power and the glory and the exaltation"; "the prayer shawl is damaged"; "evil winds [spirits] blow"; "and they know they are naked"; "wandering and howling"; "groans and cries"; "darkest melancholy—Mercy shield us!" acquired different meanings at different moments in sacred literature—from the midrash through to the late mystic literature of the Hassidim.

There is no need to review each concept nor to make a detailed analysis of the compounding of several concepts into units. But as these multiple perspectives come together in Agnon's text—indeed, as they exist separately within different midrashim—they hint at a relationship of reciprocity between the heavenly and the secular, between the Congregation of Israel, or the *Shekhinah* (the Heavenly Spheres), and the Holy-One-Blessed-Be-He (or other spheres in the scheme of spheres) as He manifests Himself in affairs of this world. As long as the stream flows from below—that is, the stream of commandments and good deeds—the stream from above continues to flow—the testing of immanence—and harmony exists. It is a harmony that the congregation as a whole, and every individual in it, feels. When this stream is impeded, generally because of an event in the lower world of the flesh, an interruption of the flow occurs. Harmony, which is simultaneously erotic and cosmic, is disrupted; there is a kind of fall in the lower world that will not be corrected until— miraculously—harmony is restored. This disharmony has multiple manifestations: in the area of personal relations (where pairing becomes separation); in the area of the spheres (where the masculine spheres are alienated from the Sphere of Kingdom, which is the *Shekhinah,* while judgments and the strength of the devil's camp increase); and in the area of the relationship between the people and their God (where exile overcomes redemption).

Some of these patterns stand out in the quotations cited previously (good deeds lead to unification of Creation, to the satisfaction of the Creator, and to the weaving of the garment that clothes the soul in good deeds), while others are to be found in the general store of meanings known to every so-called ideal addressee—that is, the reader who is intimate with this literature. Therefore, Agnon's pseudo-midrashic opening is both a précis of a sacred text and a narrative of a cosmic story. It suggests that a state of harmony, which originates in the reciprocal relations between the two heroes of the drama (God and the Congregation of Israel or the Sphere of Glory and Majesty and the Sphere of Kingdom), gives way to the destruction of this harmonic state because of some negative, human factor and to a condition of longing for restoration of the original state (as in the romantic longings for lost perfection). Agnon accepted the premise that in sacred literature are found the permanent and known laws of the cosmic drama. These laws govern the strange interplay between the midrashic assumption that all is foreordained and the concept that we are free to choose. The cosmic process is realized in human action, just as every human action is an expression of the cosmic process. The reciprocal relation between the two processes is re-expressed in the relationship between the opening and the tale.

The traditional elements in "Agunot" reveal the profound connection between Agnon and the Jewish tradition. The traditional elements also indicate the significance of the rebellion against tradition that is implied through the use of these materials. Perhaps here I should emphasize that direct reference to the sources is less significant than the fact that the midrash as presented is not actually in this form in the sources. Agnon pieced the sources together, joining them in mythopoeic fashion to create his own midrash. He neither imitated midrashic texts nor used them as they were. He grappled with them and interpreted them for his own purposes, thus pointing out the abyss between the tradition of the past and the present.

The story "The Overcoat" ("Hamalbush") borrows from such traditional texts as *Midrash Jonah* and *Masekhet Hibut Hakever* (The tractate on punishment in the grave tomb) or the "Story of the Splendid Cloak About Rabbi Joseph the Gardener," from the collection of stories *Hibbur Yafe Meyeshua,* by Rabbi Nissim of Kairouan. However, that borrowing is not in the authentic spirit of the texts but is rather parodic and is sometimes even grotesque.[40] Agnon did not displace the simple meaning of a quotation; instead, he exposed new aspects of its meaning—often even its opposite. For example,

"Edo and Enam" is related both to the stories of Rabbi Benjamin of Tudela that describe his travels in the second half of the twelfth century in the land of the Kurds[41] and to midrashic and kabbalistic sources.[42] Agnon's work is not, however, an interpretation of these sources; nor did he make historical or geographical use of them. Rather, he attempted to understand their function after they had lost their validity in the new context of a Jerusalem on the eve of the War of Independence.

When the dog Balak in *Only Yesterday* uses the language of *Bereishit Raba* (the midrashic commentary on Genesis) to describe the Creation from a dog's point of view[43] or when the fish use midrashic language to describe the trap in which the "king" of the fish is caught in "Pisces," in *A City and the Fullness Thereof*,[44] the passages do not merely secularize or profane the text. They are an absolute disorientation of the relation of the addressee to the traditional texts—which have devolved from the sacred books into the mouths of demonic animals. The tradition has become a kind of "antitradition." What began as innocent—although often acerbic—parody in the works of Mendele Mokher Seforim became grotesque parody in the works of Agnon. Agnon no longer made fun of the ancient text. He created an "antitext" that appears to retain the traditional form, but the content has been replaced by high explosives. Works that seem to be "readerly," traditional texts prove to be "writerly," contradictory, and ambiguous.

Agnon did not relate to traditional materials merely as semantic fields. Instead, he borrowed entire forms from the tradition, such as the letter, the midrash, the sermon, the anecdote, and the fable. These borrowings appear in concentrated form in "And the Crooked Shall Be Made Straight," one of Agnon's first works written in the Land of Israel.

The story itself derives from the European tradition from Odysseus to Balzac's Colonel Chabert, but the short introduction and the anecdotes attributed to the Baal Shem Tov in the body of the story are borrowed from Jewish tradition. The anomalous combination negates the religious content of the sources, although it binds Agnon—both positively and negatively—to past generations of Jews, [45] making him the most Jewish of writers.

The borrowing of Jewish forms and combining them with European ones recures in many of Agnon's works, such as *A Guest for the Night,* "Until Now," "The Tale of Rabbi Gadiel, the Infant," and *The Bridal Canopy.* Literary scholarship has addressed primarily the way in which Agnon draws upon the tradition, [46] without always noting that his borrowings are also an outstanding expression of movement in the opposite direction. Agnon borrowed from tradition in order to tear it down, not to strengthen the beliefs of pious Jews.

Like Hayim Nahman Bialik, Agnon was an avid collector of cultural arcana, which he stamped with his own original style. His bonds with Jewish culture actually deepened during the time he spent in Germany (1912–24). There, he associated with Jewish scholars, such as Martin Buber and Gershom Scholem, and served as the secretary of the Mekitzey Nirdamim (sleeper's awake) Society, which reprinted and published old books. The first work reprinted under his aegis was *Megilat Hamegale* by Rabbi Abraham Bar Hiya Hanassi. [47]

Agnon also published three volumes of Jewish stories and

legends: *Yamaim Noraim* (Days of awe, a collection of customs and legends for the Days of Mercy and Penitence and for the New Year and Day of Atonement and the intermediary days); [48] *Sefer, Sofer, veSippur* (Book, scribe, and tale), [49] which contains only part of the material collected by the author and was published later in *The Books of the Righteous (One Hundred and One Stories of the Disciples of the Baal Shem Tov and the Disciples of His Disciples);* [50] and *Atem Reitem* (You have seen), [51] a collection of stories about the giving of the Torah. That material demonstrates Agnon's enormous erudition regarding the sources and explains the richness of his own work and the character of his multilayered style.

Western Culture

One must be careful not to turn Agnon into a prayer shawl woven only of Jewish threads. He was as well versed in Western European culture as he was in Jewish culture. Moshe Kanpfer, who came from Buczacz and was almost the same age as Agnon, writes of the young people of Buczacz:

However those revolutionaries themselves used to read Schnitzler, take pleasure in Altenberg, and they were particularly susceptible to the mighty spell of Hamsun. I remember the great impression made by *Mysteries* on the young Agnon. Like a madman he raced around the city, speaking constantly of that book. [52]

Additional proof of the place occupied by Knut Hamsun in the minds of the Galicians was that in 1907 his story "The Trapper" was translated and published in an issue of *Haet.*

The young Agnon was familiar with many authors from various European cultures. In his youth, for example, Agnon published a collection entitled "Fragments," which contained quotations and apothegms taken from Mirabeau, Dumas, Wilde, Montesquieu, and others.[53] His affinity with Scandinavian literature is evident in his translation (apparently, from German and Yiddish) of "Dust" by Bjornstjerne Bjornson (1832–1910).[54] In yet another example, Na'aman, the hero of "Tishrei," takes it upon himself to translate *Niels Lyhne* by yet another Scandinavian author, Jens Peter Jacobsen (1841–85). In a letter to Yeruham Fishel Lachover, Agnon mentions that translation again: "Regarding the translation of Jakobsen [Jacobsen], that refined poet, I will look into it again and try my strength, and if I succeed in the translation, I'll send it to you, sir, so that you can judge whether the work is well done."[55] In that respect, Agnon is close in spirit to the authors admired by the Second Aliya (particularly the anti-genre writers) who drew on similar sources.

However, unlike his fellow writers, Agnon did not depend only on that source of influence; and he also superseded it rather quickly. While in Germany, from 1913 to 1924, he reworked what he had previously written in the Land of Israel during the years 1908 to 1913. Although at the time he was influenced by the Scandinavian writers, he took care to counterbalance their influence and to change the form and style of the stories. Indeed, Agnon "betrayed" his sources and formed his own image of himself.

The Scandinavians were not alone in earning his praise. In letters later written to Salman Schocken, he sang the praises of Gottfried Keller (1819–90), preferring him to Balzac.

However, Agnon's major literary idol was Gustave Flaubert. He claimed, "Every writer should read him before writing and after he writes, and then there would be no more barren books." In other letters he also refers to the pseudonymous Ossian, to English ballads, and to August Strindberg.[56] In any case, there is no question that he was more than just a *"shtetl* boy" who was familiar only with the Talmud and its commentaries. One can sense the influence of European romantic ballads on stories such as "The Dance of Death" and "The Black Bridal Canopy," just as one can see the influence of Flaubert's ironic control of point of view throughout Agnon's work (although these are merely possible influences that are difficult to define with precision).

In Agnon's early writings, the influence of Scandinavian neoromanticism is prominent, as represented by writers such as Jens Peter Jacobsen and Knut Hamsun (1859–1952), both of whom wrote extensively of love and death. Agnon's stories "Tishrei," "Nights," "Miryam's Well," and "Sister" are all centrally concerned with these topics. Even "Agunot: A Tale" can be interpreted as a text mainly treating the themes of love and death.

Hamsun's influence on Agnon seems to have been stronger than the influence of the other Scandinavian writers. It could be that his afflicted and miserable character Minutte, in *Mysteries* (1892), became Agnon's unfortunate Ovadia the Cripple. There are also clear parallels between the two festive balls in which the strong mock the weak.[57] The romantic triangle of Lieutenant Gran, Edvarda, and the Baron that is at the center of Hamsun's *Pan* (1894) is not unlike that of Na'aman (Hemdat), Yael, and Shamay in Agnon's "Tishrei." The gloomy atmosphere in stories such as "The Black Bridal Canopy" or "The Dance of Death" is close to the atmosphere of Scandinavian stories and ballads.

Agnon's German period distanced him from the Scandinavians (although neoromantic subject matter did not completely disappear), and he drew closer to the moderate and controlled realism of Gottfried Keller and Flaubert, and perhaps also to Thomas Mann. That realism and the new style it produced counterbalanced Agnon's neoromantic sources from both world literature and Hebrew literature.

From 1932 onward Agnon began publishing surrealistic stories, such as those in *The Book of Deeds,* and critics have found a resemblance in them to the works of Franz Kafka. Agnon himself, in a speech in honor of Dov Sadan, denied such a connection categorically.[58] Nevertheless, some critics have labored hard to find a link between the two authors (for example, Gavriel Moked, Kurzweil, and Barzel), while others (most prominently, Band) have denied any connection.[59] The elements typifying *The Book of Deeds* are also found in Agnon's other works—in one form or another—even before 1931. Kafka describes a world out of time and place, making the unreal become real. Agnon, however, used real materials rooted in a concrete time and place and then deprived them of reality. The effect is that the familiar world becomes distorted and alien. In that respect, Agnon's writings are actually more similar to Gogol's.

Agnon and Kafka are actually the converse of each other—the latter makes the alien seem real, while the former makes the real seem alien. In the works of both authors, grotesque effects are achieved but through the use of opposite techniques. Perhaps it would be best to take Agnon at his word:

Kafka is not from the root of my soul, and I cannot absorb anyone who is not from the root of my soul, though he be as great as the ten elders who wrote the Book of Psalms. I take joy in reading Homer, Cervantes, Balzac, Gogol, Tolstoy, Flaubert, Hamsun, even their minor works, but not Kafka.[60]

Agnon admits the influence of the great realists and impressionists—like Hamsun—who marked him at the start of his path; but he rejects, with some justification, the influence of Kafka's nonrealistic expressionism. Be that as it may, Agnon achieved his own nonrealism that derived more from his own inner development than from external influences.

Hebrew Fiction

I have traced the lines of comparison between the writers of the Second Aliya and the young Agnon. But to sum up the description of Agnon's function in the literary field and the fusion of diverse powers in his literary achievements, it is necessary to review again his literary relationship with his contemporaries—who inherited only partly what Agnon received abundantly from a variety of cultural and social sources.

Indeed, it is not difficult to extend the lines between Agnon and the major Hebrew authors who were writing at the turn of the century, such as Berdyczewski, Shofman, Uri Nissan Gnessin, Isaac Dov Berkowitz, and especially Brenner.

At the start of his career, Agnon borrowed motifs from the romantic tradition without resorting to the style of David Frishman, Berdyczewski, or Peretz. On the contrary, stylistically Agnon is actually closer to Mendele and Bialik. One might say that he brought their well-balanced style to its "rhythmic" fulfillment by developing his own way of constructing sentences and linking them together.

Agnon went beyond that careful style, known by historians of Hebrew literature as the *formula*, which features balanced rhythms and semantic equilibrium among the various layers of the Hebrew language, especially the biblical and Mishnaic idioms. In Agnon's writing, the world of imagination, which is related to Berdyczewski's romantic style, is played off the use of materials taken from the social setting. In that world of reality and imagination, Agnon's deracinated and hopeless heroes wander—related, apparently, to the heroes of Brenner, Gnessin, and Shofman.

What made Agnon so radically original and what gives his work incomparable value is his relationship—although in a negative sense—with the whole of the literary world, the contradictions and problems of which he assumed absolutely. The two social and the two literary fields that shaped Agnon's work are contradictory: Buczacz versus Palestine, or Israel, and Jewish tradition versus Western culture and modern Hebrew literature. The tension between these pairs is the source of the paradox of "revolutionary traditionalism." Agnon depicted Buczacz from the ironic point of view of the Land of Israel, and he secularized the tradition from the point of view of modern literature.

However, the ironic outlook was not one-sided. The so-called revolutionary poles were ridiculed from the opposite poles. The ambiguity of Agnon's work in its totality is that there was never a clear-cut and unequivocal decision between the alternatives. This ambiguity is one of the major sources of the complexity and intensity of his oeuvre. All the rivers of Hebrew prose flowed into the sea of Agnon, and that marvelous mixture produced his character as an artist and laid the foundations for his poetics.

CHAPTER 2

POETICS, DEVELOPMENT, AND RECEPTION

Poetics

IN CONTRAST to many of his colleagues, such as Brenner, Kimchi, and Reuveni, Agnon seldom wrote literary criticism or made statements about his poetics. However, we can glean something of his theoretical views from incidental statements made in articles and speeches or from the works themselves.

Agnon, who began as a romantic in theory (as evidenced in his essay on the sentimental poet Mordechai Tsevi Maane [1859–86])[1] and in practice (as seen in most of his first stories about the Land of Israel, written in the years 1908–13),[2] increasingly tended toward a classical, formal view of literature. Different traditions pass through Agnon's work in dialectical fashion. The Jewish tradition and the tradition of a balanced style became a protective wall erected against

46

the instincts and emotions that were the young neoromantic's stock in trade.

The rigors of classical form imposed upon the writer by the literary tradition were expressed in a speech called "Letters and Authors," delivered by Agnon in 1963 at the Hebrew University in Jerusalem upon receiving a prize awarded by New York University:

When it is decreed that a person will be a writer, the Holy One, blessed be He, takes just so many letters out of his treasury and gives them to the writer.

The Holy One, blessed be He, is not one to compromise, and what He gives, He gives in good measure. If the writer is clever he calculates and measures and counts every single letter before putting it in his work. If the writer isn't clever, he wastes the letters on worthless things. There are some among us who are called writers who waste all their letters on vanity and foolishness. May the Lord preserve me from them and their books.[3]

The demand for formal perfection no matter what the content may be is an expression of the need to contemplate from a distance what is torn and ravaged. The relationship between formal excellence and romantic and modern content is one source of Agnon's irony, in that it creates a gap between the balanced view and the disjointed contents.

The remarks that follow explain what Agnon learned from the tradition and why—from his beginnings as a young and rebellious romantic—he came to bind himself in the thick cords of its style.

Ancient literature *saw* first, and what it saw *moved* it, therefore we too are moved when we read it.[4]

I have already mentioned that my poetry was high-flown. Gradually I abandoned the whole heavenly and exalted host, and I and the queen of my poetry descended lower and lower, writing poems about the humble of the earth and things that not every versifier wastes rhymes on. That quality persists within me still: everything small is lovely in my eyes.[5]

Agnon viewed classical literature as an artistic ideal. In principle, classical literature was for Agnon Jewish sacred literature; everything that came afterward was a decline from it. In fact, despite his admiration for classical Jewish texts, Agnon was unconsciously bound to the classical Greek tradition in which there is a preference for the visual over states of mind.[6] Agnon's few statements on poetics indicate that in his view a literary work that is not sufficiently *concretized* cannot be a well-made work. Concretization in depiction and a balanced style constitute the Homeric ideal.

It is astonishing that Agnon made use of the formal Homeric ideal to depict the precariousness of modern society and to present the nostalgic and sentimental existence of characters who have lost their connection to the world of the past. Agnon's characters are people who pine to return to a certain place, but the gates of their destination have been locked because the world behind the gates has been destroyed.

Agnon is a decidedly *sentimental* writer (in Schiller's sense of the term), but one who uses the literary stratagems of naive writers. The contrast between naive literary stratagems and modern or sentimental content is the principal source of Agnon's irony. It is also a formal expression of the contrast between revolution and tradition that is implicit in Agnon's work—the style represents the tradition, and the content embodies the revolution. From another point of view, it could be said that Agnon combines sophisticated mimetic manipulation with textual simplicity. However, the phenomenon of parodic intertextuality creates an ironic subtext that prevents the attentive reader from being seduced by the facade of textual simplicity.

Agnon was acutely aware of the pathetic fallacy typical of modern Hebrew literature in the nineteenth century and at the beginning of the twentieth, in the sense that the emotional-pathetic impact was more important than was the "showing" of human situations. He knew that the young Czaczkes (Agnon's family name), who was close to Maane (a sentimental, pathetic poet of early Zionism), was trammeled by that pathetic fallacy and neglected to measure out his words with precision. Agnon's first stories written between 1908 and 1913 in the Land of Israel ("Miryam's Well," "Sister," and "Nights") were emotionally overwrought, and their excesses exemplify the "main trouble of modern Hebrew literature," which, according to Agnon, was *moved* before it *saw*.

Agnon believed that to descend from romantic pathos the writer must pass through the seven circles of realism. (Was this Brenner's influence?) According to Agnon, what set his course toward the artistic ideal was an unmediated approach to the low mimetic mode. When romance was passed through the fire—or ice—of realism, it shed the dross of pathos and was restored to the classical formula, which Agnon viewed as the closest to perfection.

By returning to classicism, Agnon sought to "show" rather than be moved by what he saw and to arouse emotions in the reader instead of being moved as a writer. He tried to follow what he took to be the creative process typical of traditional literature: first, the world must be made real—that is, a world in which, retrospectively, emotional content was inherent. In approaching the real, Agnon strove to concretize experience, which is at first naked and disintegrated. An artistic consciousness that demanded concretization and the restrained use of the so-called holy letters guided him in shaping his works. Agnon's poetic attitude is entirely different from that of the romantics, as expressed in the essays and writings of Berdyczewski.

That attitude implies a constant struggle to give classical, or balanced, form to romantic, realistic, and modern contents. In Agnon's story "The Tale of the Scribe," he writes that the scribe (the writer of religious parchments) "must be like a man who stands in icy water on a snowy day"[7] before setting to work.

By overcoming the pathetic fallacy, Agnon attained breadth and power of significance in his works. A sentimental work transmits an unambiguous emotional message. Hence the development from the sentimental to the visual mode is also the development from a single level of meaning to multiple meanings and from "readerly" texts to texts that become increasingly "writerly." While Agnon himself never advanced such a theory in his writings, he applied it effectively in his fiction.

Development: Czaczkes in Buczacz and Agnon in the Land of Israel

The poems and stories published by Shmuel Yosef Czaczkes in Hebrew and Yiddish in Buczacz before moving to the Land of Israel (or, as the critic Arnold Band writes, by "Agnon before he was Agnon")[8] are not important. They are written mainly in a pseudonaturalistic style similar to Brenner's first stories. Only here and there is the power of the future master evident.

The early stories were published in *Hamitspeh* in 1906 under the general title of *Types*. These include "The Landlord," "The Light of the Torah," "The Broken Plate," and "The Daughter's Trouble." These stories describe the troubled lives of humble figures: Feibush-Mendl, the teacher who, for his whole life, wanted only to attain a roof over his head; Asher-Borukh, who learns Torah from smugglers; Hayml, who dreams about cantorial art and breaks his plate; and Hirshl, who was snatched from his father-in-law's table.

Another story, "The Letter," also published in *Hamitspeh* in 1906, is similar to Agnon's other early stories and was inspired by the tragicomic epistolary novels of Shalom Aleichem (1859–1916) and Isaac Leib Peretz (1852–1915). In "The Letter," the widow of Moyshe-Aharon the tailor writes to her son and recounts her sorrows to him in detail. Other stories of that period, such as "Avrum Laybush and His Sons" and "The Dealer in Flesh," both published in *Hamitspeh* in 1905, and "The Story of a King and a Queen," published in *Hamitspeh* in 1906, are all populated by characters whose lives are miserable—having been defeated by the irony of fate. Avrum Laybush has two sons, one is studious and the other is an artisan. The first, of whom Avrum is proud, leaves the straight way; the second, for whom he has contempt, supports him in his old age. The main character in "The Dealer in Flesh" consecrates his harlot's pay to the Torah. In "The Story of a King and a Queen," Malka (meaning queen), who is a servant, has a child by her husband who has fled overseas. When the husband returns they live together happily, whereas Malka's masters have no peace in their home. (There is a close connection between this story and one by Shalom Aleichem.)

Other stories, such as "At the End of Autumn" or "Present," both published in *Ramat Hamitspeh* in 1907, are social tales in pre-Agnon style, containing nothing of the writer's later style. Only a few stories, such as "The Lantern," published in *Haet* in 1907, or "Toytentants" (Dance of death),[9] contain some of the romantic elements typical of the later Agnon. "The Lantern" is the germ of the later Hebrew story "The Dance of Death." The lantern witnesses a nobleman abducting a bride on her wedding day; it shines on night watchmen, on perpetual scholars, and on those who mourn for the destruction of the Temple. They all depart, leaving only the young poet. The lantern collapses because the poet leans on it in a time of pain and suffering. "Toytentants" is the romantic, sentimental source of the later Hebrew story "The Tale of the Scribe," published in 1919, and appears in another version in "Miryam's Well," published in 1909.

As a young man Agnon was closer in his Hebrew writings to Peretz and Shalom Aleichem than to Brenner, Shofman, and Berkowitz, who also began publishing at that time. One might almost say that he was merely a marginal epigone in Hebrew and Yiddish literature. It was only upon his arrival in the Land of Israel that he took the huge leap that transformed him into one of the greatest of writers. That was the result of two works: "Agunot: A Tale" and "And the Crooked Shall Be Made Straight."

Even "Sedarim,"* a medley of stories; "Shlomo Yakov's Bed" ("Ha-Seder"), published in *Hatsefira* in 1913; and "Yakov-Nahum's Dream," published in *Yizreel* in 1913, are not particularly original, being derived from the works of Shalom Aleichem. Similarly, Agnon's stories of the Second Aliya are close in subject matter, structure, and style to the other writers of that generation. For example, see Arieh Yaffe's "Tirtsa," "The Sephardic Woman," and "Tsionia"; Levi Aryeh Arieli-Orlof's "Pale Heinrich" and "Young Bunya"; and Aharon Reuveni's "In the Thick" and "Miniatures." Agnon's stories describe the flirtatious loves of alienated immigrants in the Land of Israel. Most of the stories are written in an impressionistic style, and they were changed progressively only after Agnon went back and reworked them both in the Land of Israel and in Germany, using "And the Crooked Shall Be Made Straight" as his yardstick.

Some of these early stories are the kernels of later ones. "Sheepfolds" (1910) precedes "And the Crooked Shall Be Made Straight" (1912); "Sister" (1910) is the kernel of "Betrothed" (1943); and "Miryam's Well" (1909) contains "The Tale of the Scribe" (1919), "Nights" (1913), and *Only Yesterday* (1945). "Yakov-Nahum's Dream" (1913) became

---

* The word *sedarim* is the plural of *seder*, which is the feast held on the first evening of Passover.

"Orphan and Widow" (1922), and "Tishrei" (1912) grew into "The Hill of Sand" (1920). The medley of stories entitled "Sedarim" (1913) was incorporated into *The Bridal Canopy* (1931). With the exception of two stories, "Agunot: A Tale" and "And the Crooked Shall Be Made Straight," Agnon's first sojourn in the Land of Israel was preparatory in nature. During that time he involved himself in experiments and experiences that paved the way for his later writings. His self-image had not yet been consolidated. However, in contrast to his Buczacz period, signs of his talent are in evidence; and his works transcend the style of the time.

Development: Agnon in Germany and in the Land of Israel

In 1912 Agnon left for Germany, where he married Esther, née Marx, and his two children were born. The German Jews were fond of him. Some of his stories were published in German translation (for example, "The Tale of the Scribe")[10] even before their appearance in Hebrew. A group of Hebrew writers established a kind of sanctuary in Bad Homburg.[11] Agnon also gained the financial support of the German-Jewish philanthropist Salman Schocken. This support allowed him to devote himself entirely to literature.[12] From the time of his stay in Germany, his work both solidified and became more varied, so that it can no longer be divided clearly into periods. One type of writing appears immediately after another, making it impossible to divide diachronically the various types of writing.

After his German sojourn, Agnon published folk tales and realistic love stories, such as "The Rejected" (in 1919, with passages called "The Ascension of the Soul" published in 1909); "The Tale of Rabbi Gadiel, the Infant" (1920); "The Hill of Sand" (1920, a reworking of "Tishrei"); and "Ovadia the Cripple" (1921). He also wrote satires, such as "Of Our Young People and Our Elders" (1920), and Gothic, balladic stories, such as "The Black Bridal Canopy" (1913), which appeared in later versions as "The Lovers' Canopy" (1922) and "The Dance of Death" (1919).

During this time his novel, *The Bridal Canopy*, was also taking shape. The first version came out in 1919 in the American magazine *Miklat*. Several stories that were later placed in the second version of the novel appeared during the 1920s. In 1931 the entire novel was published; in 1953 a second, expanded edition came out. Agnon's return in 1924 to the Land of Israel, now Mandate Palestine, led to no substantial change in his way of writing, although in the 1930s a turning point is evident. From 1932 on, Agnon began publishing *The Book of Deeds*, a collection comprised of nonrealistic stories that do away with the dimensions of time and place and reveal the unsettled and unconscious world of the believer. Here is a technical innovation, although not entirely so, for we find the seeds of this pattern as early as "And the Crooked Shall Be Made Straight."

While Agnon continued to write in the realistic tradition, he also published surrealistic stories, such as "A Whole Loaf" and "Metamorphosis," both of which were published in 1933. During the 1930s, the major novels also took shape. Some appeared in full, without preliminary versions, such as *A*

Simple Story (1935). Others, such as *Only Yesterday,* which was published in its entirety in 1945, had appeared earlier in parts ("Rabbi Grunem 'May Deliverance Come,' " in 1931, and "Yitzhak's Beginnings," in 1934) and were gradually knit together. At the end of the decade, Agnon's masterpiece, *A Guest for the Night* (1939), appeared.

Throughout the 1930s and 1940s, stories of various kinds continued to appear. There were legends, such as "The Pipe of My Grandfather—On Him Be Peace" (1941); love stories, such as "The Doctor's Divorce" (1941); modernistic stories, such as "The Orchestra" (1946); and decidedly realistic stories, such as "Between Two Cities" (1946). The same trend continued in the 1950s and 1960s. Along with chronicles about his native town—which were collected posthumously in 1973 in *A City and the Fullness Thereof*—and parts of the novel *Shira,* also published posthumously in 1971, more complex modern stories began to appear. These include "Edo and Enam" (1950), "The Overcoat" (1950), "Forevermore" (1954), and "Footstool and Throne" (1958).

Since Agnon's death additional collections have been published, including writing previously published at least in part, such as "Footstool and Throne," *Within the Wall,* and the lion's share of his stories of Buczacz in *A City and the Fullness Thereof.* Works that had remained in manuscript form have also since been published, such as *In Mr. Lublin's Store* (1975); *Opening Remarks* (1977); and *The History of Our Houses* (1979). Some of the posthumous publications show Agnon at his best, such as several of the stories in *A City and the Fullness Thereof,* whereas he had not managed to put the finishing touches on others or else they were not sufficiently formed, such as sections of *Opening Remarks*.

The individual stories and types of writing described here are in most cases merely names for the reader who is not well versed in Hebrew literature and in Agnon's works in particular. I mention them here in order to emphasize the variety of his writings and his development. One does not find clear diachronic progress in Agnon's work, and it would be difficult to claim that he began as a traditional writer and ended up as a modern one.

As I shall discuss later, interesting developments took place in Agnon's style that changed the stylistic character of the work and its messages. However, from the point of view of genre, these developments are less extreme than one might think. Modern elements are found in Agnon's works from the start. "Agunot: A Tale" and "And the Crooked Shall Be Made Straight" are no less modern than the stories in *The Book of Deeds*. In Agnon's first stories, the inner revolution that destroys the image of the traditional world is already in evidence. Under Agnon's traditional guise, both true and apparent revolutions take place. In "Agunot," two couples marry because of the pressure of the Jewish society around them, and one of the marriages ends in divorce. Jewish society becomes a source of abandonment, the deprivation of interpersonal happiness. This ingenuous tale reveals an existential chasm, which has general meaning because the author indicates that his intention is not to describe one particular situation but rather an underlying condition.

This is also the case in "And the Crooked Shall Be Made

Straight" where the social situation leads to a violation of Jewish law (a woman marries a man and bears him a son while her first husband, from whom she is not divorced, is still living), indicating the precariousness of society. The society in the story trusts in miracles, which will not take place, and depends on a welfare system that does not function properly. Agnon's traditional literary style, taken from Hassidic and pious literature, once again conceals the tottering foundations of society's existence.

Early in Agnon's career the inner tensions of the depicted society were hidden, implicit, and concealed both thematically and formally; but these tensions gradually became more evident both in his thematics and in his increasing use of modern surrealistic techniques. What had been hidden and implicit in Agnon's writings completed during his first years in the Land of Israel became more open during the time he spent in Germany. The deep modern structure of his fiction became evident during the 1930s in *The Book of Deeds.* In the 1940s and 1950s the author achieved a new synthesis, and the revolutionary element is once again well hidden beneath the stylistic camouflage (see "The Overcoat," "Edo and Enam," and "Forevermore").

Agnon's first stories and novels (until the mid-1930s) seem to be more unequivocal and direct and seem to be open to "readerly" interpretations. However, a second look shows that they are as ambiguous and multivalent—in other words, as "writerly"—as the later stories and novels. The only change was one of technique. From the mid-1930s on, especially in the stories collected in *The Book of Deeds,* the multiple meanings of Agnon's texts became more overt. Paradoxically, the modern surrealistic technique made the demand for "writerly" interpretations more evident but did not, in fact, deepen or enrich the complex meanings of these stories.

Agnon, a supremely Hebraic writer, has been remarkably successful in translation. In 1910 Ernst Mueller translated "Agunot: A Tale" into German.[13] Since then, Agnon has been translated into almost every European language. Agnon's works have been translated into English, French, Italian, Yiddish, Spanish, Swedish, Turkish, Dutch, Danish, Norwegian, Finnish, Hungarian, Japanese, Russian, and Arabic. A particularly strong impression was made by Max Strauss's 1918 German translation of "And the Crooked Shall Be Made Straight," which helped to introduce Agnon to young German Jews. As noted previously, "The Tale of the Scribe" was actually translated into German prior to its publication in Hebrew. Unfortunately, reading Agnon's works in translation precludes savoring their full flavor, for Agnon's greatness as a writer depends to a large extent on the intertextual force of his Hebrew style.

Development: Inner Development in Form and Style

After an account of Agnon's outer development, it is important to discuss the inner changes that took place in Agnon's work from his Buczacz days to his years of artistic maturity in Germany. One may trace that development by comparing versions of stories first written in Buczacz or the Land of Israel with later ones composed in Germany. "Tishrei," "The Hill of Sand," "Miryam's Well," and "The Tale of the Scribe" could all exemplify Agnon's metamorphoses from a "readerly," pseudorealistic writer to an emotional, neoromantic writer and, ultimately, to a "writerly" author with a restrained and moderate style of his own—a "revolutionary traditionalist."

I shall, however, begin my comparison with an early story, "The Broken Plate," first written in Buczacz and published in *Hamitspeh* in 1906 (the Yiddish version, "Der Tserbrokhener Teler," appeared four months earlier in *Der Juedische Wecker* in 1906). The second version, "Yakov-Nahum's Dream," was published in 1913 in the Land of Israel in the publication *Yezreel.* The third version, "Orphan and Widow," appeared in 1923 in Germany in *Rimon.*

These three versions mark the three stages in the development of Agnon's narrative art. What they all have in common is the character of an unfortunate, fatherless boy. Aside from that subject, the content changes from version to version. The differences are expressed first in the titles. In the first version, the broken plate holds the reader's attention. The story is an anecdote in which there is no central character. The most important element is the development leading to the breaking of the plate, which rouses the boy Hayim from his dreams. The second version, "Yakov-Nahum's Dream," centers on the character of Yakov-Nahum. In this version, the anecdotal point has become secondary to the psychological description of the dreamer. The emphasis has shifted from the story—a dream and an awakening—to the explanation of the dream. The author asks, What made Yakov-Nahum daydream? What are the qualities of his reveries? What is their erotic, social, and personal cause? The story offers answers to these questions. In the third version, the protagonist's individuality is suppressed. "Orphan and Widow" describes neither an object nor a unique character but rather a human situation. The vision has become more general; psychological and social causality are de-emphasized; and the author seeks to grasp the human condition.

The changes in the presentation of the central character are revelatory of the development that took place in Agnon's conception of humanity from one version to another. The first version begins:

> When Hayim—a boy of about thirteen, redheaded, with two curly earlocks—came home from synagogue on Friday night to his widowed mother, his brain was very perturbed, his head was full of thoughts, and fiery visions danced in his little head.[14]

This opening sentence is close to the Yiddish version.[15] Agnon does not try, as he did later, to avoid the rather long parenthetical phrase separating the subject from the predicate. That phrase, in apposition modifying the protagonist's name, is meant to present him to the reader, providing information about his age and including two bland synecdoches: the character's red hair and curly earlocks, which neither distinguish him nor represent psychological traits. At most, the sidelocks indicate his social origins. The redness of his hair hints, without any internal justification, at his beauty or erotic charms. (The reader is reminded that King David was a redhead.) The description neither advances the plot nor creates assumptions that will later be confirmed or refuted. The author, whose intention is to write an anecdote, uses the character only to reach his punch line, and the descriptive details detract rather than contribute.

The picture is entirely different in the description of the second boy, Yakov-Nahum, at the beginning of "Yakov-Nahum's Dream":

Yakov-Nahum is a sickly, weak child. His body is scrawny and his shoulders, stooped and slender. But whoever sees him is not indignant, perish the thought, at the Creator for creating him that way, nor does he wrap himself in pity at the boy's fate, as is customary when seeing a frail and infirm creature like him, but rather one shakes one's head and continues on one's way, saying to oneself: "The Holy One, Blessed be He, was charitable in creating him thus, for if his body were not scrawny and his shoulders slender, his legs could not carry him. For even now, with his body as it is, how hard it is for his legs to bear him." [16]

The author no longer limits himself to the facts, adding a few synecdoches to make the character's age and social origin clear. In this passage Agnon opens with a declarative sentence defining the figure with parallel expressions indicating characteristics that are likely to affect the child's fate. The physical description has a psychological function here, in contrast to the first description, which does not go beyond identifying traits. After introducing the child, the author presents a new character: "whoever sees him," the observer who views the child from outside, relates to him, and estimates the fate in store for him. The observer is an ironic, cruel figure whose function is to thwart the reader's pity for the frail cripple. The first sentence and the words about the anonymous observer create an ironic relation toward the boy, toward the observer himself, and, to some extent, toward fate. The author links body and fate, but he is not willing to arouse the reader's sympathy for the unfortunate boy or allow the reader to identify with him. The viewer is a rather clumsy stratagem for regulating the ironic attitude.

Parts of the following passage from "Orphan and Widow" also appear in "Yakov-Nahum's Dream," but they appear later in the story to describe the character's conduct. However, what is subordinate in the earlier story performs a primary task in the later one. This is how the character is presented in the later story:

The orphaned son of a widow was in our city. His body was like an ant's, and his legs were like two toothpicks. All winter long he would be shut up in the house. A large High Holiday prayer book was in the house, it was his mother's and had been his mother's mother's before her, and he used to read the story about Rabbi Amnon in it. Sometimes he would take an apron and cover his head like a cantor and sing the Yom Kippur hymns by Rabbi Amnon, "Let Us Affirm" and "Behold I Am Like Clay." Once a day a tutor would come and teach him some Bible.[17]

Here the characterization is different from those in earlier versions. At first the hero has no name; only toward the end does the reader learn that his name is Yakov. The narrator defines him tautologically as "the orphaned son of a widow." He also localizes Yakov in a time and place known to the narrator. In contrast to the objectivity of the earlier version ("when Hayim . . . came home"; "Yakov-Nahum is a sickly, weak child"), in "Orphan and Widow" the character is presented through the testimony of the city chronicler who observes from a distance. The tautology and remote point of view fulfill the same ironic role as does the previous description of the observer. The narrator then uses two images to describe the figure: "like an ant's" and "like two toothpicks." The purpose of these two images is to illustrate the character's weakness and helplessness. In contrast to the description in "Yakov-Nahum's Dream," the synecdochic image—based on comic similes—rather than arousing sympathy for the character evokes a slightly derisive attitude. The narrator tries to arouse mixed emotions regarding his character and tries to control the reader's reaction to the main character by implanting within the body of the characterization stimuli for ambiguous emotional reactions.

In the course of the story we learn about the character's habits. That he remains secluded in his mother's house and reads the prayer book are presented in a rather ironic fashion, which is heightened by the repeated use of the verb *to be* and the possessive "mother's." Later, the character is presented as a kind of Rabbi Amnon in miniature who reads about the martyred author of the hymn "Let Us Affirm." Legend has it that Rabbi Amnon composed the hymn after his body was cruelly mutilated by the Crusaders and that he died in the synagogue after reciting it. Both of the hymns for the High Holy Days treat the insignificance of man and the acceptance of judgment, and they obviously are particularly meaningful to a child whose body is like an ant's. However, that meaning is undermined by the end of the passage, which diminishes the force of the earlier words by introducing the tutor. Thus, this passage produces complex parodic parallels and tensions between the orphaned son of a widow and Rabbi Amnon, the author of hymns. The character who tries to raise his voice in song like a cantor is half ridiculous, half pathetic; he is a kind of "modern" version of Rabbi Amnon.

The reference to Rabbi Amnon, a medieval martyr, also ties the figure into the archetypal cycle of suffering, martyrdom, and redemption—thus, transcending the concrete figure. The boy's anonymity reinforces the tension with that cycle, as does the metaphorical characterization, which does not give the figure distinguishing features but rather a generalized image. The connection with Rabbi Amnon in this version is far more vital and significant than is the connection in the earlier version. There too the narrator makes reference to Rabbi Amnon, but the interaction between figure and archetype is robbed of the psychological, sentimental interpretation of Yakov-Nahum's relationship to him:

He would read the story of Rabbi Amnon in the Yiddish commentary and bend his soul to him and his fate. His eyes too flowed with tears like the dew of autumn upon the withered leaves, and his soul was in a turmoil within him. [18]

The version published in *Yezreel* presents the actual relationship of a pathetic figure to a mythical one. By contrast, in the final version the reciprocal relations are between an anonymous figure, still lacking any particularity, and a mythical one. The portrayal in the final version gives far greater importance to the association of the figure with Rabbi Amnon than does the earlier one. The figure is no longer realistic but rather stands for something beyond particularity; we are no longer interested in the character's motivation but in the principle that the character represents through his actions. That is to say, it was only during Agnon's third stage—during his stay in Germany—that he found his unique way of creating a character that possesses simultaneously an actual dimension and a symbolic one.[19]

Substantial stylistic changes took place from one version to another. Without exaggeration one can state that in the first version signs of Yiddish are still evident, and the text reads like a free translation of the Yiddish. In the second version, the typical features of Agnon's style are still missing: the punctuation is heavy-handed; the sentences are complicated; the vocabulary lacks any clear stylistic direction; and the imagery is cumbersome. Statistical analysis shows that the number of "rational," hypotactic structures in "Yakov-Nahum's Dream" is far greater than in "Orphan and Widow," thus creating the impression that the world portrayed in the story is more fragmented than unified.

It is also interesting to note the lexical changes between the second and third versions. In "Yakov-Nahum's Dream," Agnon wrote:

Morning after morning his mother would prepare a cup of chicory and some black bread for him, cut up two or three half-apples, and, after removing the rotten parts, polish them nicely. They were for the noon meal, then she left the house, sighing, going out to work.[20]

But in "Orphan and Widow," he wrote:

In the morning before the widow went out to the market she would give him a cup of chicory and some coarse bread and half an apple from which she removed the rot.[21]

The most evident changes in vocabulary are the replacement of "morning after morning" *(baboker baboker)*[22] by "in the morning"; "rotten parts" becomes "rot";[23] "black bread" becomes "coarse bread";[24] and the "two or three half-apples" become "half an apple."[25]

With the exception of the first change, all the others come from rabbinical Hebrew. The author replaced those terms that appeared in rabbinical Hebrew, but no longer had its special character, with expressions of a far more stylized character. Conversely, Agnon purposely forwent the biblical connotation of *baboker baboker* and its connection with manna, which is unnecessary in the context of the story and detracts more than it contributes. The formulaic expressions play a role similar to that of the rhetorical phrasing of the sentences. The world appears to be more consolidated, more balanced, and more distant. Agnon removed the fragmentary, emotional quality of things found in the earlier version. Rhetorical balance and formulaic consolidation are a sign of the third stage of the artist's development.

Having discussed the style, let us turn our attention to the changes in the overall structure. In "Orphan and Widow," several motifs have disappeared and others occupy a different place in the structure. For example, the erotic element has disappeared entirely—the orphan's heart no longer yearns for his "Eve." The character's ambition for social status (that of a cantor) is also diminished. A change has also taken place in the mythic figure of Rabbi Amnon and in the importance of the orphan's prayer with the dead. In "Yakov-Nahum's Dream," Rabbi Barukh intones the sabbath hymn "Come, Beloved," and the chorus responds. However, the cantor does not recure later as a motif. In "Orphan and Widow," the motif of the verses sung to the Lord of the Universe by the orphan returns when he prays with the dead, and his mother hears him through the locked gates of the synagogue. "Yakov-Nahum's Dream" ends with an ironic awakening; whereas the final, revised version of "Orphan and Widow," published in *Rimon,* ends this way:

> She stood and peeked through the hole and began whimpering and crying out, "Lord of the Universe, there he is, standing among the dead, there he is on the pulpit, wrapped in a prayer shawl." At that moment the woman's legs gave way, and her heart was shaken. The voice, Yakov's voice, called out melodiously, "Too long hast thou sat in the vale of tears, and He shall have mercy upon thee." Then that woman's heart filled with joy, and her two ears pricked up to hear her son's voice, as he stood in the house of God and sang, "Redemption is near to my soul." [26]

Various references to aspects of Jewish culture that in the earlier contexts were transmitted through psychological explanations and sentimental images here receive new power. In this version, Rabbi Amnon is incomparably more important. [27] Although the beginning of the story of Rabbi Amnon —which describes his martyrdom by having his limbs cut off—is inappropriate to the story of the orphan, the end—"when he finished that entire sanctification he departed and disappeared and was no more, for the Lord took him" [28] —does apply. The metaphor implies that the orphan is a miniature version of Rabbi Amnon, becoming what he does without having to undergo the heroic trial.

Both the end of the story and the middle part are studded

with verses from the hymn "Go, Beloved," which is repeated by Rabbi Barukh, the cantor, and the orphan. That hymn, written by a Safed kabbalist, has received various mystical interpretations. The interpretations in *Etz Yosef* and *Anaf Yosef* are generally accepted, tying the hymn to the relationship between God and the Divine Presence, on the one hand, and exile and redemption, on the other.

Moreover, the story of a boy who prays with the dead is found in the *Sefer Hassidim*,[29] and it was also a familiar folk belief. In fact, the story is filled with references to Jewish customs of the past, which expands the meaning of the story and no longer allows the reader to interpret the story simply as a psychological story about frustration, art, and eros.

Toward the end of the story, the author spreads a thick net of references to biblical verse: "the child is no more" (Gen. 37:30, in reference to Joseph); "Yakov, my son, Yakov, my son" (an echo of David's mourning for Absalom) (2 Sam. 19:1 and 19:5 [18:33 and 19:4 in Christian translations]); "let me hear your voice" (Song of Songs 2:14); and "the voice is the voice of Yakov" (Gen. 26:22). These biblical resonances and others, which are clearly evident to the Hebrew reader, increase the story's depth, obliging the reader to pay attention to a latent and intricate text. The orphaned son of the widow, lacking vital power, is a nonheroic metamorphosis of Rabbi Amnon and demands an explanation. The martyred rabbi justified his fate. The boy, however, remains in this world as someone abandoned by his father in heaven; he is a grotesque figure, wandering about in the lower realms like a withered limb.

The development of the story is connected with yearnings

for redemption that go unrequited. The cantor chants a song of longing, but the orphan cannot be redeemed in this world. Therefore, he joins the dead. The verses "Too long hast thou dwelled in the vale of tears" and "Redemption nears my soul," from the mystical sabbath song "Go, Beloved," raise that polarity to the level of the grotesque. Only someone who prays with the dead will be gathered up with them and find redemption from his exile in death. Therefore, what is said about the widow, that her "heart was filled with joy," is astounding. The exaltation of a person's soul when "his body is like an ant's and his legs are like two toothpicks" is extraordinarily grotesque.

The latent text of the story suggests, in a grotesque fashion, the orphaned state of the Jewish people—"like orphans were we with no father" (Lam. 5:3)—and the widowhood of the Congregation of Israel. However, the latent text does not take the place of the explicit one. On the explicit level, the reader encounters a grotesque version of Rabbi Amnon. The orphan's soul pines for his father, and that yearning, audible in the hymn "Go, Beloved," draws him to his death. In the language of Freudian psychoanalysis, we would say we are dealing with a person whose libido has been crushed and stifled and who finds redemption in the realm of thanatos. This is the cruel story of someone who desires death because he is not fit for or worthy of life.

"Yakov-Nahum's Dream" was transformed from an explicit, realistic, "readerly" story to a symbolic, "writerly" one and from a psychological story to a mythical one. The narrator gives up sentimentality and concentrates on the dominant motifs (Rabbi Amnon, "Go, Beloved," and the prayer of the dead), consolidating and stylizing them to produce a work about the basic Jewish condition, which can be interpreted in many different ways. The contribution of style to the metamorphoses undergone by this story is indeed great. The style creates the distance and balance that give the story's structure the monumentality necessary for a mythical interpretation.

Hence, we find that Agnon constantly changed—from a pseudorealistic author to a romantic, and from a romantic to a metapsychological, or mythic, writer. While the real and psychological factors that appear in the first stages of his writing are present in the later stages, they are shunted from the foreground to the background. This process is not one of exchanging one style for another but rather the reconfiguration of elements. The realistic and the romantic-psychological elements move to the background, while the mythic and metapsychological elements advance to the foreground. Although no extreme thematic changes take place, Agnon's treatment of the subjects is deepened and their significance is altered, since the shift in the formal configuration changes the depth and breadth of their meaning. The stories have been opened up to multivalent, "writerly" interpretations. That change takes place in the constant revisions of older works, as well as in works published since the 1920s.

Reception

A writer as varied and multifaceted as Agnon is not merely himself; he is also what generations of readers have taken him to be. Like most scholars who attempt to examine a writer's reception, I have, to my regret, no other evidence regarding the author's reception than the way in which he was received at various stages by the critics and by his primary reading public, which consists of readers of Hebrew. At various stages of Agnon's development, different and limited aspects of his work were discovered. Only a few critics, mainly Yosef Hayim Brenner, recognized from the beginning Agnon's full powers. Agnon's reception generally produced a rather distorted picture of him as a writer. The first critics viewed him as a naive and folkloristic writer, although he never was. Later critics discovered the sophisticated, demonic, and ironic aspects of his work. These critics sometimes set aside the naive mask, which was not merely camouflage but was also a part of Agnon's complex literary persona.

The following account seeks to describe the way Agnon was received during the sixty years of his literary career, as well as since his death. Agnon entered upon the stage of literature at a time when it was concerned with the struggle between the writers who adhered to a formalized, traditional style and the writers who broke with that formula and rebelled against it by depicting a new deracinated hero. Criticism was defined in terms of the traditional Odessa style (identified with Mendele Mokher Seforim), as opposed to the more romantic and fragmented Warsaw style (identified with Peretz), and in terms of literature that was sometimes semidocumentary, as opposed to literature that was freed from the bonds of immediate realism. When Agnon's first works were published, they were read in the context of the conventions of his generation. His detractors argued that his works were anchored in conventions that they despised. (Berdyczewski, for example, called him a folkloristic imitator.)[30]

Yeruham Fishel Lachover (1883–1947) misunderstood Agnon's uniqueness, believing it derived from Agnon's need to reaffirm the traditional lineage, beginning with Bialik and continuing through Berdyczewski. Lachover linked Agnon "to the eternal source of our soul of souls, to things which, in any case, have existed for centuries and which cannot but be preserved by us, within us, for centuries to come."[31] According to Lachover, "And the Crooked Shall Be Made Straight" confirms Agnon's affinity with the treasures of Judaism, and he interpreted it (as opposed to "Agunot: A Tale") as "another kind of love, not the love of a lad for a lass, but devotion between a husband and his wife."[32] Another anonymous critic believed that the story was merely "a charming story in the pleasing style of Mendele Mokher Seforim." But he ultimately rejected the story because it does not affirm the "values of Judaism."[33] This critic voiced a complaint similar to Lachover's, although his interpretation of the story was different.

Jacob Fichman (1881–1958) praised "Agunot: A Tale" but took exception to what is most original in it:

The most poetical and best work in *Ha-Omer* * is "Agunot: A Tale" by Sh. Y. Agnon. That elegant work is written in the style of the folktales found in Hassidic literature. However that style is not unified and harmonious throughout. Modern lines creep into the broken Hassidic style, which is all hints and secrets, and that does great damage to the unity of the work.[34]

---

*A Hebrew periodical published in the Land of Israel in the early years of this century.

Among those who welcomed Agnon, only Brenner understood that the power of Agnon's work is to be found in the
implicit contradiction between the innovations it introduced
and the literary tradition of Berdyczewski and Rabbi Nachman
of Bratslav. Brenner was extravagant in his praise of "Agunot:
A Tale" because "the element of the Land of Israel, in the
technical sense of that term, does not occupy an important
place at all." [35] That is to say, it is a story from the Land of
Israel that broke through the limitations of immediate reality
and reached "the mystic desertion between loving souls." This
was in contrast to the legends of Berdyczewski—"in this
legend of life there are no miracles or supernatural things." [36]

Brenner had an intuitive grasp of the ambivalence of "Agunot:
A Tale," which is simultaneously mystical and realistic. Because of that ambivalence, the story overcomes the boundaries
of the literary tradition, breaks through the limitations of
Agnon's generation, and tears open a curtain upon "new
horizons." [37] It is not surprising that Brenner greeted "Agunot:
A Tale" and "And the Crooked Shall Be Made Straight" with
enthusiasm, while rejecting stories such as "Yakov-Nahum's
Dream," "Tishrei," and "Nights," calling them "sentimental
tear-jerkers" without clear contrasts and subtle meaning. [38]

After Brenner, the critics who have sensed the greatness of
Agnon's oeuvre have tried to accommodate it to the expectations of their generation. Generally, they have attempted to
eliminate the contradictions (Fichman: modernism versus tradition; Brenner: mysticism versus realism), either confirming
or denying that Agnon's works belong to the lineage of Hebrew
literature. In an article full of praise for Agnon and for his
major early stories, including "Agunot: A Tale" and "And the

Crooked Shall Be Made Straight," Shmuel Streit wrote: "Hebraic love, Hebraic sighs, a Hebraic view of life, the vision of a Hebraic heart. Different, a completely different atmosphere from other nations."[39] However, Aharon Abraham Kabak attacked Agnon. According to Kabak, the fact that Agnon wrote "a story about the life of the ultra-religious in the language of the Hassidic books"[40] did not yet give him status in the history of literature. According to this view, Streit had given Agnon more praise than was his due. German critics, including Martin Buber and Fritz Mordechai Kaufmann, reiterated the importance of Agnon because he fulfilled their expectations of an eastern European Jew who drew deeply upon Jewish sources.

Rabbi Eliezer Meir Lipschuetz, a most interesting critic, tried to circumnavigate the contradiction in the works of Agnon:

The life which he depicts is innocent, and, with marvelous ingenuousness, he gave it a name and a memory. Just as the deeds are innocent, so too is the writer and his story. That innocence characterizes him, and I wonder whether there is innocence such as that in our generation among the Jews or other nations. However it can hardly be believed that that innocent man is a great artist, carving out and shaping forms, that everything here is conquest of form and creativity, control over form and style. Life does not burst through here to disturb tranquillity and unity (that was the greatness of Brenner, who did not control his creativity, which ruled him and forced itself upon him, and therefore he did not conquer form). How do innocence and art join together and complement each other here? It is by standing both above the subjects and within them.[41]

In Rabbi Lipschuetz's view, Agnon is a *naive* writer in the sense Schiller gave to that term. Moreover, Agnon is the epitome of naiveté of the writers of his generation. His writing is the embodiment of traditional conventions, and that is his greatness. Lipschuetz tried to resolve the inner contradiction—that is, the place of irony—by arguing that the irony in Agnon's works derives from his naive point of view. The source of the irony, according to Lipschuetz, is not the author's ambivalence but rather the unequivocal standard by which he judges the world and his protagonists:

It is the virtue of irony that it measures its subjects against a great human ideal which is the hidden truth by which one judges warped and twisted, contraries and opposites.[42]

The critics who opposed Agnon, such as David Aryeh Friedman and Aryeh Leib Mintz, also tried to dismantel the inner contradiction. Friedman argued that Agnon is static and monotonous rather than dynamic and innovative:

It would not be too much of a generalization to say that Agnon's world is all of a piece. The white slippers his Jews wear come in only one size. Only one kind of spot is on their clothes, spots of fat and snot. And their life has but one measure, perpetual comfort, a world resting in its mire.[43]

Mintz argued that the elements of Agnon's stories are not integrated but rather appear singly, in exaggerated fashion.[44] In response to *The Bridal Canopy,* the critics frequently spoke of the need to "criticize" the author for his ingenuous plainness of meaning.[45]

It was not until the mid-1930s that the critics began

finding other aspects in Agnon's works. They no longer denied the originality of his contribution, and they tried to elucidate the contradiction in his work from various points of view. Agnon, in the opinion of the new generation of critics, was no longer the naif writer of the past—for better or for worse. Now, he brought out the contribution between past and present, faith and heresy, art and life, and naiveté and irony. Freud's influence and the growing awareness of the crisis in Jewish life expanded critical horizons, bringing readers to a different understanding of Agnon's work—closer to that of his "discoverers," Brenner and Fichman.

Dov Sadan, in his articles "Human Perplexity and Its Metamorphoses" and "Beyond Simplicity" (both in Hebrew), called attention to the ambivalent irony in Agnon's work and to its many strata and inner tensions ("Story Within Story").[46] From another point of view, in 1938 Gustav Krojanker argued that it was the rift between the yearned-for unity and the possibilities of existence that were the true "central problem in Agnon's work."[47] Baruch Kurzweil did more, perhaps, than any other critic to increase Agnon's audience. He created an Agnon that satisfied the expectations of the Israeli intelligentsia of the 1940s.

Following Kurzweil's lead, the intelligentsia, detached from the experience of the past and from the roots of faith, discovered in Agnon an accurate expression of modern man's crisis of faith—the opposition between the demonic and the holy.[48] On the other hand, Meshulam Tochner was among those who argued that the contradiction in Agnon's works is merely an outward manifestation. These critics believed that inwardly Agnon expressed the happy innocence of "pious Hassidim."[49]

In the first sequential account of Agnon's work, Band used the words "nostalgia and nightmare" as the subtitle of his book; thus, he suggested two emotional attitudes by which the reader may understand Agnon's basic life experience, encompassing such contrasting stories as "Tehilla" and "Edo and Enam."[50] David Canaani addressed the social aspect of Agnon's hero. Canaani even tried to describe Agnon in terms borrowed from the deracinated generation of writers of the Diaspora. Like the heroes of Brenner, Gnessin, and Shofman, Agnon's heroes are also uprooted—but in a special way.[51]

It was at a relatively late stage that Agnon was shown to be a revolutionary who took traditional materials and wrote in a traditional style in order to transmit revolutionary messages. Agnon was rediscovered by Dov Sadan and was disseminated by Baruch Kurzweil, but his main acceptance came from the writers and critics of the 1950s. For them, Agnon became the principal modern writer of their generation.

The younger critics sought to alter the balance of interpretation and to dispose of the contradiction within Agnon by emphasizing only a single side of it. Gavriel Moked tried to argue implicitly that Agnon's roots are in existentialism and that he is a faithful exponent of modernism.[52] Hillel Barzel tried to bring Agnon nearer to modern society by comparing him to Kafka, the master of modernism. (Moked also linked Agnon with Kafka.)[53] Shlomo Tsemakh opposed Agnon because of his modernism, preferring the premodern author to the one who emerged in the 1930s: "How and why did it happen that a Hebrew writer who had always written beautiful things just as they are should suddenly turn from his proper course and begin wandering, feeding from a trough other than that of his master?"[54] In Tsemakh's opinion, the root of the evil already is evident in *Only Yesterday*.

In conclusion, the history of Agnon's reception—or the changing ways in which he was read—shows that the essential qualities of his work were not understood at once but were revealed gradually. Nor can one possibly state that all the treasures have been discovered. Much still remains to be done[55] in the area of interpretive descriptions and in the exploitation of critical insights.[56] What stands firm is what the critics Brenner and Fichman discovered from the first: Agnon's work is a mixture of essential contradiction. It is not unequivocally traditional or modern nor realistic or nonrealistic. It contains many things and their opposites as well.

Various methods, including psychoanalytical and mythological criticism as well as various types of New Criticism,[57] have sought to reveal the treasures of Agnon's works. In a general way, one could say that the strength of Agnon's works rests in their thematic, structural, and stylistic unity—the elements that characterize the works from the 1920s onward. Their unity does not restrict their variousness. On the contrary, it reveals oppositions and contradictions that bring together Agnon's entire body of work in its various forms and diverse structures.

The accumulation of contradictory and complementary interpretations seems to be symptomatic, showing that most "readerly" readings of Agnon were actually misreadings and that he always has been a "writerly" author. As in the past and in the present, Agnon will continue to be read, misread, and recontextualized in the foreseeable future.

CHAPTER 3

UNITY AND DIVERSITY

Place and Time

FROM NOW ON, I shall attempt to describe Agnon's work synchronically, as though it had all been produced at the same time. The various influences have been well digested; and a literary unity has emerged, full of variety and constant tensions among its components—the stylistic unity and its variants, the fictional world, the variety of narrative types, and the diverse social classes and ethnic groups depicted. However, we shall also find that interesting changes take place in the development of the plots.

Agnon's diversity derives first from the broad expanse of time and place and the many cultural groups included in his works. Abraham Yacob Brawer notes:

The historical ground of Agnon's fiction extends from 1775 * until 1950. The geographical setting is Galicia from east of Lwow and

---

* That date is actually erroneous, resulting from the faulty deciphering of a date in Hebrew letters in "The Rejected." The correct date is 1815.

north of the River Dneister, especially the city of Buczacz (Szibucz) where the author was born and raised; it includes several places in Germany and its close vicinity, the Land of Israel, Jaffa, Tel Aviv and its surroundings, and Jerusalem.[1]

To a large degree, Agnon's works describe Jewish emigration from eastern to western Europe and to the Land of Israel. He portrayed three geographical areas that he knew well, although each had a different significance in his life. There is no region in its historical depths that he knew better than Galicia. Within the historical area of Galicia, taken as representative of eastern European Jewry, a great revolution took place that brought about the disintegration of the tradition. Referring to the phrase coined by Arnold Band, "nostalgia and nightmare," Galicia was the place where the "nightmare" of decline took place. It is the place for which Agnon's heroes yearn when they think of a historical time before the crisis.

In this regard, Agnon shares affinities with other Hebrew and Yiddish writers of his generation, such as Isaac Dov Berkowitz, Asher Barash, Shalom Aleichem, Israel Joshua Singer, and Isaac Bashevis Singer. However, in contrast to most of the writers of that generation, Agnon also was capable of describing German Jewry from within, both in its place of origin and after immigration to the Land of Israel. However, when contemplating German Jewry he does not find a society distinguished by revolution but a world emptied of tradition.

In contrast to the unambiguous descriptions of German Jewry—devoid of its tradition—the descriptions of the Jews of the Land of Israel are far more complex. From the beginnings of the renewed Jewish settlement of Palestine, tensions had emerged between those who advocated revolution and those who believed in tradition, as reflected in this pioneering song:

> Here in the land of our fathers' delight
> All our hopes will be fulfilled
> Here shall we live and here shall we create
> A life of glory a life of freedom
> *Here the Divine Presence will dwell*
> Here too the language of the Bible will flourish.

Agnon mainly was interested in the line that I have emphasized, following which, as it were, he might have placed a question mark:"Will the Divine Presence dwell here?"

In the Land of Israel Agnon was more familiar with the various elements of the Jewish community than was any other writer of his generation. He portrayed the entire range of Jews in Palestine, from the Russian and Galician immigrants in *Only Yesterday* to the German Jews, the Oriental Jews, and the native-born Jews in *Shira;* from members of the ultra-Orthodox community in Jerusalem to the young pioneers in Jaffa and of the settlements. In all of these areas, the question is asked again and again: was the secular pioneering society capable of living without any connection to Jewish tradition, which draws upon the world of the *shtetl* from which it came?

Agnon's ability to penetrate the worlds of the various settlers makes him without doubt the most important writer in describing the social conflicts and psychological problems accompanying Jewish settlement in Palestine from the beginnings of the Second Aliya, in "The Hill of Sand," through the 1960s, in "The Covering of Blood."

If we pass from geographical extension to historical continuity, we find that Agnon's works treat some of the most important turning points in modern Jewish history. Some of his works (for example, "The Rejected") deal with the early period of Hassidism. Others describe the mid-nineteenth century (*The Bridal Canopy*), the early twentieth (*A Simple Story* and "Of Our Young People and Our Elders"), the First World War ("Until Now" and *In Mr. Lublin's Store*), the period of the Second Aliya in the Land of Israel ("The Hill of Sand," *Only Yesterday*, and "Betrothed"), the history of Buczacz from its origins to the period between the two world wars ("And the Crooked Shall Be Made Straight," *A Guest for the Night,* and *A City and the Fullness Thereof*), and Mandate Palestine before the War of Independence ("Edo and Enam" and *Shira*). It should also be noted that Agnon did not deal with these expanses of time and place as an outsider. He was as involved in the early nineteenth century as he was anchored in the mid-twentieth. The canopy of his writing extends over figures born and raised in eastern Europe and in Germany ("Between Two Cities," "Metamorphosis," and *In Mr. Lublin's Store*), as well as over characters born in the Land of Israel (*Shira*).

Agnon's depiction of time and place is characterized by a shifting angle of vision. Sometimes the setting is described from within, as in "Between Two Cities," and sometimes the setting is treated with a strange sort of counterpoint, in which the observer has a dual status—he is uprooted from one setting and finds himself in a new one, which is revealed to him both from close at hand and from a distance, as in "Agunot: A Tale," "And the Crooked Shall Be Made Straight," and *In Mr. Lublin's Store*. In *Only Yesterday* whenever the hero seems to be involved in his life, the narrator or another secondary figure, such as the dog Balak, comes between the hero and his setting, creating alienation. That contrapuntal point of view causes the hero to observe one setting—in this case, Jaffa—from the point of view of another—the hero's father's home. Later, he sees yet another place—Jerusalem—from the point of view of Jaffa. The dog's walking tour in *Only Yesterday* is Agnon's technique for guiding the reader through a description of the city.

That strange counterpoint also is found in *In Mr. Lublin's Store,* where three points of view interact. The narrator, who is the central character, regards Leipzig from the point of view of Buczacz and the Land of Israel; Mr. Lublin sees Leipzig as a citizen of the city whose roots go back to Buczacz; and Jakob Stern, a resident of Buczacz who appears toward the end of the story, has a particularly acute confrontation with the German city.

Historical time is occasionally depicted contrapuntally as well. The narrator sometimes appears as a chronicler observing Jaffa or Buczacz from the ironic viewpoint of the present (for example, in *Only Yesterday* or in *A City and the Fullness Thereof*). The gap in time is a source of both explicit and implicit irony (like the shifts in the narrative point of view in *The Bridal Canopy*). Thus, it is not sufficient merely to note that Agnon's writings cover both a long period and a broad geographical expanse. It must be emphasized that these extensive circles of time and place were what enabled Agnon to create his characteristic ironic counterpoint.

One Language and Many Tongues

Agnon dwelt upon various settings and times; but he described all of them with his own particular style, which unifies all times and places. The unity of his stylized diction has disturbed literary critics and researchers. As Eliezer Meir Lipschuetz observed:

He learned to speak the language of the day before yesterday's generation. That particular rhetoric—of tales and Biblical exegesis, of legends and prayers, of chronicles and scrolls commemorating catastrophes, of community registers and books of customs—left echoes of its language and its distinctive features in that style, which is Hebraic and vernacular in its origin, the Hebraicness being its vernacularity.[2]

The richness brought with it the varied meanings of Hebrew culture. Like the style of Mendele Mokher Seforim, Agnon's style is based on a symmetrical organization of linguistic patterns—particularly in the use of synonymous expressions and the rhythm of the sentences. However, unlike Mendele Mokher Seforim, Agnon did not create frequent clashes between semantic levels of speech to attain comic effects (biblical diction in contrast with the language of the sages), nor did he always keep to the rhythm of that style. Instead, he imposed an original organization of his own upon the linguistic material. Agnon's diction, constructed by means of the oblique connections between the visible text and the implicit one, creates a reciprocal relationship between the surface and the inner strata, hinting at various cultural sources that expand the meaning of the visible text—whether through parody or by intensification.

In contrast to Mendele Mokher Seforim's style, Agnon's is not of a piece. In keeping with his subject matter, Agnon constantly tried to avoid routine patterns and was always looking for the proper objective correlative. Israel Iser Seidman has dealt with this topic extensively, comparing the biblical style of "In the Prime of Her Life" with the entirely different style of "And the Crooked Shall Be Made Straight," which, according to Seidman, is a "pastiche, mosaic-like style." Seidman also points out the use of various levels of diction: the language of the pious, the language of rabbinical literature, and the language of the Bible. In *The Bridal Canopy,* according to Seidman, the style of the sages is prominent, taking the form of rhymed prose when necessary. But there, too, Agnon used biblical style; and when it suited him, he did not forgo the use of spoken Hebrew mixed with rhymed prose, as in *Only Yesterday.* Seidman has made a detailed examination of the linguistic elements in Agnon's work, concluding that Agnon was not an extreme purist. Agnon used Yiddish calques (bringing him close to the vernacular), sought neologisms, coined his own expressions, and made a home for foreign material.[3]

On the semantic level, Agnon sometimes played with the linguistic and artistic function of the single letter (for example, *'ayin* in the titles of "Ido Ve'Enam" ["Edo and Enam"] and "Ad Olam" ["Forevermore"]), which is partially alliterative and partially a semantic field hinting at the meaning of the work. Hebrew grammatical roots play a similar stylistic and structural role.[4]

Most critics speculate on the role played by the stylized diction in Agnon's work—such as the choice of words, the archaic combined forms, and the like—as well as the balanced rhythm of the syntax. These critics attempt to determine the meaning of that style, which creates distance between the author and his audience. The question is what precisely are the substantive functions of that distance? Hayim Rabin believes that Agnon mainly used a medieval stratum of the language (the Hebrew of the Ashkenazic diaspora) because that language arouses a feeling of archaism in the reader, and the author can thus be said to have been seeking an archaic distance.[5]

Benjamin De Vries addresses the inner literary functions of a language that

is erected like a shield against the danger of foreign and opposing worlds and consciously developed for a specific purpose: to give a precise meaning to what was written through oral expression. That language serves the author as a shield against threatening, violent invasions from the modern world, which cannot be avoided. Clearly his incomparable talent allowed him to attain that fulfillment, but the motivation was identification with the unequivocal positions taken by the rabbis and their goal of creating a precise world, the world of scholarly hair-splitting.[6]

Boaz Shachevitz, who attributes literary significance to the syntactic rhythm (after a statistical analysis of the punctuation), argues that Agnon's syntactic rhythm emphasizes the epic side of his writing, playing down the dramatic and lyrical aspects.[7]

Most scholars concur that the rhythm of Agnon's works

plays an ironic role, creating distance between materials taken from close at hand, that is, modern life, and those taken from far away, as in *The Bridal Canopy*. The extreme use of the style in reference to the past is no different in function from its use regarding the present. (Here, I disagree with the one-sidedness of De Vries.)

Nevertheless, style is without doubt a unifying element in Agnon's works. Despite all of the variants, the fundamental pattern remains in place. The stylized "verse" establishes a kind of balanced norm from which the author can then deviate. Intensity occasions the main deviations; the sentences become exaggeratedly rhythmical and violate the epic tranquillity (in Shachevitz's terms), raising it to lyricism — if the intensification is justified in relation to what is signified — or debasing it to grotesque comedy — if there is not internal justification for the intensification, and a gap is created between the excessive balance and the subject. The following is an example of Agnon's lyric intensity:

I dwell alone all day / Salsavila's steps unheard. / Though I cry, "Salsavila," / she comes not. / Only my voice is heard and never the sound of her feet. / I sit like a man forlorn, and I take my head in my hands / saying, "Salsavila" comes not.[8]

In contrast:

And thus that man, ill starred / Came to the library, where knowledge is stored / and the wisest of wise men are seated learned and for scholarship much feted / editing and restoring phrases / also postulating hypotheses, / writing notes, pen in hand / while tomes before them stand / booklets and notebooks, thicker than thick / growing and multiplying, multiplying and growing.[9]

In neither of these passages does the style create balance and place the narrator or the audience at a distance from the subject. In the first case (for semantic reasons the passage is in biblical Hebrew), the style heightens the emotional content of the passage; in the second (for semantic reasons the Hebrew contains homonyms and excessive balance expressed in rhyme), the style shows the subject in a comic light.

Agnon's style may serve many purposes, but the main function is to have vision quell sentiment by taking an ironic, distant viewpoint. The emotions pass through "ice water on a snowy day," until they are "chilled." That style is what recollects emotions in tranquillity. Like other components of Agnon's writing, in his style there is a constant tension between the solid core and the departures from it. That tension creates the uniqueness of the works as a whole and of individual passages within the works.

In other words, Agnon's oeuvre displays powerful tensions between a homoglossic classical norm and the heteroglossia of genres, themes, and characters. The stylistic norm is coherent and strong. Hence, each and every deviation from it immediately and intensively defamiliarizes the stylistic norm created by the author. That which had seemed to be balanced and coherent is actually deeply diversified and enormously disrupted.

The Structure: Continuity, Parallelism, and Digression

The syntactical and rhetorical pattern characteristic of the tissue of Agnon's style also marks the overall structure of his work. Just as Agnon avoided using everyday, spoken language and instead filtered it and stamped it with the pattern of art, he avoided presenting events in their *Sturm und Drang*. In contrast to Yosef Hayim Brenner, Agnon did not attempt to give the impression of creating "nonfictional" art.

Brenner preferred placing literary works within the framework of memoirs or journals. His intent was to create the effect of a pseudodocumentary literature. The narrator is generally a protagonist or a witness, or else a character who sees to the publication of a manuscript written by someone close to him.

In contrast to Brenner, Agnon tended to use an omniscient narrator, distancing the work from the fictional illusion of "nonfictive" art. The fictional world has its own rules and regulations, completely different from the extraliterary world. The fictional world is convincing in its own right, not because of its similarity to the extraliterary world. The literary connections in Agnon's works are intratextual, intrinsic, and self-referential and are less dependent on extraliterary information than are the works of most of the writers of his generation.

Agnon created an independent literary world that exists as a model standing on its own strength, independent of reality. The power of that model lies in its being so convincing that, despite its intensified fictionality, sometimes the extraliterary world is measured against the fictional model, rather than vice versa. When Agnon presented material from chronicles and used extraliterary materials in his work, he did so in a stylized fashion, so that the chroniclelike materials are swallowed up within the fictive world and lose something of their documentary character. Nevertheless, the power of that fictional world is more convincing, apparently because of its wholeness and its closedness, than the actual world, which resembles a chronicle in every respect. One of the most interesting examples of this quality of Agnon's work is that the *Hebrew Encyclopedia* refers readers to Agnon's *Only Yesterday* for an account of the tribulations of the early construction of Tel Aviv. While such a description is indeed to be found in Agnon's novel, it is extremely stylized and does not pretend to be a pure chronicle. However, the fictive reality is so complete within itself that it is more convincing than the account in any history book based on constant reference to signified reality.[10]

In other words, the rules of art in Agnon's works are imposed on the flow of life. Paradoxically, the result is that life is shown to be more complex and varied in meaning because of the patterns imposed by the artist.

Every literary work displays an equilibrium between linear continuity, on the one hand, and the characters and setting, on the other. The work must both present the sequence of the plot and also view the work as a unity beyond linear continuity. Thus, the reader must actively link up the details that are revealed as points along and beyond a line. The equilibrium within the work brings out connections in the material.

Agnon's works demand spatial readings,[11] for he preferred intratextual connections among various literary phenomena— as motifs—to sequential, linear exposition. As he developed as a writer, Agnon increasingly chose to disrupt the balance between the linear plot and the spatial connections within the structure. At the beginning of his career, in works such as "Agunot: A Tale" and "And the Crooked Shall Be Made Straight," there are tight, complete plots. However, in the late 1930s, after *A Guest for the Night,* stories proliferate where the analogous links become the dominant element. In works published in the 1950s (for example, "Until Now") and post-humously (for example, *Within the Wall, In Mr. Lublin's Store,* and "The Covering of Blood"), linearity declines in importance relative to spatial form. In "Until Now," the structure is based on extremely elliptic connections that are mostly parallel in nature—if related at all. *In Mr. Lublin's Store* presents the space where the store is situated rather than a story with a plot about Mr. Lublin and his relationships with other characters. The message is no longer a recollection of the plot but rather the product of an agglomeration of a number of subplots that all happen in the same fictive space.

The Linear Plot

Can the reader find repeated plot structures in Agnon's works? Is there any connection between the writer's way of organizing the plot and his conception of fate? It seems to me that the plot models of Agnon's early works, such as "Agunot: A Tale," "And the Crooked Shall Be Made Straight," and "The Hill of Sand," do indeed recur in variant forms.

In "Agunot: A Tale" the protagonists, Ben-Uri and Yehezkel, are placed in problematic situations. They flee from their circumstances in the wrong direction because they prefer to accept the norms of society over personal fulfillment. The story becomes entangled when the protagonists are ensnared in a predicament where they must decide, and their release from that predicament discloses the punishment incurred by their decision. In a general sense, that predicament is viewed as the inexorable decree of fate, and the decision is a necessary outcome. The protagonists' punishment appears to be a result of their decision; but, in fact, they are victims of the predicament. The main character is an immigrant in a new land, and his decision only heightens the feeling of alienation that gradually becomes part of the release-punishment.

The stages of becoming ensnared, deciding, and being punished also mark "And the Crooked Shall Be Made Straight." In that story, Menashe Hayim is caught in a situation of decline (because of an impersonal economic crisis), but it seems as though he has resolved to enjoy being caught. His effort to get free of his predicament leads to ever deeper entanglement—a loss of identity—and release comes only indirectly. Menashe Hayim's punishment is the loss of identity and the loss of the purpose of his journey.

In "The Hill of Sand," the hero, trapped in unfamiliar surroundings, is incapable of adapting to the norms of those surroundings and of making true contact with them (for example, in his relations with Yael). The plot thickens with a description of incapacity and impotence. Release comes with the revelation of the impotent person's punishment. The hero has no grip on reality, and his life becomes a kind of hill of sand.

This plot pattern—the predicament, the decision, and the punishment—generally is connected with the figures of immigrants in a new land or with heroes who become alien outsiders in their own world. The plot lines consist of journeys and emigration (in "And the Crooked Shall Be Made Straight," *The Bridal Canopy, Only Yesterday,* and *A Guest for the Night*), or else they are centered on the hero's alienation from his surroundings (in "The Rejected," *A Simple Story, Shira,* and "Edo and Enam"). Moreover, the two plot patterns sometimes combine into one (as in *Only Yesterday*). All the plots are designed to be fleshed out with varied and diverse emotional content—from tragic pathos to comic farce—and with materials from many places and periods.

Some of Agnon's works have what appears to be a plot based on wanderings. The hero drifts from place to place for economic or social reasons. The existential problems generally crop up during his wanderings, and these problems are connected to the primary impetus that compelled him to set out on his path. Thus, Menashe Hayim sets out on his journey because he has lost his fortune and because he cannot cope with his wife. The untoward event takes place because he wishes to acquire property to enable him to return and deal with his wife and to return from a condition of impotence to one of potency. The gap between his desire and his ability brings about his final downfall, and the punishment is his utter hopelessness, which becomes apparent when he discovers that his wife has had a child by another man. Thus, he remains bereft of both wife and property.

Three of Agnon's major novels, *The Bridal Canopy, A Guest for the Night,* and *Only Yesterday,* are all stories of wandering, as are some of the novellas and short stories that will be discussed at greater length elsewhere. Nevertheless, I must emphasize that, along with the dominant plot, there are also other plots, which cannot be subsumed under the main plot type just described. Agnon is far too varied and complex to permit his conception of plot to be contained within a single, basic pattern.

Intratextual Connections: Parallelism

A linear plot is usually schematic; to enrich it, Agnon had to shatter this linear pattern. An example of such a strategy is the technique of parallelism and analogy, by means of which bonds of significance are woven among the characters and among various linguistic phenomena, motifs, and events within the plot. Differences and analogies among the parallel elements deepen the meaning of their interrelations. Of course, this technique was not invented by Agnon. It has been used extensively by some of the giants of world literature, such as Shakespeare and Dostoyevsky,[12] but Agnon placed it in the foreground of several of his works. Thus, he took a technique that other writers had kept in the background and made it dominant.

Parallelism plays an equilibrating role with regard to the aesthetic structure. However, the subject is not distanced but rather deepened. As early as "And the Crooked Shall Be Made Straight," Agnon employed such a stratagem and called the reader's attention to its essence:

Behold and note well that what *happened* to Menashe Hayim *happened* to the beggar [emphasis added], for he drank and became drunk, for after obtaining the letter of recommendation he did not think about money, for in his heart he felt blessed at having found a proclamation of exemption for the future in that he possessed the recommendation of the Sage of Buczacz. [13]

Some of the main ironic passages of the story are created by means of contrastive parallels. See, for example, the conflict between the believing innkeeper and Menashe Hayim, who lacks faith. [14] Even the narrator ironically draws the parallel between them:

By the Lord on High, I did not do that except to show you that the deeds of the fathers are signs of the sons' actions. What happened to the first servants of the Lord could also happen to the latter ones. [15]

The confrontation between Menashe Hayim and the Hassid, who was ordered to steal for a living by the Holy Magid of Kuznicz, "may his memory protect us," is also an ironic parallel. [16] The thief who steals in the name of the rebbe is successful because of the rebbe's blessing. Menashe Hayim fails because his generation is no longer worthy, and in his time miracles no longer take place such as took place in the olden days. These parallels are parodic, emphasizing the contrast between tradition and revolution. The parody is a revolutionary manifestation of the traditional motif; and being its opposite, it is actually a negation of the tradition. The religious miracle, which previously was conditioned on the social circumstances of a society of faith and on true, naive believers, becomes grotesque in the present—where faith is shaken and the foundations of existence have been undermined. These parallels enrich the work since they are based on the figure of the *Doppelgaenger* (the beggar) and on the gap between the traditional plot and the plot in the present.

In *A Guest for the Night*, the number of parallels has grown inestimably. Parallelism has systematically invaded the entire work, interweaving various strands with the main plot line, contradicting it over and over again. Here we have a new configuration of the elements of the novel, which represents a structural revolution throughout the entire work. This was not only an innovation within Agnon's work but was also an important contribution to the European novel.

The parallels in *A Guest for the Night* are not merely between the central plot and the subplots. There are parallels among the various plots, and between them and an additional, implicit plot that takes place in the mythic past, as it were, or in the nation's collective unconscious. Some critics maintain that the central plot in *A Guest for the Night* is that of the forlorn son's return to his decaying hometown.[17] The first parallel is between the plot that recounts the return of the main character (the narrator) and the secondary plots that are centered on a similar subject. Mr. Zommer and his wife were driven from the city during the First World War and have returned to it. That is also true of Daniel Bach and his wife. Yeruham Hofshi Freeman, like the narrator, is also a "guest for the night," for neither has found a place for himself in the Land of Israel—the first because he wished to "establish a temple and built a house" (representing the gap between the ideal and the reality); the second because he has not been absorbed in the Land of Israel. Rabbi Hayim returns from Russia, another land of exile, where he was a prisoner of war. He, too, tries in vain to sink roots. Schuster and his asthmatic wife have returned from Germany. Schuetzling has come back, and his return is secular and cynical: "When a person sees that he is fond of no place in the world, he deceives himself and says he is fond of his hometown."[18] Jacob (Kŭba) Milch returns to bring back a divorced woman, waging a quixotic battle for a life that will never return. Here is a dense texture of analogous parallels between the return of the main character and those of the secondary characters—thus, giving the story additional depth. The First World War is the impersonal force that has trapped the characters. Each protagonist's plot is his struggle for release from entrapment.

In each case, the character's return to the solid world of faith is unsuccessful, as were all the other efforts to return. An entire world is built upon the failure to return. The wheels of time cannot be turned back, and time cannot be vanquished. A major event—the war—created distortions that cannot be repaired.

The main function of the parallelism is to present seemingly unique events as general ones, which are manifest in various forms and embodiments in the characters. The function of the parallelisms is ironic; it offers an ironic counterpoint to every melodramatic event. The parallelism among numerous melodramatic plot lines causes an ironic trivialization of the melodramatic event.

A similar, but less evident, pattern is found in *Only Yesterday*. Here, I will mention only two central parallels: the one between the main character, Yitzhak Kumer, and the dog, Balak, and the one between Yitzhak and Rabinovitz, a secondary character. The first parallel juxtaposes a human being and an animal, with the human representing the individual and the animal symbolizing the demonic, brutish forces of the generation ("the face of the generation is like that of a dog," say the sages). Many critics have noted the parallel development and connection between Yitzhak and Balak, including the horror of reality and the feeling of persecution by an absurd, grotesque power that both of them share. [19] However, I wish to emphasize that this parallel should be viewed not as a unique literary device but as part of the author's repertoire of structural devices.

The second parallel, which greatly expands the social significance of the novel, is between Rabinovitz and Yitzhak Kumer. Yitzhak Kumer abandons Jaffa and ascends to Jerusalem because he does not succeed in establishing roots in the new society and yearns for his father's house. Yitzhak's failure makes us aware of human failure in the dynamic conditions of a society lacking tradition. His second failure derives from his inner bond with his demonic generation (represented by Balak) and the insecure character of Jerusalem's Meah Shearim neighborhood. Thus, he is also unable to gain a foothold in the old society. Parallel to him is Rabinovitz, whose problems are solved on the external level. Rabinovitz leaves the country and returns to it, but now he lives there with a diaspora frame of mind, having become a storekeeper rather than a pioneer.

The technique of analogous parallelism also can be found in a work portraying two structures that are distant from each other yet relate to each other as a tenor to a vehicle or as a symbol to what is symbolized. Two structures of that kind can be combined in a grotesque, unlikely mixture that can be both threatening and ridiculous.

"Pisces," in *A City and the Fullness Thereof*, is a story built on such a principle. The story brings together a man whose name, Fishl Karp, links him to the zodiac sign of Pisces and to a gigantic fish caught by a fisherman and sold to Fishl. Fishl devours things like a fish, and in the end he is as quiet as a fish. The fish swallows things like Fishl, until Fishl is swallowed by the fish rather than the fish winding up in Fishl's stomach. Finally, an artist, Betsalel Moshe, whose name recalls the master craftsman of the Book of Exodus, comes and consummates the grotesque union by drawing a portrait of the fish on Fishl's head phylactery (and the dead fish takes the place of the living Fishl) and by putting the final seal on the macabre union by carving the word *Pisces* on the monument over the grave shared by Fishl and the fish.

Here, the intratextual parallels appear contiguously in space and are brought together by the continuous time line, thus becoming one. In contrast, in *Only Yesterday* the two antonymic parallels are brought together in a final dramatic encounter (when Balak bites Yitzhak Kumer); and unification is produced in the continuity.

In both of these texts, the "reunion" between the divided parallel metaphors—the characters are metaphors for each other—which function as vehicle (the fish and the dog) and tenor (Fishl Karp and Yitzhak Kumer) or as ego and alter ego, leads to a catastrophe for the protagonists in the "drama."

Intertextual Connections: Tradition and Canon

The technique of parallelism is a syntagmatic structural technique constructing parallels of paradigms acting within the literary continuity. Agnon used it to create relationships among the thematic units and motifs, or characters, of the inner literary and textual space. Through a different technique, semantic in character, he established a parallel between a given text and ancient texts, or between a given text and others within his own canon—which is highly paradigmatic. I already have noted this effect in stories such as "Agunot: A Tale" and "Orphan and Widow," which seem realistic although they are actually mythic and symbolic.

In this context, it is appropriate to return for another look at "Agunot: A Tale," which I previously analyzed with regard to Agnon's relationship to the Jewish tradition. Now, however, I will discuss the way in which intertextual connections, both distant and near, function in this work.

"Agunot" is the story of characters who do not establish themselves in the Land of Israel, about redemption that has not transpired, and about the failure to grasp at a chance for human fulfillment. These themes are epitomized by the artist, Ben-Uri, who because of his work does not devote himself to the human connection that might bring harmony into the world. The failure of potentially harmonious relationships, which does not permit the community to fulfill its social and national objectives, is figured in the reciprocal relationship between the tale itself and intertextual elements that appear in the tale. The obstruction represented in the paradigm of the fall—which causes cosmic or metaphysical disharmony— also causes social disharmony and the delay of national redemption.

Underlying both the opening myth and the human tale is a text that, even as it does not appear explicitly, is implied both in the opening and in the tale. Finally, this text is rendered implicit in the epilogue, which once again introduces what might be called a superreal component into the story and, in fact, creates the deepest connection among the different elements of the text. In various midrashic commentaries we find a motif of the perfect pairing, similar to the one in Plato's *Symposium*. Thus, for example, the development of the well-known parable in *Genesis Rabbah* 8:

Rabbi Jeremiah, son of Eleazar, said: "At the hour that the Holy-One-Blessed-Be-He created the first man, he created him as an adrogyne, as it is written, 'male and female created He them.' " Rabbi Samuel, son of Nahman said: "At the hour that the Holy-One-Blessed-Be-He created the first man, He created him with two faces, and sawed him through, and made him double-backed, one facing this direction and one in the other."

And in the continuation of the same chapter:

He said, "in the past Adam (man) was created from earth and Eve created from Adam (man)." From here onwards it is said: "in our image and after our likeness." There is no man without a woman; there is no woman without a man. And both of them do not exist without the Shekhinah.

And in *Genesis Rabbah* 68:

A matron asked R. Jacob son of Halafta: "In how many days did the Holy-One-Blessed-Be-He create the world?" He said unto her: "In six days, as it is written (Exodus 31) 'For in six days the Lord made heaven and earth.' " She said unto him: "What has He been doing from that hour to this day." He said unto her: "The Holy-One-Blessed-Be-He sits and makes matches, this man's daughter with that man. That man's wife with this man."

These early sayings are elaborated in mystical ways in later midrash, frequently endowing the relations between man and woman with cosmic meaning. The following well-known example of such elaboration is from the *Zohar* 1, 5b:

Another explanation refers "His fruit was sweet to my taste" (Song of Songs 2:3)—to the souls of the righteous who are the fruit of the handiwork of the Almighty and abide with him above. Listen to this: All the souls in the world, which are the fruit of the handiwork of the Almighty, are all mystically one, but when they descend to this world they are separated into male and female, though these are still conjoined. And look at this: the desire of the male for the female, and his clinging to her, bring(s) forth a sour; and he incorporates the desire of the female and takes it in; and the lower desire is taken up into the higher desire and becomes one thing, without separation. And then the female takes in all and is impregnated by the male; their two desires are conjoined. And because of this all is mixed together, this in that.

When the souls issue forth, they issue forth as male and female together. Subsequently, when they descend (to this world) they separate, one to one side and the other to the other, and the Holy-One-Blessed-Be-He mates them—He and no other, He alone knowing the mate proper to each. Happy is the man who is upright in his works and walks in the way of truth, so that his soul may find its original mate, for then he becomes indeed perfect, and through his perfection the whole world is blessed.

And for this reason it is written: "His fruit is sweet to my taste" because He blesses through making whole, and "that the whole world will be blessed through him," because everything depends upon the actions of the human being, if he is righteous or not righteous.[20]

Even without a detailed description of this passage, it is clear that its meaning is based squarely on a quotation from the Song of Songs and on several of the chapters of the midrash quoted previously. The topics have been transposed from a conceptual exegesis, backwards one might say, to a level of understanding that is concerned with the movements of the Heavenly Spheres. Here, abstractive commentary has been recycled into the processions of phenomenal-noumenal being. Thus, for instance, Yeshaya Tishby explains the first portion: "Souls are created in the coupling of the Holy-One-Blessed-Be-He—Glory—with the Shekhinah. And of the over-abundance given to the Shekhinah by the Holy-One-Blessed-Be-He for the creation of souls, she says: 'And his fruit was sweet to my taste.' "[21]

In the next section the chapter describes what results in the world of human souls as a consequence of the events in the Heavenly Spheres. The coupling of the Holy-One-Blessed-Be-He, says Tishby, brings about the coming together of the souls that were united above in the world of spirits, but those who are not deserving may lose their rightful partner, the one created with them in the holy coupling (see "he becomes indeed perfect"). And the perfect couple brings blessing to the *Shekhinah* and draws her blessing to the world in their coupling. Of them, the *Shekhinah* says: "And his fruit was sweet to my taste,"[22] which means, the coupling of the souls that are the fruit of the Holy-One-Blessed-Be-He gives me pleasure.

This is the harmonious and phenomenological understanding of the erotic ideal, which connects perfection created in the Heavenly Spheres with perfection in relations between men and women. In a properly ordered world, all species would have existed in permanent pairs, but Adam and Eve's sin caused a breakdown of this harmonic order. The coming together of split souls in this world is fraught with manifold difficulties. Only he whose acts are desirable can be blessed in coming together without hardship with his ancient partner, with the help of the Holy-One-Blessed-Be-He.[23]

This myth is at the foundation of "Agunot: A Tale" and is perhaps more important than all the other implied texts, both in the opening myth and in the tale's plot. This myth determines that the ideal coupling is the desired state, while the imperfect coupling is the state of the world. The plot itself does not tell an unusual story; it reflects a given, everyday situation. The need to correct this situation creates the eternal longing for harmony, which characterizes all "deserted" souls ("Agunot"). Ben-Uri's music, a social order that creates improper matches, and the conflict between art and reality—all are necessary obstacles through which the myth, which hints at a desired harmony but points to the reality of disharmony, is concretized. In Agnon's hands, this myth expresses romantic agony and romantic irony—the suffering of deserted souls, those who cannot find their partners, and the irony created by the gap between longings and the frustration of those longings. It re-creates the internal connection between the opening myth and the tale itself and between the paradigm and the concretization of the paradigm, which in itself incorporates the mythic foundation of the same paradigm.

The intertextuality created among the midrashic texts, the mystical text (the *Zohar*), and the "modern" text—which is divided longitudinally between a quasi-midrashic introductory passage laden with traditional connotations and a secular love story—also is endowed with traditional implications. These reciprocal relations sometimes create vertical relations within the text. Thus, the vertical relations give the text a different meaning than that implied by the horizontal relations created by the development of the plot. One cannot understand Agnon's work without taking account of the complex interaction among the various levels of the text—which are synchronic—and the syntagmatic development of the text as a continuum.

However, some of Agnon's stories are patently nonrealistic; and in them, reality is stood on its head. Realistic works in general, and those of Agnon in particular, may be rich in connotations; but one may also interpret them on the basis of the explicit text alone. However, the meaning of nonrealistic works can be deduced only after the hidden, connotational text has been deciphered—that is, only after intertextuality has become an active part of the act of reading.

One such story is "The Overcoat," which cannot be properly understood without help from the sources: *Masekhet Hibut Hakever* (Punishment after death) and *Midrash Yona*.[24] The reciprocal relationship between the hidden and explicit texts reveals that the task given to the tailor—to finish a garment for the lord within a certain deadline (which the tailor fails to keep)—hints at the complex relationship between a man and his soul and between a man and the Lord of the Universe.

Again, I must emphasize that the contrasts between the explicit text of the story and the implicit traditional text create parodic effects and also expand the story. The relationship between traditional connotations and allusions and the explicit text of the story points to the revolution that took place in Agnon's language and worldview. Throughout Agnon's works the tension exists, whether the traditional text is embedded in the infrastructure of the explicit text—as in "Agunot: A Tale"—pointing to secondary meanings that change the principal significance of the explicit text, or whether the explicit text barely exists at all, unless one decodes the secondary meanings implied by the underlying traditional text—as in Agnon's other modern stories. In these works, the secondary meanings alone endow the explicit text with significance. Only through the secondary meanings do the plot and the function of the characters make sense, as in "The Overcoat," most of the stories of *The Book of Deeds,* and stories like "Edo and Enam" and "Forevermore." In stories of the second type, the revolution is there for all to see because the structure of the story is dreamlike, indicating its modernity through its form. In both types of stories, the revolutionary traditionalist is in evidence.

There are also enriching intertextual references taken from Agnon's own texts, as noted by Lipschuetz:

There is yet another great unity in his work: warp strings run through the volumes from story to story, from life to life: the grandchildren of Kreyndl Tsharny and her relatives return ("Of Our Young People and Our Elders"); R. Gadiel the wonder child is mentioned by (Reb) Raphael's wife; Reb Yisrael Shlomo the pillar of the community and his cat appear in several places. That shows that the characters have attained independent life in his spirit, and we have here an ambition to bring the project to completion. Everyone views his individual works as chapters of a great composition.[25]

According to this view, every story exists in itself and as part of an entire canon. The whole sheds light on the part, just as the part elucidates the whole. Several examples are sufficient to indicate the frequency of the phenomenon. As noted, the character of Kreyndl Tsharny, the heroine of "And the Crooked Shall Be Made Straight," is mentioned in "Of Our Young People and Our Elders": "On the way, one of my friends found me. His name is Hofmann. Mr. Hofmann is the son of the son of Kreyndl Tsharny the abandoned woman." [26] Only someone who knows the circumstances under which Kreyndl's son was born will catch the hint that Hofmann is, from the point of view of Jewish law, a bastard. Another character, Jacob Rechnitz of "Betrothed," makes an appearance in "Edo and Enam": "But as I stood gazing the colors altered before my eyes into the tints of seaweeds drawn from the depths, such weeds as Dr. Rechnitz drew up from the sea of Jaffa." [27] Only if one has descended to the depths of the meaning of the symbol of seaweed in "Betrothed" can one understand the parallel reference in "Edo and Enam." Thus, we find an intertextual parallel between the protagonist of "Betrothed" and the protagonist in "Edo and Enam."

Here, I would also mention the many links between *The Bridal Canopy* and *Only Yesterday* (Reb Yudel Hasid, the hero of the earlier novel, is the forebear of Yitzhak Kumer, the hero of the later one); between "In the Prime of Her Life" and *A Simple Story* (Blume Nacht and Akabia Mazal); between "The Hill of Sand" and *Only Yesterday* (Hemdat); and between *Only Yesterday* and "Pisces."

For he could have painted on the fish's skin, like Yitzhak Kumer, who painted on Balak's skin, but Balak was a dog, whose skin absorbs color, which is not the case with a clammy creature full of fluid, where the paint spreads through the fluid and retains no shape.[28]

I chose the last example because it creates a multivalent parallel among Betsalel Moshe, the painter, and Yitzhak, and between the fish and Balak (the demonic dog), illustrating both the source story — "Pisces" — and the one taken from the canon — *Only Yesterday*.

Despite the multitude and variety of characters and motifs, the connections within the canon imply that unity rules over the inner multiplicity. The intratextual connections create links of similarity across time — that is, syntagmatically — obliging the reader to regard the structure spatially. In that way, the forward motion of the plot is held in abeyance. The intertextual connections create bonds of similarity along the axis of choice — that is, the paradigm — and expand the meaning of each single unit. Thus, bundles of meaning are passed from unit to unit without making the connection among them only metaphorical. They force the reader to pause and step out of the time line in the pursuit of continuity.

Decoherent Structures: From Digression to the Spatial Story

Intertextual parallels are latent suspensions of continuity. Another kind of suspension is that conditioned by the relationship between the expectation of unbroken continuity and the frustration of that expectation by various digressions. One such digression is that the plot (as forward movement in time, assuming that the units linked to each other lead to some ending) is interrupted.

Here, I refer mainly to the subplots that delay the main plot. In such a structure, secondary elements acquire autonomy out of all proportion to their relationship to the principal elements. This often produces metaphorical and comic relationships among the various minor elements and between them and the main plot. The segments of the plot may be strung together formally but are not bound to each other meaningfully. *The Bridal Canopy,* for example, is structured as a mass of digressions—an agglomeration of stories secondary to the main one. In fact, the entire structure is a digression. What had been intended as a voyage with a goal, to collect money for the dowry of Reb Yudel's daughter, becomes a voyage of digressions, dinners, and stories. Between the main story and the secondary story are parallels of synonymity and antonymity, but the entire structure is little more than a digression leading to a finer goal than it is a goal-oriented journey. "Of Our Young People and Our Elders" also is structured as a voyage with a goal and a digression from it. As one of the protagonists, Mr. Deichsl, says: "From the bitter comes the sweet. We came because of a pogrom, and in the end we have a party."[29] The secondary has become primary; and delay has become an independent structure, producing an ironic effect.

The hidden connection between the digression—the task that the hero has taken upon himself—and the threatening purport of events creates the grotesque effects of stories like "A Whole Loaf" (1933), "To Father's House" (1941), "Friendship" (1932), and "Quitclaim" (1945). That pattern (in this case, an asymmetrical one) appears frequently in Agnon's works and can serve many purposes.

The pattern of digression also is typical of *A Guest for the Night,* gaining constantly in strength as the status of the plot is reduced and the place of impeding factors is expanded. "Until Now" is based on two aimless movements: the narrator-hero's journey within the city of Berlin from rented room to rented room and his trips between cities to Leipzig and its surroundings to save Mr. Levi's library. The implied author lays bare his devices through the narrator-hero's words:

I set aside the things that happen without our notice. Only He who makes them happen knows why they occur. I don't know. Sometimes, it seems to me, they are like the things that link one dream to another and which are forgotten as they are experience, so we find ourselves viewing our dreams as though there were no connection between them.[30]

The journey within the city is a Sisyphean task in which the narrator wanders through Berlin, winding up in a number of rented rooms that are synecdoches for German society during the First World War. They represent various features of the signified geographical space—women without men and families that have been dismembered. The stations along the way stand for the setting, and the main character illustrates human estrangement in that setting. The story describes the relationship between man and his setting rather than the hero's development toward any goal. The trips between cities, to Leipzig, are also pointless. The trips are not a rescue expedition but rather are encounters both with victims of the war (orphans, widows, bereaved parents) and with those who will profit by it (the Schimmelman family). The turning point at the end of the novella, when the hero returns to the Land of Israel and Mr. Levi's books reach him, is coincidental; it is a kind of deus ex machina. The story simply stops, although the hero's wanderings might have continued ad infinitum.

Hence, one might say that "Until Now" is decoherent with regard to continuity—that is, the logic of the plot is not dominant. That is also true of *In Mr. Lublin's Store,* in which the structure is also fundamentally decoherent, as it is composed of two situations of entrapment. Mr. Lublin was caught in Leipzig in his youth. The narrator-protagonist also was detained there as a result of the war. The narrator describes the limited extent of Mr. Lublin's existence (his store and the ones around it), and through it he describes German society in general, and the Jews in particular, before and during the First World War. The estrangement of all those who are caught in that place—the narrator, Mr. Lublin, Yakov Stern, the German Jews, and perhaps also the Germans themselves—is the subject of the story, which, like "Until Now," does not end but is cut short (in this case, without a deus ex machina). In this work, representing a synecdoche of the setting, the parallels among the secondary plots are no longer important. The story's main concern is the multifaceted portrayal of the setting. That is to say, a new pattern of entrapment has become the source of the plot; it contains the punishment, and release is no longer important. This pattern is suited to the feeling of fate. A person is caught in a setting; that setting becomes his fate because the setting is the pathetic product of historical time. Therefore, personal fate results from the historical fate of the setting. A similar view is to be found in *A Guest for the Night,* but there it had not yet found such an extreme correlative as in the two works just discussed.

Agnon was cognizant of the novelty of his literary form and perhaps also of its causes. In the following he revealed his device and explained its decoherence:

Now that I have specified the time and place, I am starting the fourth chapter, in which I tell about my conversation with Mr. Yakov Stern and a few other things, some of which belong to the heart of the matter, and others are peripheral. But don't say that if they're peripheral, they don't belong, and if they don't belong, what do they matter? You should know that everything is peripheral to everything and revolves around everything, and there is not difference between cause and effect except the first cause.[31]

Agnon's coherent novels, in which the structure and meaning are expanded by both intertextual and intratextual means, already contained the possibility of decoherence. After *A Guest for the Night* and *The Book of Deeds,* in a very complex fashion a new unity is consolidated, which is characteristic of some of the later stories—such as *Within the Wall* and "The Covering of Blood." This unity is no longer based on the logic of the plot, in the Aristotelian sense. At its peak, this unity creates its own wholeness, as in "Until Now"; in decline, it brings the structure to the verge of disintegration, as in *In Mr. Lublin's Store.*

Diversity: The Figure of the Hero and Its Characterization

In describing the structure of the novels, stories, and novellas, one discerns certain basic premises that, in various guises, underlie Agnon's works and place the stamp of unity upon their multiplicity. However, it is more difficult to find such a pattern in his characterizations.

Contrary to the opinion held by the critic David Aryeh Friedman, little in Agnon's works is more impressive than the great variety of characters who populate the stories. They extend over four or five generations: from Reb Yudel Hasid, Yitzhak Kumer's grandfather, to Zohara and Tamara, who could be Yitzhak's grandchildren. They extend over many countries and nationalities: from Buczacz in Galicia, to Germany, to the Land of Israel. The spectrum of characters knows no ideological or social limits. It includes penitents who return to piety (Reb Hayim-Ignatz and Reb Shlomo in *A Guest for the Night*); God-fearing and Hassidic Jews (Reb Yudel from *The Bridal Canopy*, Hananya from the novella "In the Heart of Seas," and Tehilla and Rabbi Gadiel, the wonder child, each in the story bearing his name); heretics (Heschl in *The Bridal Canopy* and Shakherson from *Shira*); Zionists (Yitzhak Kumer in *Only Yesterday*); assimilated Jews (Steiner and Fernheim in "Fernheim"); and ultra-Orthodox fanatics (Reb Grunem, "may the redeemer come," in *Only Yesterday*). The list of Agnon's characters encompasses various strata of society: petits bourgeois like Tsirl (from *A Simple Story*); poverty-stricken men like Ovadia the Cripple; ignoramuses like Shammay (in "The Hill of Sand") and Sarini (in *Shira*); great religious scholars like Rabbi Shlomo and Rabbi Abraham (in "Two Scholars Who Were in Our City"); professors like Manfred Herbst and Weltfremd (in *Shira*); and scholars like Yakov Rechnitz (in "Betrothed") and Ginat (in "Edo and Enam").

There is no standard *commedia dell'arte* figure who does not appear in Agnon's works. There is the pedant (the denizens of the "house of lips" in "On Taxes" and Weichsl and Deichsl in "Of Our Young People and Our Elders"); the femme fatale (Helena in "The Lady and the Peddler," Sonia in *Only Yesterday,* and Shira in the novel named for her); and the ingénue (Toni in "Metamorphosis" and Shifra in *Only Yesterday*). There are some nonfictional characters, such as Brenner, and others that refer to historical prototypes, such as Bakhlam, who stands for the late Professor Joseph Klausner. In contrast are figures taken entirely from the world of imagination (such as Gemula in "Edo and Enam"). Also, Agnon included psychological types from every extreme: introverts, such as Ben-Uri (in "Agunot: A Tale"), Hirshl (in *A Simple Story*), Hanokh and Reb Hayim (in *A Guest for the Night*), Ginat (in "Edo and Enam"), and Adiel Amzeh (in "Forevermore"); and extroverts, such as Deichsl and Weichsl (in "Of Our Young People and Our Elders"), Schpaltleder, Rabinovitz, and Askanovski (in *Only Yesterday*), and Pincha-Arieh (in *A Guest for the Night*). Between the extremes, of course, are balanced individuals like Menachem Ha'omed.

Some of the characters are depicted realistically (see, for example, *A Simple Story* and *A Guest for the Night*); some are fantastic (see "The Lovers' Canopy" and "Edo and Enam"); and yet others are farcical caricatures (see "The Frogs") or are grotesque (see "At Hemdat's"). Nevertheless, one primary character is dominant in most of the works. David Canaani argues that the roots of this character go back to the world of the Torah scholar who lost his way in the new society, becoming a marginal figure seeking to get a grip on life. In any case, this character is passive, lacks the capacity for theoretical statements, stands at a crossroads, and does not know how to escape his cul-de-sac. Whenever the characters seem "whole" —such as Rabbi Yosef in "The Story of Rabbi Yosef, or Torah for Its Own Sake," Reb Nehemia Cohen in "Priest of Truth," Yehezkel Cohen in "The Stones of the Place," and Tehilla or Reb Yudel Hasid in *The Bridal Canopy*—the narrator appears and, in ironic fashion, points out the characters' ingenuousness.

The passive attitude to life, that of someone unable to articulate the conflicts to which he is subject, typifies Menashe Hayim ("And the Crooked Shall Be Made Straight"), Rabbi Yehezkel ("Agunot: A Tale"), Yitzhak Kumer (*Only Yesterday*), Reb Hayim and Hanokh (*A Guest for the Night*), Hirshl (*A Simple Story*), Adiel Amzeh ("Forevermore"), Yohanan the guardian of the graves ("The Lovers' Canopy"), Leah Mazal ("In the Prime of Her Life"), and the hero of *The Book of Deeds*. All of these are deracinated figures. The existential, social, and religious conflict in which they are caught is beyond them; they are ruined.

The characters' passivity is what seals their fate. They are dragged along by events and have no control over their own actions. Menashe Hayim, who sells the rabbi's letter of recommendation to a beggar who happens along, is no different from "that man" whose soul thirsted for a "whole loaf of bread" (in "A Whole Loaf") or from the tailor, Yisrael, who is attracted to an inn to drink and to engage in pleasant conversation and who therefore does not complete the task assigned to him (in "The Overcoat"). The main causes of the characters' downfall generally come from outside of them. At a certain point they cease struggling against danger. They are dragged along but also hasten the process of decline. The "original sin" increasingly becomes a decree of fate. So it is with Yitzhak Kumer in *Only Yesterday* and Dan Hofmann in "The Disappeared." The reader should interpret characters like Hirshl from *A Simple Story* in that way and also Manfred Herbst, from *Shira,* whose lust is stronger than he is. That is to say, the portrayal of the character is what creates the plot line.

Such characters also were created by Brenner and Gnessin. They used introspection, internal monologue, mixed direct speech, or stream of consciousness to portray the inner lives of the heroes' souls. However, that is not the case with Agnon's characters. Most are not depicted introspectively because it is not their way to ratiocinate about their own essential being. They do not confess nor are they laid bare. They disclose their inner worlds through their actions and by means of recurrent but changing habits. Even dialogue conceals more than it reveals. (See the dialogues in "Fernheim"[32] or "Metamorphosis.")[33] Agnon's heroes are eternally mute and passive but are opened up by the author to expose their doubts and inner rifts.

To understand the protagonist the reader must take an active role. The author does not decipher the characters for the reader; rather, that task is given to the reader himself or herself. The text is "writerly" since most of the characters' lives are mysteries that the reader is asked to solve. Whether the protagonists are realistic or metarealistic and allegorical, they always pose a riddle to the reader. The plot is often a process of deciphering a character who is the riddle of the story.

Agnon's method of characterization is generally complex and conceals more than it reveals. The protagonists are, as noted, riddles that the reader must solve. For the secondary characters, however, the author uses simple methods of characterization, which often are transferred partly to the main characters as well. In portraying the secondary characters, direct and simple characterization diminishes the breadth of their significance. In the characterization of the main, complex characters, the same means are used to expand and deepen their "secret" characterization.

To begin with the most external technique, Agnon used traditional names or nicknames to sketch a character's likeness. For example, Ben-Uri recalls Betsalel Ben-Uri, the master craftsman of the tabernacle; Reb Yehezkel refers to the prophet Ezekiel; Blume Nacht is German for night flower; Yitzhak refers to the patriarch Isaac, and his last name, Kumer, means newcomer in Yiddish. Daniel was rescued from the lion's den, and the letters of Bach, his last name, *beit heit,* are the Hebrew abbreviation for two parts. (He has a wooden leg.) Fernheim is German for far from home; Hartmann is German for a hard man; Askanovitz comes from the Hebrew *askan,* or a Pooh Bah; Hecht is a pike in German; and Hillel was a famous sage.

Sometimes Agnon exploits a name's Yiddish or German meaning (for example, Fishl Hecht, Kumer, Fernheim, Hartmann) or the connection between the name in its new context and the same name in its original, traditional context.

For instance, the biblical Hanokh (Enoch) did not die but was taken by God;[34] Hillel was known as a human sage; and Yekutiel Neeman's name refers to Moses.

These names are taken from various stories by Agnon, and the characterization is based on the *nomen omen* technique. Some of the names refer to the most external feature of a protagonist, but others embody a character's secret fate. For example, the name Menashe Hayim means that the hero causes life to be forgotten. His impotence makes him forget life, bringing about his virtual death in that his wife has a son by another man (see "And the Crooked Shall Be Made Straight"). The names of Helena and Joseph in "The Lady and the Peddler" expand the significance of the story. She seduces him and is about to devour him, but his return to faith saves him at the last minute. The relationship between the two protagonists is not merely between one man and one woman but also symbolically between Hellenism and Judaism. Joseph is an avatar of Joseph de la Reina, a kabbalistic hero who struggles with the powers of darkness, particularly with the demonic power of Lilith. Helena represents Greece, or Helen of Troy whose face launched a thousand ships, as well as the figure of Lilith. The story also refers to the biblical story of Joseph and Potiphar's wife, as well as to the midrashim that embroidered upon that story.

However, Agnon's main points are made with more complex techniques—that is, by using "style indirect libre," dialogue, and the like—which are means of characterization that force the addressee to fill the gaps and to interpret what is polysemous. The presentation of people in motion, ambiguous style indirect libre, and dialogue rich in emotional expanses—all produce a profound depiction of the protagonists. One notes a tendency, particularly in the novels, to give the characters a split portrayal—that is, to deploy information about the character over a broad expanse, with every comment providing insight into a new aspect of the character. The author frequently does not offer concentrated analyses of the character but rather leaves that task to the addressee, for whom the character is revealed in both the microtext—motion and speech—and in the macrotext—entry into a structure of relationships.

Moreover, the economy of the characters is organized in such a way that each is accompanied by synonymous and antonymous doubles that expand the meaning and reveal aspects that do not emerge when the characters are introduced simply. Thus, along with Reb Yudel (*The Bridal Canopy*), there are figures such as Reb Yudel Nathansohn, Reb Yudel who is not Reb Yudel, and the actor who plays Reb Yudel as a synonym and Nuta as an antonym. Getzl Stein (*A Simple Story*) is a synonym for Hirshl, and Scheinbard is his antonym. Rabinovitz (*Only Yesterday*) is a synonym for Yitzhak, and Balak is his antonym. Synonymic and antonymic connections among the characters are typical not only of Agnon but of many novelists. However, Agnon made the structure of parallels and contrasts among his characters into an art in its own right.

It is appropriate to add a few comments about some of the characters previously mentioned. Agnon used the similarities between names—that is, homonyms—to intensify the antonymic relationships between characters. Characters may have similar names but belong to contrasting social classes, such as

Reb Yudel Hasid and Reb Yudel Nathansohn in *The Bridal Canopy;* thus, the homonym creates comic effects. Of course, the main character represents itself as it develops in a work; but a character may also acquire certain traits from synonymous figures, as with Hirshl and Getzl in *A Simple Story.* The synonymous character, which is a secondary one, also is illuminated by the main character.

In *A Guest for the Night,* one could interpret the characters returning to their native city as synonyms for the narrator Reb Hayim, Yeruham Hofshi, Schuetzling, and finally Elimelekh Kaiser. The work is constructed on what the characters have in common and on what distinguishes them from each other. The story is deepened and expanded, while each character sheds light on the others and is illuminated by them as well.

Beginning in the late 1930s Agnon began writing stories that might be termed *narcissistic stories.* In these stories, the characters do not stand only for themselves; the author hints, through their names, that they are part of the biographical person of the actual or implied author. These figures function as though in a dream, in which every character is a part of the implicit personality expressed by means of representatives. In order to signal his intention of using the characters to stand for the different aspects of his personality, Agnon divided his given name, Shmuel Yosef, into two synonymous figures or had the names of many of his characters begin with the first or second letter of his family name, *a* or *g.* This method of characterizing the figures gives the stories close affinities with the expressionist school, in which characters are generally projections or emanations of the ego. Shmuel and Yosef in "Until Now" and in *Knots Upon Knots* are a synonymous pair.

(Here the technique borders on the technique of the *Doppelgaenger.*) The narrator, Greifenbach, Gamzu, and Ginat in "Edo and Enam" are also synonymous figures. In the latter two stories, and in others such as "Forevermore," the characters do not fulfill synonymic or antonymic functions alone; they represent various aspects or elements of a single personality. Agnon created a complete and varied world in his works. However, his power does not lie only in its quantitative richness but also in the quality and depth of the portrayals.

CHAPTER 4

THE NOVELS

Chronicle, Psychological Novel,
and Myth

WE FIND four types of implied author in Agnon's novels—that is, four aspects of literary expression: (1) the author as a chronicler who places extraliterary situations in a structure implying a philosophy of history; (2) the author who presents his hero in various contexts and discloses his human reactions to changing social circumstances; (3) the author who, in confrontation with a protagonist and the times, transcends time and place; and (4) the author who combines a historical situation with a personal one, revealing various segments of the myth of Jewish and human existence in the modern age.

Galicia in the early nineteenth century, the *shtetl* in the early twentieth century, Galicia between the two world wars, the Land of Israel during the Second Aliya period in the 1930s and 1940s, and Germany during the First World War—

these are the times in which the novels take place and the time of the author's life and his observations. The materials are drawn from worlds that Agnon knew at first hand, and they are integrated within the figure of the narrator, who functions as a chronicler following the heroes' actions in historical time and interpreting historical time by means of the heroes.

Agnon's novels are always social novels. The ironic ingenuousness of Reb Yudel Hasid is primarily an interpretation of the social geography of Galicia. One cannot understand *A Simple Story* outside of the context of the Zionist and socialist revolution that opposed the Jewish bourgeoisie that had dominated the *shtetl* before the First World War. *A Simple Story* is a psychological novel with pronounced extraliterary, social aspects. *Only Yesterday* is a novel that mixes a chronicle of the Second Aliya with a chronicle of the Old Yishuv (the non-Zionist, Orthodox communities). Similarly, *A Guest for the Night* is a rather accurate slice of social life combined with extraliterary, historical materials about the decline and fall of the *shtetl* between the two world wars.

Agnon's heroes wander and search. They do not accept their situations and try—usually, in vain—to bring about some change. In the end they succumb, in one way or another, to the old world (as in *A Simple Story, Only Yesterday,* and *Shira*); or else they discover there is no returning to it, and they must accept the new world as it is (as in *A Guest for the Night*). Their lives are made possible only by the miracle of faith (as in *The Bridal Canopy*). The heroes repeatedly discover that by changing one's place one does not change oneself (as in *Only Yesterday* and *In Mr. Lublin's Store*). Although the novels are all enmeshed in historical time, they bear a message that transcends time, as we shall discover through a detailed discussion of them.

THE BRIDAL CANOPY:
The Journey of a Great Believer

Agnon's first novel, *The Bridal Canopy,* is a picaresque epic. The kernel of the novel was published in 1920, and it appeared in full in 1931. It is a "tale of the pious" about "a righteous man who had neither food nor a living"[1] who raises money to marry off his three daughters as commanded by the Rabbi of Apta. But it is also a story based on the European tradition of the wandering picaroon who discovers civilization —such as the tale of Don Quixote and Sancho Panza—which passed through Mendele Mokher Seforim's *Travels of Benjamin the Third* into *The Bridal Canopy* and was metamorphosed into the character of Reb Yudel Hasid, who removes himself from worldly matters, and Reb Nuta the driver, whose main drives are practical. In addition to these two traditions are also traces of the static background story (as in *The Decameron* and *The Arabian Nights*), which is composed of a chapter within a chapter and a story within a story—all placed in a framework. However, here it is linked to the dynamic tradition of the travel story.

We also find the European tradition of the *Doppelgaenger.* Some of the comic elements of the plot depend on the interplay between the different characters of Reb Yudel Hasid, the

Reb Yudel who is not Reb Yudel, and Reb Yudel Nathansohn.

The story begins with poverty and sexual barrenness (associated with Torah study) and ends with wealth and sexual fertility, with the hero retaining his knowledge of Torah. The story begins: "Once there was a Hassid who was greatly poor and oppressed with poverty, may the All-merciful preserve us, and he used to sit and study Torah and pray, far from worldly matters."[2] It ends with a carnival of feasting and drinking, when Reb Yudel celebrates the marriage of his eldest daughter.

Four antitheses run through the entire work, and the effort to overcome them results in a comic and paradoxical mixture. They are

    a. fasting (1) versus gluttony (2);
    b. Torah and poverty (1) versus wealth (2);
    c. story (1) versus travel (2);
    d. quotation (1) versus reality (2).

At the start of his trip, Reb Yudel is on the left-hand side of these antitheses (1); as it progresses, he leans toward the opposite side (2). By the end, he overcomes the oppositions and combines them through the power of his faith. The miracle of that combination is possible primarily because the story has many meanings, and in such a situation every option remains open. Here is the story of a journey, during which a legend about the story itself is embroidered; and the Purim *shpil* (a comic skit traditionally presented on Purim) about Yudel's journeys becomes a part of folklore even before the trip is over.

The novel hovers between reality and imagination and between source and parody (for the Purim *shpil* is a parody of
the story of Reb Yudel). The plot is partially realistic, partially legendary, and partially a parody of its own legend. The
narrator presents various versions, including those of other
poets and those of the *Broder zinger*. But the narrator himself
sometimes uses eloquent, rhymed diction like the poet of
Brod, until it appears that even the principal version—the
one presented to the reader—is merely one composed by
various poets about the legend. Even its reliability becomes
doubtful and causes surprise.

The novel consists of a tissue of stories told at the various
stations at which the hero lingers. The stories include synonymic and antonymic parallels that delay the progress of the
trip and sometimes foreshadow its conclusion.[3] The plot is
based mainly on a comedy of errors. Reb Yudel manages to
find a groom for his daughter because the future in-laws are
certain he is none other than the wealthy Reb Yudel Nathansohn
(his double). According to the principles of a comedy of
errors, the mistake ought to be revealed and Reb Yudel
punished. The logic of the plot ought to lead to a comic
catastrophe. However, Reb Yudel's daughter, with the help
of Rabbi Zerah, the rooster, discovers a treasure that raises
the poor from the dung heap and makes Reb Yudel both a
Hassid and a rich man at the same time.

All occurs as a result of the advice of the Rabbi of Apta,
who orders Reb Yudel to set out on his trip and prophesies
that all will end well. The magic plot overcomes the comedy
of errors; the power of the Rabbi of Apta is greater than that
of degraded reality. His merit stood by Rabbi Zerah, the

rooster; Reb Yudel; and Reb Yudel, "the rooster"—all of whom are not doomed to slaughter but are privileged to be fruitful and multiply. In *The Bridal Canopy*, the money that cannot be raised in a normal way is found miraculously:

But how fine and sweet was the sitting of the fathers-in-law together, both the real fathers-in-law and Reb Yudel Nathansohn, the supposed father-in-law. And when folk stood behind them and called out, Long life to you, Reb Yudel, both of the Reb Yudels would turn their heads around together and reply, Long life, long life.[4]

As can be seen from this passage, which appears in the carnival-like conclusion of the novel, the two Reb Yudels are fused together into a single character. The miracle that takes place removes the barriers between the two characters, who are homonymous in name but antonymic in their social positions and in the values that they represent. After the treasure, which is to be his daughter's dowry, is found, Reb Yudel's Torah becomes—as the Yiddish lullaby says—the "best merchandise." Matter and spirit and poverty and wealth are combined in the marriage ceremony, which becomes a kind of fertility festival.

How were the comic errors circumvented, permitting the joining of the sundered parts and the contradictions—that is, fasting and feasting, poverty with Torah and wealth, life and quotation, story and reality? It does not appear to have been accomplished through the magic power of the Rabbi of Apta, who is presented in an ambivalent light toward the end of the novel as a teller of wildly exaggerated tales. The power of the Rabbi of Apta does not violate the logic of the plot for Reb

Yudel's sake, causing expectations to be violated, deviations to be forgiven, doubles to become one flesh, and the antitheses to be united. All that was a product of Reb Yudel's own character.

Reb Yudel is found innocent where others would certainly have been condemned because he is a kind of Don Quixote of theodicy—a hero who accepts the trail of woe as the best path that could have been chosen by the Master of the Universe for mankind. He emerges victorious because he is not split between the antitheses but rather surmounts them.[5] The source of the comic celebration is Reb Yudel's miraculous power of faith. He—who represents the antithesis of masculinity—merits the treasure because the treasure is buried within him. The treasure is not to be found at the end of the world but in Brod itself, from which he departs and to which he returns. On his way, Reb Yudel proves himself—like heroes from time immemorial, such as Odysseus, Theseus, and Heracles—as a hero who conquers his instincts.[6] Even his antonymic doubles (Nuta and the others) do not overcome him.

The Bridal Canopy is a comic myth of Jewish faith, one that is dependent upon the power of the believer. If you take away the quixotic, utopian dream of faith and the theodicy, you have undone the believer. This is an ironic hymn of praise for a great believer who once lived and is no more. It is ostensibly a traditional story that confirms traditional innocence and contrasts it with the social conventions of the Jewish bourgeoisie, where a great scholar will marry only the daughter of a wealthy man. Here, because of the miracle, the father's faith overcomes the customary practices of the society. The young scholar marries the daughter of poor parents, although he is certain she comes from a rich family. Miraculously, her family is actually a wealthy one.

The revolutionary factor implicit in *The Bridal Canopy* is expressed in the confrontation between value systems. The implicit assumption is that only by a miracle can the society overcome its bourgeois Jewish norms. If the plot had unfolded in the usual fashion, it would have ended with a comic catastrophe. The comic intrigue would have been visible for all to see, although it stemmed from an error and not from malice on the part of the protagonist. By granting a treasure to the indigent Reb Yudel and turning the tables on everyone, the author—who manipulates the deus ex machina—is both ironic and revolutionary, knowing full well that, left to itself, the tradition in the negative sense of the word would have won out. Even the return to innocence before the consolidation of the bourgeois norms of Jewish society is ironic and revolutionary. The revolution returns to the precivilized past, just as it seems to point toward a better future.

A SIMPLE STORY:
The Surrender of the Romantic Dream

Several years after the publication of Agnon's picaresque epic *The Bridal Canopy,* a work that is close to both the Jewish religious tradition and to the European literary tradition of the Renaissance, *A Simple Story* (1935) was published. *A Simple Story* is related to the psychological novels of the beginning of this century (such as Knut Hamsun's *Pan, Victoria,* and *Mysteries* and Thomas Mann's *Buddenbrooks*).

At one time the critics rightly emphasized the work's linear plot and the place of the hero in its development. Dov Sadan sees Hirshl as a character who has become involved in affairs of the heart and giving them up drives him to insanity. Hirshl becomes a pendulum swinging between "fate" and "decision" or between "psychological explanation" and "the horror of pathos."[7] Baruch Kurzweil emphasizes the social conflict derived from the battle of the generations. In his opinion, A Simple Story demonstrates the struggle between "collective experience" and "individual experience." The hero flees to a "pre-cultural" situation, struggling against "all the expressions of culture and civilization."[8]

A Simple Story details the conflict between the individual and the bonds of a bourgeois family. The orphan, Blume Nacht, a poor relative who becomes a maidservant for the family, liberates the forces that had been repressed in Hirshl, who, like most of Agnon's heroes, lacks the means for "containing" his soul. The family tries to tame Hirshl through the institution of marriage (to Mina Ziemlich, whose name means almost), but the repression leads to a mental breakdown (the stage of dramatic crisis).

The mad scene is the peak of the novel. Hirshl is placed in Dr. Langsam's clinic, in the attempt to dull the sting of the forces of his soul. The tension relaxes, and the hero is cured of "his soul." Hirshl looks more and more like the catatonic soldier his father meets when he travels to bring Hirshl home.[9] Hirshl returns and resumes his role in society. He no longer demands a place of his own (the last dramatic stage, that of punishment). He no longer tries to reconcile his situation with his being; instead, he adapts his being to every situation.

His claim, originating in the world of his soul, has become routinized and subject to derision.

The author does not identify with that process, but he portrays it as a necessary and inevitable development. Not surprisingly, the novel ends with an expression of the hope to return to the narrative material—to describe the life of Blume Nacht in a future story. That is a fictional promise, as when the narrator promises to write a novel called *The Field* in *Only Yesterday*. Perhaps this is a hint that in another distant and mysterious realm, a purer existence is possible. Romantic ideals cannot be realized in this world; they shatter upon the ground of reality and are a locus of yearning and mourning for the narrator and the readers.

Intratextually, in terms of spatial structure, the novel's conflict is actualized in two series of motifs: novelistic motifs describing the outer world and attempting to epitomize the human condition by means of bourgeois life ceremonials and romance motifs, expressing the hero's yearnings in fantasies derived from the world of imagination. The main novelistic motif is a series of descriptions of family dinners as real ceremonies standing for bourgeois social life. The meal is given symbolic content in the hero's mind:

Being hungry has made me realize that it's time I made something of myself. Only how can I make anything of myself when I'm still so dependent on my parents? [10]

The latter part of this passage clearly shows the son's dependence on his mother, and the connection between that dependence and the contrast between satiation and hunger—or the opposition between that which is flawed and cannot be repaired and the improvement of manners:

Though everyone except Hirshl was bursting at the seams, the aroma proved irresistible. Even Hirshl took a large slice and ate it with gusto.

"You must admit, Hirshl," said Tsirl, flashing him a smile, "that this pudding is delicious." Hirshl blushed. After priding himself on his self-restraint, here he was being a pig like the rest of them. Nor was that the worst of it. The worst of it was that his mother's words were the same as those he had spoken to her on the day of Blume's arrival in their house, when she had brought with her the most delicious home-baked cakes.[11]

Within Hirshl's consciousness a structure of identifications has been created. Taking part in a dinner is identified with dependence on his mother, as though eating implied the betrayal of some hidden purpose and the surrender of independence. A second identification, between the dinner and the erotic circle, is created by the parallel between the meal in the present and one that had taken place in the past. The meal described here is testimony to the son's loss of independence. He has become part of the family dinner, eating at the table of a society that does not give him a place of his own. The identification with the family framework returns him to the condition of nursing:

Hirshl ate a great deal despite his lack of appetite, for the fresh air and his mother-in-law's cooking had given him one just in time. Indeed, his stomach seemed to have expanded since his arrival in

Malikrowik, and his interest in vegetarianism and the simple life was a thing of the past.[12]

Hirshl finds refuge in madness. The family and wealth, together embodied by the symbol of the dinner, are the only reliable certainties in a precarious world. Anyone departing from that blessed framework enters the dubious realm of dread, where the only reward is pain.

In contrast to the realistic motif, based on the bourgeois ceremony, the romance motifs shed the trammels of time and space and redeem the hero from his environment. One example is intratextual, apparently lacking any connection with other matters in the plot. Indeed, this motif expresses some of the deepest meanings of the work. It appears in the rural idyll shared by Hirshl and Mina after their wedding:

But Hirshl was not Mina's teacher and had no interest in astronomy. He sat lazily on a wooden bench with his feet barely grazing the ground, half listening to the snatches of voices that drifted from the village. Some peasant girls were singing a song about a mermaid who married a prince. What did the prince do when he realized that his bride was half fish? The village girls were far, far off, and their voices barely reached him.[13]

This motif is repeated elsewhere in almost identical language.[14] It appears in yet another context, with an ironic tone: "Did Blume expect to be carried off by a prince on a white charger? In fact she did not."[15]

It is not clear whether the motif of "the princess whose skin was like a fish's" is presented in the narrator's name or Hirshl's, as his own inner speech. The opening question "What did the prince do when he noticed it?" also could be either Hirshl's romantic material waning in his soul or else the narrator's. In this case, implicit speech (style indirect libre) tends to blur boundaries and extremes by the use of ambivalent expressions. Agnon expressed the laden atmosphere through the repetition of words with an emotional function (for example, "broken and fragmented," "far away," "from afar"). The blurring of the listener's figure, the emotional language, and the ambiguous question create a drowsy, half-slumbering atmosphere, in which it is unclear whether the hero is listening to his inner voice or to voices coming from the outside. The prince is a leitmotif for Hirshl himself, as is the princess for Blume. The relations depicted are a metaphorical embodiment of the actual relations between the two: Hirshl is like the prince who was nauseated every time he approached the princess.

Irrational forces, which can only be represented in poetic language, act upon the hero's soul and direct it. The novel is illuminated by the light of the world of imagination, and in that light Hirshl and Blume are merely human incarnations of superhuman forces. Hirshl is the reincarnation of eros, and Blume is the reincarnation of the eternal beloved who cannot be possessed in this world (the fish skin). Hirshl, the son of merchants, and Blume, the orphaned servant girl, wear social masks; but behind the camouflage are hidden irrational forces that break down the boundaries of time and space within the small town. Such forces have laws of their own and are not subject to the customs and morality of the provincials of Szybucz.

These two motif structures create an intratextual pattern hidden beneath the overt plot, which is based on entrapment (Hirshl, with the appearance of Blume), a decision (marriage to Mina), and punishment and release (the process of going mad and the recovery of sanity). The structures of the motifs create a mythification—in polar opposites—of the psychological and social novel. The melodrama about the landlord's son and the servant girl becomes more profound, and the chronicle about the society and mores of a small Jewish town in Galicia in the early twentieth century transcends the limitations of everyday life.

But *A Simple Story* is also a typical bourgeois social novel, which can almost be described in Marxist social terminology. It is closely related to the European family novel and, similarly, describes social power struggles through family power struggles. The great mother represents the family and the tribe, which view marriage outside of one's class and without family permission as an infraction of the rules. The son struggles against the taboo that requires him to marry according to the terms of the totem. But he would rather remove the bourgeois obstacles. In this novel, Jewish bourgeois society overcomes the hero's personality and his romantic dreams, thus forcing itself upon him. The mother's dinner overcomes the romantic dream about the princess or the mermaid.

The author does not identify with the victory in the plot. The victory comes through the intervention of the modern witch doctor—the psychotherapist—who exorcises the dybbuk of revolution from the rebellious son. The author views this as an ironic victory, and he condemns it. Thus, the author's attitude is revolutionary—that is, opposed to the plot—and he condemns the victory that he himself arranged. The revolutionary hides behind the Pyrrhic victory of tradition.

A GUEST FOR THE NIGHT:
The Culpability of the Artist in a Collapsing World

In *A Guest for the Night,* published in 1939 just a few months before the outbreak of the Second World War, Agnon's artistic abilities reached their peak. Everything that had existed in potential in the earlier works is realized here. The parallelism, which previously had been a stratagem accompanying the plot, becomes essential; and the plot becomes secondary. Digression, which had been a comic technique in earlier works, becomes here a pathetic technique, appropriate to the subject.

Until *A Guest for the Night,* the explicit and implicit contents were intermingled, and the equilibrium between the two varied from work to work. Here, the implicit penetrates to the very heart of the explicit, which is laden with hints that only active reading can resolve. While in earlier works Agnon had tried to distance art from reality, here he sought to produce—as had Brenner—a fictional depiction of nonfictional reality. Agnon's text is ultimately different from Brenner's because the special stamp of Agnon's style is imprinted upon it.

The intratextual factors expanded in this work create a unity that is different in kind from the unity of plot (a continuous, logical structure). The logic of spatial analogy supplants the logic of continuity. What the reader supposes to be a travel story about wanderings instead becomes a story of gathering testimony. The narrator-hero listens as a witness to the stories of the refugees from the First World War. That testimony accumulates in his consciousness and changes his attitude to the world. The one who had arrived in order to change and reform learns that the world is flawed and cannot be repaired and that he himself is in need of improvement.

Agnon contributed a new structure to the artistic repertoire of the modern novel. What had been marginal in the traditional structure becomes central in *A Guest for the Night;* and, as happens often with literary development, the new structure twists the kaleidoscope of received norms and renews the tradition.

This new development is the result not only of Agnon's inner growth (the actualization of existing structures) but is a formal response to the problems of the hour—to the global condition between the two world wars and to the Jewish condition before the Holocaust. The standard plot, from which literature often deviated, is no longer valid in this story. Routine life is no longer routine. Henceforth, the author must use new forms to express accurately the new relationship between reality and art.

Agnon sought to create an objective correlative to the disintegrating social reality of people brought together against their will by a unifying, impersonal, historical fate. Every family has its own fate, and each individual faces his or her own destiny. All of the characters are pursued by the repercussions of the war, and the sword of destruction is brandished over everyone's head. As the protagonist-witness passes from family to family, a member of each household confesses to him—telling what happened to him or her and to the rest of the family during the war, who was killed by fire and who by water, and how those who survived managed to do so. Most describe a loss of faith; but certain outstanding individuals, such as Reb Hayim, try to regain their faith and to bring others back to it.

Every person faces his or her own fate, but a stern and terrible decree threatens them all—for there is no way of reversing history. The protagonist-witness tries to roll back the wheel of pure faith, but he discovers that he has no chance of success because history is stronger than the believing person. The following is an outstanding example of this experience, in which the author uses the dream technique to express a historical and religious situation:

I do not remember whether I was awake or dreaming. But I remember that at that moment I was standing in a forest clearing, wrapped in my prayer shawl and crowned with my tefillin, when the child Raphael, Daniel Bach's son, came up with a satchel under his arm. "Who brought you here, my son?" said I. "Today I have become bar mitzvah," said he, "and I am going to the Bet Midrash." I was overcome with pity for this pitiful child, because he was docked of both his hands and could not put on tefillin. He gazed at me with his beautiful eyes and said, "Daddy promised to make me rubber hands." "Your Daddy is an honest man," said I, "and if he has made a promise he will keep it. Perhaps you know why your father saw fit to ask me about Schutzling?" Said Raphael, "Daddy has gone to war and I can't ask him."

"Between ourselves, Raphael," I said to him, "I suspect that your sister Erela is a communist. Doesn't she mock your father?" "Oh, no," said Raphael, "she cries over him, because he can't find his arm." I asked him, "What does it mean, 'he cannot find his arm'?" "He lost his arm," said Raphael. "If so," said I, "where does he put on his tefillin?" "Don't worry about that," said Raphael, "those for the head he puts on his head, and those for the

hand he puts on someone else's arm." "Where does he find someone else's arm?" said I. "He found a soldier's arm in the trench,"
replied Raphael. "Do you think he can meet his obligations with
that one's arm? Isn't it written that the dead are free? When a man
becomes dead, he is exempt from religious precepts, and anyone
who is exempt from a precept cannot exempt anyone else." "I don't
know," he replied. "You don't know," said I, "so why did you
pretend you knew?" "Until you asked me I knew," replied Raphael, "once you asked me I forgot." "From now on," said I, "I
will not ask. Go, my son, go." [16]

This passage is composed of scraps of reality pieced together
like a mosaic in the dream of the protagonist-narrator. The
participants in the dream's story appear in the plot of the
novel itself: the boy's father, Daniel Bach, lost his leg in an
accident after the war, but he told a story about an experience
similar to putting tefillin on someone else's arm, which happened to him in the trenches during the war. The boy is
sickly and visionary, and Erela, the sister, is a Communist.
The materials are "real" but are recombined into a new form
within the dream.

In this novel, as well as in others by Agnon, the dream
appears as a compressed expression of the main message. The
protagonists are not conscious of the message; but it is quite
evident to the implied author, who presents it as the dream of
his "I," the narrator as witness. The dream consists of a
normal-sounding, well-balanced dialogue between the narrator and the child. This balanced dialogue makes the conversation sound natural and comprehensible in a way contradictory to its contents—a contradiction that is intentionally
created by the author. The idea is to portray a world where

horror has become trivial: the narrator and the child talk about rubber hands in the same way they might talk about a wooden rocking horse during normal discourse in the rational world. The father's promise to obtain rubber hands for his son seems like a father's promise to buy a rocking horse for his son in normal life. But in this unexceptional atmosphere, the two interlocutors speak of the connection between a young person and his faith. Members of the younger generation cannot assume the obligation of observing the commandments because they lack the physical ability to do so. They are incapable of belief because society has taken from them the physical and spiritual instruments of belief. Fathers are even incapable of giving substitutes for belief to their sons, who seek faith and find none. The naive tone of the conversation emphasizes that horror has become trivial and normal. Death is a part of life, and children and old people are so used to stories about the trenches and death that the stories have lost their significance.

It must be recalled that this novel was written in 1939, before the holocaust of the Jews in Europe. Agnon foresaw the destruction of the *shtetl* even before it was condemned to death by outside forces. He wanted to find an objective correlative for the trivialization of horror; for the destruction of the *shtetl;* for the loss of faith; and for the fate of the individual, condemned by an impersonal decree.

Using conventional literary techniques would not have done justice to the subjects conveyed in the passage just cited. The new image of the world no longer allowed the artist a calm, disinterested viewpoint. The aesthetic value of depersonalization and the noninvolvement of the narrative figure in the plot are concepts that are no longer beyond doubt. The artist's ironic viewpoint, as he looks from the distance of "ice water on a snowy day," which existed potentially from Agnon's very first steps as a writer, here becomes an essential thematic problem. The author deals ironically with the viewpoint of the artist who looks at the approaching holocaust without being involved in it.

The story recounted in *A Guest for the Night* is composed of digressions and retreats in narrative time, although there is order in these elipses (*analepsis,* in Gérard Genette's terms) because each refers to stories about the First World War. As mentioned previously, each of the speakers has his or her own fate, and all share a common fate—that of the citizen in the rear as a victim of the war—and secondary features—some of the family members have been killed, and the survivors are trying to make their way in the world.

The structure that had disintegrated is restored through the use of intratextual techniques typical of all of Agnon's works. The substance of the parallels is revealed through the words of the narrator-hero as he thinks about the world he has created:

I said to myself: Another old man also had two sons, and the news came to him that their blood had been shed on one day. And Freide had two sons, and their blood was shed on one day. The Holy One, blessed be He, always measures out abundantly, both for good and for evil. When He gives, He gives double, and when He takes, He takes double.[17]

Here, the technique of parallelism reaches an almost infinite degree of fragmentation: each figure has several synonymous parallels, and each situation has several parallel situations. At times it seems as if the author has lost the thread of the main plot, except that the reader finds that the loss itself is one of the main themes of the story.

The story does begin and end, but both the beginning and the end are conditioned by a framework that does not belong to the plot. The narrator-hero arrives in his hometown and leaves it; he is exiled from the Land of Israel, and he returns to the land. Between the two framework dates he wanders, and the author tries to fill that aimlessness with some sort of task, which gradually disintegrates as the plot advances. The plot framework reveals that the narrator-witness has taken upon himself a task that he is unable to carry out. Because the secondary plots are more important than the main one, they overwhelm the apparent central action of the protagonist.

The narrator-hero returns to his city in order to build his faith and to be rebuilt in his faith. However, in step after step he finds that he cannot raise the ruins of Szybucz (that is, Buczacz). His inability to restore lost glory and to bring the old temple back to life is symbolized by the key motif: the narrator has reopened the old house of study but then loses the key. After much difficulty, he has a new key made. Nevertheless, he fails to attract people to the house of study once the winter is over, and they no longer need its heat. Upon his return to the Land of Israel, he discovers the old key among his belongings.[18] He is also unable to help the miserable poor: Hanokh, Reb Hayim, Daniel Bach, Zommer, Schuster and Freide, and the invalids from the First World War who have no economic or social support. He must abandon the effort at spiritual revival in the house of study because of the need for actual and immediate physical assistance.

143

Agnon's narrator is an author and eyewitness whose discoveries weigh upon him and oppress him like a yoke. His burden is symbolized by the motif of the overcoat—the narrator has a handsome coat made for himself but then feels guilty because most of the poor in the town are hungry and virtually naked. Thus, the most personal events have national significance, and national considerations have a human dimension.

The narrator-author treats imaginary figures as though they were authentic. He uses autobiographical materials—his relation to the town, his wife and children, emigration from the Land of Israel—thus placing his entire being as a biographical and creative personality in the work. He is not merely a narrator but a narrator-writer, with his existential totality, with the life of the imagination and reality side by side.

The narrator was to accomplish a purpose in his hometown —to revive the old values of Jewish learning. He is forced to set aside that intention because he finds that helping the poor and the afflicted is more important than his original goal. The narrator is not unequivocal regarding himself but directs constant, harsh criticism against himself. The world revealed to him in the chain of testimony causes him to admit that life is more important than literature and that *an aesthetic viewpoint is not a moral one.* The narrator's feeling of guilt grows as the testimony about the suffering of the world accrues. The "faith" that confronts the suffering has committed a capital crime, for it contemplates without being truly part of the experience of suffering.

It is impossible to restore a world where children cannot put on phylacteries because they have neither physical nor

spiritual arms—depending on whether the dream is interpreted literally or metaphorically. It is impossible to make
moral demands or artistic claims upon a world where a father
places a phylactery on someone else's arm. The claimant here
is less moral than the defendants. The novel is thus a multifaceted chronicle about the disintegration of a town between
the two world wars and is also a work that places the artist's
guilt and responsibility as a human being in that situation.
As in other works, here we have a mixture of the existential
stratum with the details of a chronicle.

This manner of representation renewed two basic elements
in the tradition of the novel: fragmented analogical structure
and presentation of the narrator as both an authentic and
fictitious author—brilliantly evoking in a new way the confrontation between art and the Holocaust before the Holocaust.

The main subject of the novel is the vain attempt to restore
the glory of the tradition. The narrator-protagonist tries to
restore the faith of the *shtetl*'s residents, who live in despair.
The implied author relates with absolute irony to the first-
person narrator's vain efforts to carry out that impossible task.
The narrator-protagonist tries to cling to the tradition, while
the revolutionary implied author proves to him, with "signs
and wonders" drawn from history and by means of the secondary characters who populate the town, that these efforts are
hopeless. The revolutionary traditionalist forces a collision
between the naive aspirations of the hero and the dreadful
irony of historical fate. History itself contains the revolution
that prevents the tradition from persisting.

The characters of the novel have witnessed a cruel, impersonal historical process; and they tell their stories to the narrator-hero, who functions as a secondary witness. They have lived through the miseries they recount; he experiences their travails only by reproducing them in his capacity as an addressee who transmits the cumulative burden of the stories he has collected. In turn, the narrator-hero's own addressee, the implied reader, is meant to react both to the sufferings of the primary sources and to the narrator's guilt feelings. Thus, the responsibility of the addressee has increased geometrically. The reader must absorb the ills inflicted by history as well as the distress of the narrator-hero who recollects that history in tranquillity.

The contrast in form between the literary tradition and the revolution reaches its peak in this novel. The literary tradition persists in the balanced rabbinical style and in the many Jewish symbols, such as the phylacteries and the prayer shawl in the dream. The revolution lies in the complex structure and composition of the novel and in the complex relationship between the implied author and the first-person narrator and witness. Agnon found a fitting objective correlative for the complex subject of the revolution implicit in the tradition and the yearnings for the tradition within the revolution.

ONLY YESTERDAY:
A Portrait of the Pioneer as Victim

A *Simple Story* is a realistic psychological novel that underwent the process of mythification. *A Guest for the Night* recounts the anatomy of a society and the confession of the narrator-hero, and the novel's composition created a new literary tradition. *Only Yesterday* (1945) is a social and psychological novel with nonrealistic elements; it is a novel striving for a mythical interpretation. The seeds of this work lie in the period of the Second Aliya. It began with two separate structures — Yitzhak and the dog Balak — that were melded together in the process of creation.[19] The story describes the immigration of Yitzhak Kumer, who tried to take part in the experience of the Second Aliya and failed because he was still tied by his "umbilical cord" to the past and to his hometown.

The story is primarily a chronicle of the Second Aliya that uses extraliterary materials in an effort to attain documentary credibility. It offers a detailed description of the social life of Neve-Tsedek, Tel Aviv, Jerusalem and its neighborhoods, and Ain-Ganim. It presents a long series of historical and imaginary types whose function is to represent the reality of the Land of Israel and to serve as a believable background for the hero's adventures in space and time.

The setting is a metonym for the psychological and social problems of the hero, creating the polar opposition that tears him from within. Jaffa is a secular city of immigrants; Jerusalem is the city of religious tradition. Jaffa is a metonymical expansion of the character of Sonya, with whom Yitzhak Kumer falls in love; just as Sonya, in her frivolity, epitomizes the city. Shifra, Yitzhak's future wife, lives in Jerusalem and represents a certain aspect of the city's naive religiosity. Yitzhak's wanderings between Jerusalem and Jaffa represent his inability to decide between Sonya and Shifra. To choose Sonya is to betray his late mother; to choose Shifra is to flee from Sonya and to betray her. The choice of Shifra is also an effort

by Yitzhak to return to his mother. Yitzhak's repressed relationship with Jaffa and Sonya is embodied by the dog Balak.
Through the dog the author represents the split that takes
place in Yitzhak's personality after leaving Jaffa and trying to
return to his roots.

The hesitation between the poles brings guilt. Yitzhak
leaves his father's house and leaves his father with debts for
his fare. "Like the rest of our brethren, the children of our
redemption,"[20] he plans to work the land, but he must
support himself and learns to be a house painter in Jaffa. This
then becomes his profession; thus, he betrays both his father
and the Zionist values for which he betrayed his father. Moreover, Yitzhak is sure he has robbed his friend Rabinovitz,
who left the country, of his fiancée, Sonya. For that, too,
Yitzhak is pursued by guilt. His penitence in Jerusalem is not
complete, for he neglects his secular being, which is embodied
in the demonic figure of the dog Balak—the embodiment of
heresy—who looks upon old Jerusalem from a satirical angle.
Yitzhak Kumer is also an artist who misses the mark. Unlike
Blaukopf, who fulfills himself, Yitzhak remains a pseudoartist
—a painter who does not create things but rather covers
them. Balak, Rabinovitz, Blaukopf, Arzep, and Leichtfuss
(literally, sweet foot) are parallel figures who play an intratextual part in the synonymous elaboration of the protagonist.

The protagonist acts not only on the psychological level but
also within the mythic infrastructure of the novel. In *The
Bridal Canopy* the myth of the great believer is embodied; *A
Simple Story* presents the mythic contrast between bourgeois
life and the Dionysian powers that seek to destroy it. The
mythic infrastructure of *A Guest for the Night* points toward

catastrophes and disintegration; *Only Yesterday* is based on the myth of sacrifice.

In order to seize the significance of that myth, the reader should view the work from the perspective of its conclusion. Agnon's readers are accustomed to conclusions that open rather than close things. Rather than words of consolation and redemption, Agnon's conclusions contain a promise that the author will one day return to the heroes of the story and will tell about those upon whom fate has smiled. The teller of *A Simple Story* hints that he will one day consider recounting a love story between true lovers (such as Blume Nacht or Akabia Mazal and his wife). Similarly, the narrator of *Only Yesterday* hints that he will one day tell "the deeds of our brethren and sisters, the children of the living God, who work the land of Israel for its glory and splendor." He goes on to promise that "the deeds of our other friends will be in the book about the meadow."[21]

Despite such a promise, the novel does not seem to point toward a promise of utopia. The latter is indeed to be found in the figure of Menachem Ha-Omed or in the depiction of Ain-Ganim; but, in fact, the realm of utopia does not make contact with the realm of this novel.

Jaffa and Jerusalem and Sonya and Shifra represent two extremes that cannot be permanently united. Yitzhak is the sacrificial victim of the eternal split between exile and redemption—between Judaism and Zionism. Like the patriarch Isaac, Yitzhak is bound on Mount Moriah, but God does not provide a substitute for him. At the conclusion of the novel there is a drought. Only after Yitzhak Kumer's funeral does a new flowering begin: "Only yesterday we were standing at prayer and pleading, reciting confessions, blowing the rams' horns, and singing petitionary hymns. Today we are singing psalms of praise with great thanks."[22]

A heavy sin lay upon the earth; only with Yitzhak's death, after the mad dog (a projection of the secular world and Yitzhak's own repressed demonic instincts) bites him, is the sin expunged and the land graced with fresh growth:

When we went out we saw the land smiling with buds and blossoms. From one end to the other the shepherds came with their flocks, and from the moist earth rose the sound of the sheep, and the birds of the heavens answered them. Great joy was in the world. Never was such joy seen.[23]

The novel is founded on a tragic conception reminiscent of the theme of *Oedipus Rex.* There, too, sin lies heavily upon the city, which cannot be redeemed from the plague until a scapegoat is found and driven out. However, the difference between the protagonist of the Greek tragedy and Agnon's anti-hero is also quite evident. In *Oedipus Rex,* the protagonist strives for consciousness of sin, is purged through that consciousness, and draws near to the gods once he has come to know himself. In contrast, Agnon describes a character who never attains self-knowledge; he is the innocent victim of an ironic situation that he himself created—his relationship with the forces of evil as symbolized by the dog—although he never knows his sin. In Agnon's novel, the nonhero is trapped in circumstances that are beyond his ability to overcome. The tragic hero of *Oedipus Rex* is exalted in the hour of truth—the hour of struggle with the sacrificing powers—and the spectators are elevated along with him. The nonhero of *Only Yester-*

day is destroyed. He bows his head before the storm, leaving the witnesses of that ironic process subdued and saddened.[24] Yet, at the same time, the process of punishment also contains rebirth—the individual is sacrificed, but the society rises to new life.

Yitzhak Kumer is the innocent and hopeless victim of a transitional period when the heroes belonged to a generation doomed to destruction. As the ending shows, the author clearly felt that by virtue of those sacrifices the cursed plague was halted and the possibilities for new life were created. The essence of that life is hinted at, not depicted.

However, the end of the novel is also a pathetic elegy for the anti-hero's pointless and unpleasant death, a kind of tragic justification of his fate. Yitzhak's connection with the dog brought death to him, and because that relationship is justified on the symbolic level—where Yitzhak is representative of his generation—the death is justified. Nevertheless, as a unique individual the relationship between Yitzhak and the dog is merely coincidental. From such a viewpoint, Yitzhak is merely a pathetic and miserable victim of blind chance. Considering it this way, we cannot justify Yitzhak's fate or our own, but we feel pity for a *schlemiel* who blundered into disaster.

The reader, reacting to the plight of the nonhero, is affected in contrary ways: he or she feels that Yitzhak's fate is justified, yet that feeling alternates and is mingled with pity. The author evokes mixed feelings toward the end of the book to purge the reader of these two reactions. Thus, *Only Yesterday* is a social novel that makes use of modern symbolic techniques and is based on a structure linking background and figure that ultimately exposes the mythical roots of the social reality.

This novel is perhaps the most extreme of all with regard to the relationship between tradition and revolution. The question here is what did the Zionist revolution do to the tradition? The dog, which in many respects is the satiric embodiment of the results of the Zionist revolution—that is, secularization and skepticism—is to some degree a positive figure. The dog immolates the man, who has become a victim of the Zionist revolution. Unable to bear the strain, Yitzhak tries to return to the tradition as a penitent, in order to escape the tensions and responsibilities of the revolution. The dog proves to the victim Yitzhak that there is no way back and that the individual who takes this path can never go home again.

The surface plot of *Only Yesterday* is a detailed historical chronicle. It could be given a "readerly" interpretation, in that some readers could imagine that the implied author has "programmed" their historical and ideological readings; but the mysterious dog and the intertextual allusions of the ending open the novel up to a wide variety of contradictory interpretations. According to the hermeneutic code—that is, understanding the riddle of the text—the reader must solve the secret of the analogy between dog and man and then, of course, the intertextual allusions of the sacrificial ending. The solutions to these encoded secrets are various, and what has been suggested here is only one of many options. The chronicle novel has been opened up to a "writerly" interpretation.

SHIRA:
Portrait of the Professor as an Aging Male

Parts of *Shira* began to appear in the late 1940s,[25] but the novel was not published in full until 1971 after Agnon's death. Like *Only Yesterday,* this novel is immersed in the life of the Land of Israel and describes a specific segment of the society—the German immigrants of the 1930s and 1940s. The main character, Manfred Herbst, has two daughters, Zohara and Tamara, who were born in Mandate Palestine.

The Hebrew University in the 1930s and 1940s is at the center of the social reality in the novel; within it is Herbst, the intellectual who has reached middle age and seeks the meaning of his life. He oscillates between the fixed routines of family life and the wondrous and dreadful adventure awaiting him outside his house. Here the chronicle functions well as part of a psychological novel.

After ranging far afield in *Only Yesterday* and *A Guest for the Night* and creating structures beyond realism, in *Shira* Agnon returned to the tradition of the realistic family novel, such as Gustav Flaubert's *Madame Bovary,* Leo Tolstoy's *Anna Karenina,* and John Galsworthy's *The Forsyte Saga.* Such novels generally describe the weakening and collapse of the family. But here, too, Agnon found a rather original formulation of that constantly repeated pattern. It should be recalled that as early as *A Simple Story* Agnon took a position different from that of European writers and awarded the bourgeoisie an apparent victory over the forces opposing it. In *A Simple Story,* Agnon overcame the crisis by introducing the psychologist

Dr. Langsam, a deus ex machina, a force invented by the bourgeoisie in order to control its wayward sons.

In *Shira* Agnon used a different pattern. Detailed examination reveals that the pattern is based on repeated descriptions of the Herbst family and its inner and external relations: "I shall take the time to note all the souls in the Herbst household, starting with little Sarah."[26] Before Sarah becomes a conscious individual the narrator does not mention her in his overviews. After she attains a certain maturity, the narrator begins to relate to her as well. This is also true of Gabriel, the Herbsts' young son; of the son-in-law Abraham-and-a-Half; of the daughter of Tamara's friends, Schlesinger and Taglicht; and of Tamara's other friend, Ursala Katz. The society of professors is also an extension of the Herbst family circle, as are the domestic workers Sarini and Firdaos. The narrator's eye surveys the family circle and returns to observe all the protagonists together and each one individually. The family framework is essentially idyllic, and what is permanent within it is more important than passing events:

Once again the patterns of life were arranged without excessive incident. Gabi was growing nicely. He was like his little sister: just as she did not annoy her mother very much, so too he does not annoy his mother very much, and it goes without saying not his father. And it is well that he does not disturb his father, who must prepare his lectures for the winter season and ought not give his attention to extraneous matters.[27]

What other situation does this resemble in Agnon's oeuvre? It is similar to the apparently fixed framework of Tsirl's or

Ziemlich's houses, in *A Simple Story*, is where everything was fine and the only danger lurking within the house was that of leaving it and losing one's mind.

In describing the family history, time advances quite slowly. This is the epic continuity of ordinary, quotidian events: a meal, dialogues between the spouses, the domestics' problems, pregnancy, birth, nursing, the work of teaching, relationships between father and daughters and between grandparents and grandchildren, and so on. Even the likely changes are part of that so-called progress: aging, new human contacts, hope for professional advancement. This bourgeois order of life finds redemption in repeated tableaux of family surveys. The term *bourgeois* is not meant here to refer to a social class but rather to the order of life in Western society from the nineteenth through the mid-twentieth centuries, based on a man's commitment to a single woman and a single profession and on reasonable causality in a person's progress through life.

The very order of life that was undermined in *A Guest for the Night* again is presented here as though nothing had happened. It is a circular, unending pattern (unless the whole world is overturned), based on the pleasant legend of "to be continued" and always ending with the same marvelous words of consolation: ". . . and they did not die but lived happily ever after."

Some of the artistic peaks of *Shira* are found in that recurrent cycle. Perhaps more than in previous works, Agnon succeeded in presenting a complex slice of life and depicting primary relationships, such as man and wife (for example, Herbst calls Henrietta "mother"),[28] father and daughters, mother and daughter, father and son-in-law. An additional cycle, moving round and round, is that of Herbst's work, as he sits with his file cards day after day:[29]

We know Dr. Manfred Herbst's work habits, which are certainly no different from those of most scholars. He sits in his room in front of his table, poring over his books and index cards, reading a book, joining cards together, and putting them in a special box. Sometimes the box gets full before his time for using the cards is filled, and sometimes the time is filled and the box is not full. When the time comes for writing a chapter or an article he takes out the index cards, culls them, orders them according to their content, and binds together the ordered ones with paper clips, reading them and writing whatever he writes.[30]

That description, which is repeated several times, offers a good example of the monotonous, routine circle of the scholar's life. That Sisyphean labor, which becomes a matter of interest in its own right, becomes comic because it is petrified and habitual. Variations in the progress of the epic time of the family's life serve to moderate the comic immobility. The monotony of the scholar's work, lacking the spark of true life, emphasizes its ridiculous wretchedness.

In contrast to these two circles—family life in the Jerusalem neighborhood of Baka'a and scholarly work—in which new events are routine innovations, the author depicts an opposite pattern, with its own fixity and, sometimes, its own ridiculous immobility. This pattern is connected to the city center, represented by Shira and the coffee houses, and to the hero's flights, which are inspired by his Dionysian impulses, from his wife and his index cards. Nevertheless, Herbst remains tragicomic both at home and in the street: "For several days he would shut himself up in the house and deal with matters he had not dealt with before, so long as he did not go to town, for if he went to town, his feet would race to Shira's house."[31] On his walks, Herbst comes to the coffee house first, then certain ties are formed between him and Elisabeth Neu but mainly between him and the nurse Shira. She becomes his mistress while his wife is giving birth to his child, who is born as Herbst enters his fiftieth year. In the end, he no longer goes to the cafés but turns directly to Shira's house.

Herbst's visits become tragicomic in that they lose their purpose. At first he tries not to find out Shira's new address. In the end, he does search and finds her address, but the house is locked. He cannot visit her while awake, so he haunts her doorstep in dreams and fantasies. The more Shira's actual presence is diminished, the more her inner being expands. Herbst is willing to listen to the inanities of the nurse Ludmilla, hoping that he will hear something about Shira from her,[32] but long before that Shira had become a fantasy.[33]

Throughout the novel Herbst has many dreams laden with frightening nightmares centered on Shira, like the dream of Elisabeth's marriage to Shira. Elisabeth, the niece of the divine scholar Neu, is an ethereal presence, while Shira is a creature of flesh and blood in whose appetites there is a potency that renews a man's virility.[34] Between these two figures who mingle in Herbst's dream there is a connection, which could be one of similarity or of contraries. Both of them cause Herbst to step out of his framework and away from immobility. With Elisabeth he is drawn to celestial love and with Shira to carnal love. Elisabeth is Herbst's dream of the springtime of his life; Shira is the dream of his autumnal years.

Along with the dream is a sadomasochistic fantasy about Shira and the Arab engineer who is about to plunge "a dagger in her heart." [35] Herbst's fantasy is an expression of his ambivalence toward Shira. He desires her, but at the same time he seeks to destroy that strange yearning.

The realistic motif becomes increasingly imaginary and demonic; it grows fainter but does not disappear. Herbst is gripped by passion for Shira until the somewhat murky conclusion of the book. Shira, the realistic figure, is overtly and undisguisedly forgotten, becoming increasingly internalized within Herbst. Thus, a novelistic motif becomes one of romance. The character continues to act upon the hero's soul, even after she disappears from the novel's realistic course of action. [36]

As the book advances toward its conclusion (but not necessarily the conclusion itself), it becomes fragmentary in its structure and sketchy in its execution. The deliquescence of Shira as the dynamic motivation driving Herbst from his Olympian tranquillity brings about the increasing disintegration of the structure. It seems as if the author and his heroes are gripped by an autumnal muse; when she disappears, so does the power of creativity. The author did well to title his book after the motivating character and not after the character motivated to follow the star that appears in his life, as a miser pursues his wealth.

Shira represents a regression in Agnon's novelistic art, a return to the realistic structure of *A Simple Story*. Like *A Simple*

Story, this novel describes a Pyhrric victory. Here, it is the victory of the academic establishment and the established family over an elderly scholar who tries in his later years to break out of these institutional restrictions. The tradition— specifically, the bourgeois tradition or the tradition of the bourgeois intelligentsia—vanquishes the man who tries to stage a revolution in his life. He fails because the power of the tradition overcomes him. He finds he is incapable of being a lover or an artist (at one point, Herbst tries to write a play about the kings of Byzantium whom he is studying), and so he must go back to being a paterfamilias and a frustrated professor. The protagonist's effort to renew himself and to break out of the restrictions of his society fails resoundingly.

Agnon took the side of the protagonist in his attempts to break out of his resignation, which is surprising for an author who presented himself as a traditional writer. What this suggests is that Agnon preferred an attempted revolution to a surrender to the Jewish bourgeois tradition.

Agnon wrote an alternative ending to the novel, which he chose to suppress; from it, he created the story "Forevermore." In "Forevermore," the protagonist retreats from the world to a leprosarium, where true suffering is found. For him, the leprosarium is preferable to bourgeois society. The alternative ending is an expression of despair, which is also a kind of victory over bourgeois society and is preferable to resignation. In both the alternative endings, the implied author regards bourgeois society with irony, showing that it represses the aging fathers as it repressed the adolescent sons in *A Simple Story.*

IN MR. LUBLIN'S STORE:
The Alien Versus a Hostile Setting

In Mr. Lublin's Store was published posthumously in 1975. Agnon did not give it the finishing touches; nevertheless, the structure of the novel reflects the line of development of Agnon's work—from coherent structure (the apogee of which is *A Simple Story*) to decoherent structure. *In Mr. Lublin's Store* is an extension of the earlier novella "Until Now," both in the background described—Germany during the First World War—and in the presentation of the narrator as the protagonist. However, while the narrator-hero of "Until Now" breaks open the structure by his futile travels, both within the city and between cities, here there is no linear development. The hero is stationary, never budging from the situation in which he is stuck.

In Mr. Lublin's Store is the story of a man who takes it upon himself to watch over his friend's store because his friend has helped him to obtain permission to live in Leipzig, where he has come to study Torah. From then on, the hero recounts the story of the members of the household, the neighbors, and the servants. The store and its near surroundings become a synecdoche for the world in which Mr. Lublin is caught, as a Jew who left the eastern European town of Buczacz for the West. The outer chapters (those that comprise the framework: chapters 1, 2, and "The Last Chapter") are devoted to two natives of Buczacz, Lublin and Jakob Stern, whose attitudes to the Western world are the opposite of each other's. The inner chapters (chapters 3 and 4) are devoted to Mr. Lublin's

German neighbors, whose stories reflect the life of the setting. Chapters 6 and 7 are full of confrontation and confession; in the final chapter, the circle is closed. The narrator-hero stands before Jakob Stern again; in contrast to him, he remains faithful to the town in life and in death.

Thematically and structurally, *In Mr. Lublin's Store* is similar to *A Guest for the Night* and "Until Now." As in those two works, the narrator-hero is a transient whose status in the setting causes him to feel guilt: "Truly I too, like him, left my city and emigrated to the Land of Israel, but what came of that, since on my own and of my own free will I have left there?" [37]

At the other end of that semantic field we have:

Mr. Jakob Stern sat and was silent. One could not say he was silent because he was tired from the trip, for even in a dream, when he heard the name of someone from our town, he would wake up immediately and converse with him, nor could one say that the progeny of that great scholar, the author of *The Eternity of Israel* were not dear to him but one might hazard that his mind was not easy about Mr. Lublin, for even gentiles who left our town had a way of returning to it, but this man, not only had he left our town when he was young, but during all those years he had not come to see it. [38]

The essential theme is the culpability of a person who willingly leaves his home and tries to settle in a place that is not his. None of the three protagonists fit in. The narrator dwells in Mr. Lublin's store and thinks about his hometown; [39] Mr. Lublin, who apparently has been absorbed into German society, fears the total assimilation of his children, so much so that he is even willing to have them become Zionists;[40] Jakob Stern recalls the relationship between Jews and Gentiles in their hometown and warns against absolute deracination. The weak bound between this structure and the other structures of the work creates in the addressee a feeling of decoherence.

Another pattern in the novel is connected to the First World War and the concept of war:

War does not cease in the world. All the nations are prepared for war. Always, always they make war. And if you see a generation without war, you can be certain it's preparing itself for war. Not you and I, but the ministers who occupy the highest posts in the kingdom.[41]

The gentile neighbors and the Jewish Saltzmann family are victims of the war. The Saltzmanns' fate is similar to the fate of the families in *A Guest for the Night*. However, the parallels among the characters' fates in this novel are not strong but are actually quite coincidental. See, for example, the connections between the fate of Lemke, his wife, Frederika, the circus manager Director Ahmichen, and Mr. Lublin who saved Lemke; or the relationship between Lisa-Lotte, Lemke, Regina Honig, Gerte Hinings, and the narrator. (The hint that Isolde and Adam Eisba look like Jews,[42] whereas Lublin or Saltzmann look like Germans,[43] only appears to be a parallel.) At any rate, the analogical material is not sufficiently convincing. Through the use of anecdotes about the German bureaucracy and the relationship between masters and servants, Agnon created *thematic spaces*—that is, elements and fragments with no direct relationship to the continuity or general pattern of the work, but whose function is to provide realistic credibility for the novel's structure.

Other examples of the weak and problematic connections among the components of this novel are found in the discussion of the theater and the relationship between reality and art[44] and in the author's dream about the Jew who presents himself to Charlemagne to write a letter for him. It is also possible to view the author's dream as the mythification of the relationship between the Jews and the Germans—as an expatiation upon actual historical events.[45] If the dream is interpreted in the context, the anecdotes become synecdoches that represent a general pattern of German society and its Jewry and the alienated status of eastern European Jews. In either case, the elements of the confrontation remain decoherent.

It could be that in this novel Agnon attempted to bring the decoherent techniques employed by him as early as *The Bridal Canopy* to a peak and to make the fissures in the plot— a kind of anti-Aristotelian technique—into the basic pattern and subject of the work. In fact, the addressee, who is called upon to bring together the pieces and grasp the structure as a significant whole, faces severe difficulties, for it is hard to find a solution here beyond the mere fact that the disparate parts are located in the same place. Moreover, if the epic setting and the detailed presentation of the anecdotes in *In Mr. Lublin's Store* rescue the structure from utter disintegration, in later works with similar structures—such as *Within the Wall* and "Footstool and Chair"—the effort to bring the fragments together is unsuccessful. It seems that the author is asking the impossible of his readers: to do without one of the basic paths of all human thought—that is, the combination of fragments of appearances into a meaningful whole.

At the end of his career, after the appearance of two complex novels, one based on a split structure—*A Guest for the Night*—and the other based on a split in the protagonist's personality—*Only Yesterday*—Agnon, who began as an exponent of the picaresque tradition and as a traditional author who continued the realistic psychological novel, wrote a fissured, decoherent novel that transgresses the boundaries of the reader's expectations for wholeness. The delicate equilibrium between readability and nonreadability and between observing and flouting the conventions of the novel confronts the reader in all its problematic complexity.

The addressee faces one of the most difficult issues for the implied reader of the modern novel: the open options of interpretation. These options are characteristic of a decoherent, "writerly" text and provoke and entice readers into finding coherent meanings in a fragmented text that sometimes has no pretensions of conveying any such thing. The fragmented, decoherent medium is the only message, and most attempts at interpretation are sterile endeavors to create a new world *ex nihilo*. *In Mr. Lublin's Store* is suspended between extreme fragmentation and meaningful messages delivered by a certain degree of coherence that is given to the sequence through the framework of the spatial setting.

To a large degree, *In Mr. Lublin's Store* sums up Agnon's thematic and formal development. This novel is also a prime example of an objective correlative for a world that is out of joint—a world where a plot is no longer possible because impersonal forces deriving from the setting where it takes place, Germany, no longer permit the development of a normal plot. Only the components of the place, which determine the fate of many individuals who live there, can be described. The entire tradition has been undermined, although many of the characters yearn for it in their nostalgia for the *shtetl* of their birth. However, there is no hope of returning home; there is no chance to rebuild the fallen tabernacle of the tradition.

Whereas in his earlier novels Agnon described the tension between revolution and tradition and made implicit his great sympathy for the tradition, here he reveals that the revolution that occurred within his society—for which he himself had presented the revolutionary model—had left him and his society in a condition of utter collapse. The tradition has been destroyed, and nothing replaces it. *In Mr. Lublin's Store* is parallel to the stories of *The Book of Deeds,* which were written in a metarealistic literary technique, and to stories like "Edo and Enam" and "Forevermore." All of these stories, as well as "Until Now," express the rule of anarchy in the world. The decoherent structure is an objective correlative for that anarchy.

Agnon developed from a revolutionary author who struggled against the tradition and blessed the revolution to an innovative author who described through a new literary form the revolution that was taking place. He revealed through form and content that the new revolutionary reality did not create a new order but rather a decoherent anarchy that places man in a grotesque condition characterized by total disorientation. In this presentation, the implied author is portrayed as someone detached from the tradition; however, now that the tradition has collapsed, in the depths of his heart or in his subconscious he yearns to return to it.

CHAPTER 5

THE GENRES AND FORMS, THE NOVELLA, AND THE SHORT STORIES

Fictional Genres

THE WEALTH of Agnon's forms and traditions emerges mainly in his short stories and novellas. In fact, one of the most surprising phenomena in Agnon's work is manifest in his short stories and novellas—that is, he is not part of the natural development of the tradition of European literature. An author who in his lifetime wrote *The Bridal Canopy,* a picaresque novel like those of the eighteenth century; social novels like those of the late nineteenth and early twentieth centuries, such as *A Simple Story* and *Shira;* and then went on to write modernistic novels, such as *A Guest for the Night, Only Yesterday,* and *In Mr. Lublin's Store,* is not part of any single literary lineage.

Agnon does not follow the trail of the inner development of the tradition of European novelistic genres. In Agnon's work, there is a constant tension between the underlying modern structure and the ingenuous surface text. In his picaresque and social novels, the ingenuous, traditional veil is in the foreground; and the modern complexity is relegated to the background. In other works, the traditional veil does not obscure the modern, revolutionary content. Most of Agnon's novels, novellas, and short stories share certain basic, underlying structures and themes; but these thematic and formal patterns are transformed by Agnon's abundant diversity of genre.[1] To indicate the variety of genres in his oeuvre, I will describe some of them below.

Along with psychological love stories in the realistic European tradition, such as "The Hill of Sand," "In the Prime of Her Life," "The Doctor's Divorce," and "Fernheim," are legends about saints and their deeds, such as "The Tale of Rabbi Gadiel, the Infant," "In the Heart of the Seas," "Rabbi Katriel the Cantor," "Priest of Truth," and "The Stones of the Place." Many stories are humorous anecdotes with grotesque tendencies, such as "The Convert," "With the Death of the Saint," "The Mother's Voice," and "Pisces." Others read like social satires, such as "Of Our Young People and Our Elders," or like feuilletons, such as "Chapters of the Book of the State." Some of the most interesting stories are on the borderline between realism and symbolism, such as "Betrothed" and "The Covering of Blood."

Agnon tended to create artistic versions of primary folk forms: the balladistic saga ("Repentance" and "Under the Tree") takes its place beside the sad tale ("The Child Who Died"), the family saga ("The History of Our Houses"), and historical chronicles ("The City of the Dead," "The Father of the Ox," and chapters of *A City and the Fullness Thereof*). Some of Agnon's works are written in the style of pious, inspirational literature, such as "And the Crooked Shall Be Made Straight" and "The Tale of the Scribe," but hint at modern fiction. Others start off closer to surrealism in structure and content, such as *The Book of Deeds*, "Edo and Enam," "The Overcoat," "At the Outset of the Day," "Forevermore," and "Footstool and Chair." Certain stories appear to be Gothic ("The Dance of Death," "The Lovers' Canopy," and "The Lady and the Peddler") but contain a complex kernel of modernity. There are legends about historical figures, such as "Pleasant Stories of Rabbi Israel Baal Shem Tov"; and there are children's stories, such as "The Story of a Goat," "My Bird," and "The Kerchief." One can also find semidocumentary stories, such as "To the Galilee." Agnon's eulogies, speeches, and memoirs are a genre in their own right. (See his speeches on Berl Katzenelson, Martin Buber, Yosef Hayim Brenner, Gershom Scholem, Yosef Aharonovitch and also his speeches at various ceremonies in his honor.)

Thus, we find a rich variety of genres that cannot be classified on the basis of the author's diachronic development, for he wrote in all of them at the same time. It is noteworthy that Agnon wrote in a rich variety of forms and genres. His ability to transmit the transformation of different messages from various points of view was indeed great. He created counterpoint within his works, as in his irony toward the protagonists and their innocent actions found in works that, on first reading, appear to be legendary tales of righteous people, such as "Tehilla," or simple love stories, such as "Agunot: A Tale." There is also counterpoint among the different works of various types, which should not be read individually but rather as part of a single canon, in which each work illustrates its fellow.

The Novella

Agnon's novellas, somewhere in length between a short story and a novel, follow the tradition established in the early twentieth century by Yosef Hayim Brenner, Uri Nisan Gnessin, and Jacob Steinberg. That tradition is different from the German novella (the prime example being the works of Heinrich von Kleist), which generally is defined as a long dramatic story based on a causal sequence with few delays.

The tradition of the dramatic novella was not typical of Hebrew literature, and Agnon's contemporaries tended more toward the lyric novella or the novella of delay, where putting off the dramatic climax is more important than the dramatic processes that lead to it. This type of novella has parallels in the lyric fiction of the Scandinavians Bjornstjerne Bjornson, Knut Hamsun, and Jens Peter Jacobsen. Typical examples of the nondramatic novella were written by three members of the generation just before Agnon's: Brenner ("Between Water and Water"), Steinberg ("On the Ukrainian Border"), and Gnessin ("At").

Brenner's novellas are fragmentary and episodic (for example, "From the Straits" and "Between Water and Water"). In the novellas of Gnessin (for example, "Before" and "At"), there is no balance between the time of telling (the *sujet*) and the time of the narrative (the *fabula*); and the time of telling and fragments of stream of consciousness produce delays that do not lead to a dramatic climax. Steinberg's novellas are similar, being lyric descriptions of the inner world of the individual and not necessarily depictions of the hazards of fate.

Agnon began with a decidedly dramatic novella: "And the Crooked Shall Be Made Straight." In it, the plot is structured upon a predicament, travel and delay, crisis and punishment, and submission to fate. In later novellas the importance of the dramatic elements changes. In "Of Our Young People and Our Elders," the satirical digressions increase. In "In the Prime of Her Life," the confessional form creates an effect more lyric than dramatic. In the later novellas, such as "Betrothed," tension is created between the dramatic structure and the lyric and epic elements that delay the course of the story. The dramatic element is diminished as a result of connections both within the text and between texts, demanding a reading in breadth—that is, delayed—rather than a linear reading.

The Psychological Novella. Two of Agnon's most interesting novellas are "Betrothed" and "Pisces." At first glance, the first of these seems to be a conventional romantic novella, but it is actually a deep psychological work that lays bare the unconscious world of the protagonist and the unconscious motivations of a whole social group. "Pisces," on the other hand, is a grotesque novella in which the border between reality and fantasy is blurred. In it, Agnon displayed the full power of his originality.

"Betrothed" is also an example of a delayed novella. This type of novella is slow moving, has a deep psychological significance, and has a hidden meaning that is more important than the presentation of any social reality. The author notes both the psychological significance of social situations and the social results of psychological situations.

On first reading, "Betrothed" ("Shevu'at emunim"), one of Agnon's later novellas of 1943, appears to be a neoromantic work similar to those commonly written in Europe, and especially Scandinavia, in the late nineteenth and early twentieth centuries. The romantic element of the novella is conveyed through the atmosphere of the setting and through the plot. Jaffa, in which the story is set in the early days of this century, is portrayed as an exotic international city with a landscape of mythic dimensions. This is not a Zionist Jaffa, quite the contrary. Its inhabitants have betrayed the pioneering ideal and have become ordinary city dwellers. A Mediterranean exoticism combines with an enchanted provinciality to recall the villages in Norway that are the settings for Knut Hamsun's provincial novels *Victoria*, *Pan*, and *Mysteries*. The difference between Hamsun's villages and Agnon's Jaffa of the late Ottoman period is smaller than one might expect. Moreover, the provinciality of the settings in the works of both authors is emphasized by the premises of the plots—the arrival of an interesting, marriageable stranger into the narrow circle of village society.

Agnon's Jacob Rechnitz, a botanist who studies ocean flora and supports himself by teaching Latin, is an exotic figure—

a helpless Don Juan who is unable to endure the company of women for fear of the "particular force" that binds the sexes. The tranquillity of the province is shattered further by the arrival of two more strangers: a father and a daughter, Austrians who have come to Jaffa from Africa. The daughter, Susan, who suffers from an unexplained sleeping sickness, had once been Rechnitz's betrothed; and the father, Herr Ehrlich, apparently wants his daughter to marry the man who had frequented their home as a boy and who was like an adopted son.

A number of thematic and formal oppositions make "Betrothed" more than a provincial love story. On the one hand, the novella includes extraliterary references to such figures as Moshe Leib Lilienblum, Ahad Ha'am, and Abraham Menahem Mendel Ussishkin (who appear under their own names)[2] and provides a description of Jaffa that closely corresponds to documentary sources. On the other hand, legendary and mythic materials abound in "Betrothed." The tale of Sleeping Beauty is an important armature for the story, as is another familiar folklore motif—the betrothal. The story ends with a strange and legendary foot race, in which a floating, dreamlike figure prevails over the "real" characters.

Another conspicuous contrast hinges on the protagonist's two sets of parents. Jacob Rechnitz's natural parents are of low social standing and hardly appear in the story at all; whereas his neighbors, the Ehrlichs (Susan's mother and father), virtually become his adoptive parents, helping him advance in life and paying for his education. They are far better remembered by him as an adult than are his biological parents. The duality in the status of Rechnitz's parents recalls the Oedipus story: abandoned by his natural parents, Oedipus was adopted and raised by foster parents; it was his return to his biological parents that proved to be his undoing. In "Betrothed" the questions that arise are a variation of this theme: What will be the relationship between the adopted son and his adoptive parents? What will be the relationship between him and his adoptive sister, his intended bride? Is she truly meant to be his wife? What is the meaning of the connection between the hero and his adoptive parents? What role does the adoptive father play in the hero's life? What role does Susan play? These questions, for which the story provides no simple answers, constitute the interpretive puzzle that readers must try to solve. A starting point is the many thematic and formal contrasts within the story.

The opposition between natural and adoptive parents is one such contrast. Another is the contrast between the hero's international status as a scientific expert in seaweed and his local status as a teacher in Palestine. There is also the contrast between his apparent success as a Don Juan pursued by many women and his failure in actual love, for he is unable to form a true bond with any woman except the woman who is afflicted with sleeping sickness, who is unable—and perhaps unwilling—to maintain an interpersonal relationship. On the formal level, the story suggests many allegorical possibilities through symbolic names, yet the allegorical hints do not fit the fictional reality—they virtually contradict their actualization. The Hebrew names of the two protagonists, Ya'akov and Shoshana, have allegorical overtones because they are linked in the familiar Purim song "Shoshant Ya'akov, Tsahala veSameha" (Jacob's lily [the Jewish people], rejoicing and

joyous). Another source of allegorical overtones is the formulaic number seven: six women versus the seventh; the lone
man and the six women surrounding him, and so on. Allegorical elements are also implicit in the work because of the
tradition that creates a bond among the secular love story, the
Song of Songs, and the mystical interpretations that have been
given to it. Sentences taken from the Song of Songs, such as
"I am asleep, and my heart is awake,"[3] the mystical connection between the beloved woman and the Divine Presence,
and the status of the formulaic number seven in the tradition
and in folklore—all of these open the door to allegorical
interpretations. Finally, there is the contrast between the
idyllic and epic course of the story on the one hand, which
usually is given a credible realistic explanation, and, on the
other, the figure of Susan as well as the conclusion of the
novella, which breaks through the barrier of realism and forces
the reader to reread the text from a different point of view.
These contrasts have given rise to diverse interpretations of
the text.[4]

The interpretation I offer for this novella is based on a
psychological reading. I would argue that "Betrothed" is
concerned mainly with the ambivalent relationship between a
passive young man and his mother. Since the mother is no
longer alive, he forms a bond with an adoptive surrogate
mother. This relationship also encompasses her daughter, who
comes to stand for the mother. The bond with the adoptive
mother is extremely positive. The hero is dependent upon his
surrogate mother and admires her. Because of his ties to her,
he is incapable of any other erotic connection. He sees many
women in order to avoid the risk of forming a relationship

with any one woman and to avoid betraying the mother of his choice and destiny.

To support this thesis, I will begin with an examination of several passages and then move outward to the general significance of the work.

At the sound of the waves, at the sight of the limitless expanse of the sea, Rechnitz closed his eyes. And now he saw his mother kneeling down before him. He was a small boy; she was threading a new tie around his collar, for it was the day Susan was born and he was invited to the Consul's house. But surely, thought Jacob to himself, she can't be my mother, and it goes without saying that she isn't Susan's mother either, because one is far from here and the other is dead; if I open my eyes I shall see that this is nothing but an optical illusion. The illusion went so far as to present him at once with his own mother and with Susan's; and since one object could not be two, it followed of necessity that here was neither his own mother nor Susan's. But if so, who was she? Susan herself, perhaps? Of course not, for Susan was ill in bed.[5]

Several other passages also point toward the identification of Susan with her mother and of her mother with Rechnitz's biological mother:

They talk about themselves and the world outside, which is not more than a small part of their own. At times the gods dwell with mortals, allowing them to see eternity in an hour. Let us then ask the gods to prolong this hour without end or limit.

Susan had laid her fine, delicate hands before her on the table. Jacob gazed at them, as he used to gaze at her mother's hands when she would place them on the table and his lips would long to touch them.[6]

The following is a final example:

At this same time, Jacob in Jaffa was picturing himself as a child again with Susan. In her short frock, she chased butterflies, picked flowers and made a crown of them for her head. Actually the Consul's house now stood desolate and untenanted and Rechnitz's parents had long since moved out of that neighborhood. But whenever his father's home came to his mind, he saw it still as standing next to the Consul's.[7]

From these three passages it is clear that the hero has forged a link among the three women of this childhood. Unconsciously and on the threshold of his consciousness, they meld into a single figure. Susan's mother becomes an adoptive mother; he relates to her as to an actual mother, becoming attached to her by a deep, oedipal bond. She is the true woman in his life, and she is a substitute for his mother or is his true, beloved mother. Susan is merely a surrogate for her. In fact, his relationship with Susan is at the same time dual and forbidden. On the one hand, she is his adoptive sister, so that any sexual bond with her is a violation of the incest taboo; and, in a kind of transformation, she is also a surrogate for the mother and in that regard comes under the same severe prohibition.

These forbidden connections to the world of the mother fascinate the hero, even though, as will be seen later, they bring him closer to the realm of death than to that of life. This unconscious level suggests the opposite of a number of commonly held interpretations, in which Susan is viewed as the ideal beloved and the six girls as characters who try to tempt the hero away from his ideal. Such an interpretation suggests that Susan is an expression of the bond that *prevents* the hero from forming a true erotic connection with any woman and forces him to regress to a pre-erotic, or presexual, stage. Susan is a mother-sister figure, and Reichnitz's relationship with her resembles the fulfillment of the wish expressed by the speaker of Bialik's poem, when he implores, "Take me under your wing / be my mother, my sister."[8]

Susan's appearance in Palestine prevents Jacob from truly becoming part of the life of the country and forming an erotic connection to it. By bringing him back to his childhood, she not only makes it impossible for him to continue keeping company with the women of Jaffa (whom he had originally been unable to leave because he was bound to all of them at once), but she also takes away his other occupation. He becomes incapable of continuing his scientific research, which had served as a substitute for interpersonal relationships as well as a sublimated expression of his relationship with his past. He is unable and unwilling to form any true bond with a wife, mother, or sister. The oedipal bond with the mother and the sister—who is a substitute for the mother—paralyzes his emotional existence.

The figure of Susan, moreover, is connected with death; and in the subconscious of the narrator and the hero a tie to her brings a man closer to death. The most traumatic scene in the story is the death of Frau Ehrlich:

Never had he been so grieved as on that night, in his awareness of her death. That Susan's mother was dead, that she was an orphan, did not evoke in him any feeling of pity; it was rather like a new motion of the soul, when the soul attaches itself at once to one who is absent and another who is present, and is taken up into both as one.

Susan wore black, with a black veil over her face, her arm in her father's arm. Both walked as if set apart from this world.[9]

These two perplexing passages are significant for understanding the story. The first passage emphasizes the identification of the survivor with the deceased and with her surviving daughter; the second emphasizes Susan's status, as she is often referred to in the text as a being who is "set apart from the world." In the "combined speech" of the passage, the figure of the mother has come to include the figure of the daughter-sister. Henceforth, the connection between Jacob and his mother-sister will no longer be a connection with the mother who has disappeared but with the mother who has passed on to another world. He will assume the role of an orphan who is unable to become engaged in life because he is bound to the world of death with every filament of his soul. His return to the mother is a return to death. The bond with the mother and the sister is a bond with the world that stands in opposition to the world of life. Thus, the bond with the mother and with Susan partakes more of thanatos than of eros. Susan is an emissary from the land of the dead to the world of the living, and her sleeping sickness is far more than a "sixtieth part of death" (as the rabbis call it). Susan's "embassy of death"[10] and her ambivalent relationship with Jacob is expressed through various forms and in many passages. It is in the Muslim cemetery that the two lovers renew their oath of betrothal.[11] As they talk of Susan's mother, a parrot is heard screeching *Verflucht!* (German for cursed). Jacob thinks about a taxidermist named Arzaf (rendered as Ilyushin in English for the play on words; Susan thinks his name is Illusion). After

their conversation about Ilyushin, they order Egyptian cigarettes; and they both see the connection between taxidermy
and Egyptian mummies.

Susan summarizes their conversation:

. . . forgetting all about the cigarettes, Susan went on, "Our
days on earth are like a shadow, and the time of our affliction is
the length of our days. How fortunate are those mummies, laid in
the ground and freed from all trouble and toil. If I could only be
like one of them!" Susan opened her eyes and looked up as if longing for release from the afflictions of the world.

"From the day of your mother's funeral, I have not seen you,"
Jacob said. "And even on that day I didn't really see you. You
seemed so distant from this world, Susan."

"No, Jacob, I felt as if the world were distant from me. And
now, here I am, still not part of the world." [12]

Susan prefers the world of the dead to that of the living. Since
the death of her mother, she has been removed from the world
—and the world from her. Afflicted with sleeping sickness
and removed from the world, she resembles a mummy from
the ancient Egyptian culture that so fascinates her. [13]

It is not surprising, then, that the hero repeats his oath in
the Muslim cemetery and that Susan is close to the mythic
figures of the mermaid or Sleeping Beauty. Both are symbols
of the eternal virgin, pre- or posterotic. For Jung, the virgin
is a symbol of the anima; for others, she is a symbol of the
unconscious itself, which awaits activation by conscious forces.
It seems to me that far from being a figure that expects to be
awakened from slumber, she is a figure (like the Sirens) who
tries to lure the hero into the world of the sea. It is after his
encounter with Susan in the guise of a mermaid that the hero

devotes his life to the study of sea vegetation. The world of the sea tempts the hero to flee from life rather than embrace it. The motif is further developed in the dream that Susan recounts to Jacob:

"Once," said Susan, "I dreamed I was dead. I wasn't happy, I wasn't sad, but my body felt such rest as no one knows in the land of the living. And this was the best of it, that I wanted nothing, I asked for nothing, it just felt as if I were disappearing into blue distances that would never end. Next morning I opened a book and read in it that nobody dreams of himself as dead. If that's so, perhaps it was not a dream but a wide-awake reality. But then, how can I be alive after my death? It's a puzzle to me, Jacob. Do you believe in the resurrection of the dead?"

"No, certainly not," Jacob said.

"Don't say 'certainly.' These certainties of yours bring me to tears." As she spoke, she closed her eyes.[14]

Not only is Susan an emissary of death, she also enjoys the experience of death, dreams about it, and sees it as a positive goal of existence and as a rescue from life's vale of tears. She identifies with the figure of her mother; and the hero, grieving for the mother figure and unable to detach himself from his mourning, sees her as an extension of the vanished mother, who also draws him into the infinite sea, once again returning to the bosom—that is, the grave, the eternal sleep before birth.

Susan arouses an ambivalent reaction in the hero because she is fundamentally ambiguous. As a mother and sister she is forbidden to Jacob; but she is also the woman to whom the hero is betrothed, and only with her is he permitted to form any kind of bond. On the one hand, she is an object of

incestuous desire, fascinating and seducing him, although—
and because—she is forbidden. On the other hand, as an ideal
figure like a mother but not a mother, it might be said that
she is permitted to him. However, she sees herself as part of
the sleeping world of mothers who have no erotic interest in
this world. In the cemetery she makes Jacob swear to be
faithful to her in the next world—to forgo eros in this world
in return for the protection of thanatos that will lead to the
next world.

The protagonist has failed to pass through an important
stage in his life. He has transferred the oedipal bond from the
mother to the daughter, who is a kind of transformation of
the mother. Ehrlich, the father, is still living, whether as a
father or as a father-husband-widower traveling through the
world with his wife-daughter-orphan.

The entire structure of the relationships surrounding the
hero is distorted. The hero perverts his environment because
his own life is warped. It is he who causes the formation of
the group of women, all of whom seek deliverance, and it is
he who perverts their personal lives because he prefers all of
them together to any single one. The connections among these
women gradually become lesbian relationships because the
man is unable to give them what they want. Something
essential has gone wrong in the town's sexual life because of
the hero's dreadful ambivalence. The girls of the town want
him to marry one of them; and, for them, this is the meaning
of the race that concludes the novella.

In the race the women attempt to decide the issue, as
did the Greeks. The winner will receive the wreath from

Rechnitz's hair. However, in that race, too, the tables are turned; and the human condition appears perverted:

> Leah insisted: "The Greeks had the men run, not the girls."
> Asnot answered, "But since all those young men are dead and we are alive, let's do the running ourselves. Do you agree, Dr. Rechnitz? Yes or no?—Why don't you speak?"
> Rechnitz answered, "I agree," and his heart quaked all the more.[15]

The race symbolically underscores the reversal that has taken place in the sexual life of the social group being described. The man is paralyzed and passive because his life has been blocked by his bond with the mother and the surrogate mother. The erotic initiative has passed, therefore, to the women. It is the figure afflicted with sleeping sickness who suddenly appears from nowhere and triumphs over the "waking" women in the race. Thanatos triumphs. The unmasculine man, who has become a woman for whom manly women fight, cannot give himself over to them even as a "woman" because he has formed an alliance with death by giving himself over to the mother and the mother-surrogate. The bond with the mother emerges as a process of emasculation, which directs the libido toward the world of its opposite. What remains to the hero besides the blue expanse of his sleeping beauty who will never awaken? He is left with his substitute activity, the study of aquatic plants, which also symbolize the dreadful and silent endless distance of the oceanic feeling that is closer to death than to life.

Susan, whether interpreted as a real person or as a dream-like figure, is not an ideal figure. She is ideal only in the sense that a child's mother is an idealized figure or in the sense that seeking shelter in the bosom of death can be idealized. She is more beautiful, gracious, and delicate than other women because angels have no evil impulses. She exists in the hero's world before entering the *sujet* of the book, and her appearance explains Reichnitz's inability to find his place and to become involved in the world. Thus, the allegorical level presents the possibility of parody. The connection between Susan and Jacob (Shoshana and Ya'akov) is far from being a source for rejoicing. On the contrary, faithfulness is paralytic and destructive and inhibits the redeeming festival of fertility.

With regard to the structure of the novella, the progression of time in the story—what the formalists call *sujet*—is not of primary importance. The main point is the relationship between the narrated time and the time of narration. In contrast, the Kleistian novella (for Heinrich von Kleist) develops mainly in the time of narration, which is generally identical with the narrated time. In this type of novella there are no flashbacks, but there are many delays. In Agnon's novellas, there is an explicit withdrawal from the present, which would be entirely incomprehensible if the author did not explain it by the past and by means of analogical characters.

Whereas the Kleistian novella is rendered convincing through its linear development, Agnon's novellas are rendered convincing through a spatial reading. The hypothesis that the source of the present lies in the past holds true for many of Agnon's novellas. Such a hypothesis expands the scope of the stories and seeks to shape their messages. The strength of Agnon's novellas depends mainly on the brilliant combination of various levels of significance. The novella has another aspect with which we have not yet dealt: the cultural and social ramifications of the oedipal dependency of the hero may in the end be as important as the psychological ramifications.

It cannot be ignored that the mother and sister from the past belong to the Diaspora and that the six women belong to the Land of Israel. The hero cannot become involved in Jaffa, "darling of the waters," because he is a foreigner who is bound by his "umbilical cord" (with all the possible meanings of that term) to another country and another culture. His warped sexual life is also a symptom of spiritual and emotional perversion in this portrait of the scholar as a young immigrant. Professionally, the hero comes from Germany and is headed for America. Emotionally, he has not left the realm of the great cultural and social mother who clutches him so close that he is unable to free himself. The attachment is not only sexual but also cultural—the culture of western Europe, of assimilated Jewry. Jacob belongs to the assimilated culture of Ehrlich, just as he is part of the mummified and enclosed world of Susan, his sister and mother.

Susan is an emissary from the land of death, and Jacob spreads the illness, which has also infected him. It is an illness of impotence, infertility, and the incapacity for masculine decisiveness, which causes women to take the sexual initiative into their own hands until they themselves become manlike in their pseudolesbian relationships with each other. Agnon discovered a basic neurosis in the young European Jewish intellectual who immigrated to the Land of Israel but failed to free himself from his mother and, therefore, never managed to put down erotic roots in his new land. [16]

In relation to his own work, Agnon wrought no innovation

here. In fact, he extended the pattern and thematics already present in his first story, "Agunot: A Tale." In both instances, the heroes are unable to achieve fulfillment in their sexual lives because their development has been halted by an attachment to a woman from another world.

With this theme Agnon penetrated beyond personal neurosis to deeper meanings. With great sensitivity, he homed in on a neurosis typical of an entire society—the Zionist society of young immigrants who sought rebirth and yet thirsted for death. Commanded to set out for a new world, they still yearned to return to the bosom of the great mother. Agnon was aware of the great conflict in this novella as well as in his novel *Only Yesterday;* and, to a degree far greater than one might imagine at first, he understood the problem of the immigrant as a young neurotic.

This story, like Agnon's novels, emphasizes the tension between the traditional and revolutionary elements. The connection with the traditional in the story is regressive and perverted. The connection with the Diaspora is oedipal and morbid, preventing the protagonist from forming healthy human bonds and normal relationships with the women of the Land of Israel. Agnon's protagonists are revolutionaries who are held back by their bonds with the tradition; they are neurotics whose neuroses derive from the inability to free themselves from the past. Agnon, the traditional revolutionary, revealed the power of this neurosis and described the deep tensions of his society through a structure of symbols and extremely complex human relations.

"Betrothed" is a lyric novella that reveals the psychological depths of the main character. "Pisces" is a comic novella, although the plot, which is macabre in its account of the deaths of a man and a fish, lends a grotesque character to the comical tall tale. Through the fate of a single protagonist, "Betrothed" portrays the basic problems of young immigrants who are separated from their parents' homes and are seeking to strike roots in the Land of Israel. In "Pisces," Agnon penetrated the psychological depths of an entire society.

The Grotesque Novella.   Agnon achieved his most interesting and complex forms of expression in his novelistic works. In the novella "Pisces," published rather late, in 1956, and included in the posthumous volume *A City and the Fullness Thereof* (1973), Agnon reached one of the peaks of his accomplishment as a writer. "Pisces" has a decidedly dramatic plot: the protagonist goes out to buy a fish; instead of filling his belly with the fish, he and the fish become one flesh in their death. However, this dramatic plot is entirely secondary; the interplay among the various elements and the digressions and delays are more important than the plot itself. In this story all of the traits of Agnon's writing discussed so far are epitomized. In fact, an examination of "Pisces" is tantamount to an analysis of most of the characteristics of his works. Every possible intertextual and grotesque element is to be found in this story. Like "Betrothed," "Pisces" is not a thoroughly dramatic novella. The story demands a slow reading. This is because the combinations among the factors implicit in the intertextual depths and the factors hinted at in the internal relations among the various intratextual elements are no less important than is the linear development of events in the plot.

As part of *A City and the Fullness Thereof,* "Pisces" pretends
to be a chronicle of the city of Buczacz, Agnon's native town.
The author also pretends that this is an authentic story,
creating a brilliant contrast between the pose of authenticity
and the fantastic elements.

> Seeing that most people don't know the story about Fishl Karp,
> or those who know a little about it don't know it all, or else they
> know the story in an offhand way, and there is no greater enemy
> of wisdom than superficial knowledge, I have taken it upon myself
> to tell things the way they happened.
>
> I know that I have not managed to batten down all the details
> and smooth out all the rough spots, and, needless to say, others
> would have told the story better, but I say that details aren't the
> main thing, and consistency isn't the main thing, and character
> isn't the main thing, but truth is the main thing. This much then
> I may say here, that every word is true.[17]

The emphasis on fidelity to the facts is quite exaggerated
and causes the reader to suspect the text. The author seems to
be hinting at the lack of historical veracity and at the aesthetic
strength of the story; therefore, he means the opposite of what
he says, which is the essence of irony.

As the story continues, the reader finds that although the
narrative is not credible on the realistic level, it has veracity
on a level beyond the real. Like the rest of Agnon's work,
"Pisces" has intertextual connections with the canon of Jewish
tradition. The story is enriched by these connections, through
the use of both explicit quotations and latent references that
expand and deepen the story's symbolic world—although the
relationship between the ancient text and the present one is
merely parodic.

"Pisces" relates to fish in many ways and in various senses of the word. The title connects the story to the Hebrew month of *adar,* in which the holiday of Purim falls. The name of the human protagonist is Fishl Karp; another of the principal protagonists is the "carp" that Fishl buys from a fisherman; and the whole story alludes to the fish eaten by the Children of Israel in Egypt.

Fish are mentioned in Hebrew legend and midrash. The following are a few of the sources that address this topic from various viewpoints. (I will note later the connections among these sources as a subtext and as an explicit text of the story.)

Bab. Tal.,* *Brakhot* 40a: He who is used to eating small fish does not become sick, and, moreover, small fish fructify and multiply and cure a man's entire body.

Bab. Tal., *Shabat* 108a: What about a phylactery scroll written on the skin of a pure fish? If Elijah comes and assents.[18]

Bab. Tal., *Yoma* 75a: In memory of the fish that was eaten in Egypt. Rav and Shmuel, one said fish, one said fornication. When the children of Israel would draw water the Holy One blessed be He would bring little fishes into the water in their jugs.

Bab. Tal., *Avoda Zara* 4a: What's the case regarding fish? The larger one swallows his fellow. That's also the case with humans. If it weren't for fear of the royal authorities, the one larger than his fellow would swallow his fellow.[19]

*Bab. Tal. is the abbreviation for the Babylonian Talmud.

Bab. Tal., *Avoda Zara* 3b: Fish in the sea, when they go up to the dry land, they die, so too human beings, when they abandon the words of the Torah and the commandments, they die immediately.[20]

Esther, *Rabbah* 7: When Haman cast the lot and it fell on Adar that month said, "Pisces. Just as fish devour, so too I shall devour them." The Holy One blessed be He said, "Evil one! Fish sometimes are swallowed and sometimes they swallow."[21]

Therefore, whether the narrator distorts or exaggerates this event or ostensibly tells things as they happened, this story—which purports to be a mere chronicle and is included in a collection of stories that declares that its purpose is to describe the history of the city of Buczacz in a series of anecdotes—does not simply recount something that happened by following the chronology of historical reality. To some degree, the intertextual connections deny the possibility of historical reality from the start because the connections emphasize that the event is an extension, in one form or another, of an existing paradigm. In other words, the new event is merely a transformation of an earlier literary model that is realized once again in a new context.

Thus, the story exists on the axis of the literary tradition no less than on that of historical continuity. The traditional element shapes the historical one and stamps it with its seal. The historical event is merely an echo of the literary model, or of various literary models. The story has ramifications both forward and backward; it existed in the past and exists in the present. The midrashic material expands the story's meaning and gives it symbolic significance.

The midrashic traditions influence the entire text and also various details in the linear development: The fish as a fertility symbol appears in other contexts and in various folk rituals. The major figure in the story expresses, in one form or another, a world of powerful instincts. The protagonist is a Renaissance figure; he is a symbol of fructification and multiplication whose excess virility is expressed in his unbridled appetite for food. He is a gargantuan figure recalling the characters of Rabelais (1494–1553) and expressing, like Rabelais's giants, the revolutionary power of a society departing from its framework and taking leave of its senses. To a great extent, this oral exaggeration is an expression of sexual power. In describing Fishl Karp's double, the fish, the author gives direct expression to the fish's sexual prowess: "Here it danced with the daughters of leviathan. Here it visited them as a bridegroom. Here it passed its days in feasts and festivities, with all its sages, the sages of snail shells."[22]

Although these descriptions are said almost in an instinctual fashion, like mechanical doggerel and, as it were, unconsciously, they have great significance because in them alone the author offers a glimpse of the hidden, sexual side of his gargantuan figures.

The comparison of the fish on dry land to Jews who have desisted from the Torah creates a hidden equation between Fishl Karp—whose main interest in the world is in eating and drinking and for whom the Torah is merely an excuse for eating and drinking—and the fish, who rises up from the depths. For both, the whole world is eating and drinking, and both are doomed to death. The strange inner connection between excessive vitality and the desire for oblivion is brought out quite sharply in this story. Insatiable eaters and men whose spiritual limitations are like those of a fish out of water will come to an end as bitter as the fish's. The midrashic legend and its modern avatar emphasize the limits of Renaissance desires. These are the boundless desires that ultimately led to ruin and destruction.

The equation between the human struggle for survival and that of the fish is also highly significant. It explains the self-destruction to which the limitless desires of the Renaissance led. The desire for prey, for power, and for sex—when it knows no bounds or law—ultimately leads to the anarchy of the strong treading down the weak. The world in "Pisces," in which animal vitality and the desire for self-destruction are intermingled, is presented as a grotesque world arousing both panic and laughter. The overblown, grotesque figure is a revolutionary force, bursting from the dialectical development produced by itself.

Nor should the reader ignore the connection between the story and the carnival atmosphere of Purim in the month of *adar*. This is the one day in the year when every Jew may play the fool. Among the Gentiles, carnival day is when the Dionysian overcomes the Apollonian. Similarly, among Jews the reins are loosened during this small-scale carnival, and they may drink until they can no longer distinguish between Haman and Mordecai. Popular custom created the Purim *shpil*, where people dress up as figures from the Book of Esther; and

Jews act in the theater, like pagans. On Purim a person may be himself or herself or someone else at the same time. Theatricality is typical of both the gentile carnival and the Jewish minicarnival. Human boundaries break down and "his royal highness"—reason—abdicates for a while. The breakdown of the distinction between man and fish and fish and man is the main quality of this story, where Fishl Karp—a fish by virtue of his name and by his gluttony—becomes a kind of fish; and the fish becomes like Fishl. The artist mingles them both in his picture of Pisces.

The midrashic materials give symbolic depth to the literary text and expand its messages, whether the text is merely a renewed manifestation of the tradition or whether the tradition echoes within it, either overtly or latently. At the same time, it should be emphasized that the story does give signs of being a chronicle, attempting to link the fantastic experience produced in the course of the plot and the extraliterary social reality of the *shtetl*. The story does not only create daydreams but also interprets, in one way or another, the social model that the author had declared, ostensibly in ironic fashion, to be the subject of his work.

As we have seen, a complex and rich network of midrash is woven through the body of the work. However, even without these references to midrash and the intertextual connections with it, we can discern the relationships among power, force (including sexual force), and eating. Fishl Karp is like a legendary giant, of whom the writer speaks with the exaggerated language of Rabba Bar-Bar-Hana.[23] In the exaggerated description of Rabba Bar-Bar-Hana, those who died in the wilderness without reaching the Promised Land were mythical, gigantic figures beyond life and death. However, Fishl Karp is not a mythical character, and he is not described in the language of eternity or as existing in eternal time. He is a figure of flesh and blood:

Fishl Karp was a certain householder. Householders like him aren't found in every generation or every place. He was a tall man, and as broad as he was tall. That is, his height equalled his circumference. And his limbs were of a size. His neck was fat, and his whole body, as they say among us in Buczacz, was truly to be measured by the hand of the Eglon King of Moab. Moreover his belly was a creature in its own right. Such a belly isn't found in our generation, but even in his generation Fishl was numbered among the wonders of the town.[24]

From the start this figure is of mythical proportions, although the myth is given a comic interpretation, for the parts of the body are described explicitly by the author with associations, formulae, and metaphors that render these comic dimensions ridiculous. "It wasn't for no reason that they used to say that his double chin, compared to his belly, was like a gizzard, compared to a fowl, and his double chin was as fat as a fireplace before Hanukkah."[25] This comic metaphor is appropriate because the living gullet is often similar to the materials that it devours; occasionally, the gullet and the things swallowed are intermingled. The sources also speak of the fish as a creature that devours and is devoured, but Agnon's text gives the connection far more emphasis. We find that the story's mythical fish is a kind of living gullet, as is the human protagonist:

Even in his youth, when he was still a bright greenish color, he was well known among the notables of the water. The fish large and small all feared him. Before he reached them they used to swim up to him and enter his mouth alive. Both the fish who float on their belly and the fish who swim on their ribs, both the righties and the lefties, by their very selves they came to be food for him. The same went for the ones whose snouts and eyes were to the right and for the ones whose snouts and eyes were to the left. The fish, whose heart was close to his cheeks, didn't let hooks into his cheek but opened his mouth wide and at his fill. Truly in our times we have not heard that such fish are found in our rivers, but because of his power and courage, in exaggeration it was said that all the fish in the sea were subject to him.[26]

The grotesqueness of description derives here from the contrast between the catalogue of the various types of fish and the common fate awaiting them all in the belly of the fish. Just as this welter of fish will lose its identity in the belly of the fish so, too, the fish and other kinds of animals lose their identity when they are digested in the belly of the fish-man, Fishl Karp. Eating means the digestion of the uniqueness of what is eaten. Since what is eaten loses its particularness, it becomes part of the eater, until the eater is eaten—by being swallowed up in the belly of someone larger than himself (like the fish that first finds its place in the net and ultimately ends up in Fishl's belly; or else Fishl himself, who finds his place in the belly of the great earth, which more than all the other bellies becomes the tomb of all living things.)

There is a strange correlation between the process of eating and the process of burial. Living creatures are buried in the belly of a living creature, which is then buried in the belly of another living creature, until all living things are buried in the belly of the earth:

With the years the gravestone *sank* into the earth. Not only do all living things end in the dust, but also the dead, and so too the things one makes in their memory. Some are lucky enough to have their gravestone stand for a generation, and some stand for two, but in the end it *sinks* deeper and deeper until *it's swallowed in the earth.* Thus Reb Fishl Karp's gravestone *sank and was swallowed* in the earth, but the inscription did not *sink* [emphases added]. One still sees two fish there. In another city they would have said a fish was buried there.[27]

The process of sinking is so overwhelming that not only does the body sink but also the memory of the body. Not only does a man's identity disappear in the process, in which everything loses its identity, but even a man's memory is liable to lose its identity.[28]

The blurring of the distinction between the one who wanted to eat and the one who was about to be eaten continues throughout "Pisces," reaching a climax toward the conclusion:

When they removed [Fishl's] clothes to let his blood they found a phylactery bound on his arm. They stopped, astonished. Was it possible that a man with a brain in his head should have laid one of a pair of phylacteries on his arm without placing the other on his forehead? Before they could resolve the meaning of Fishl's action, they were stumped by the fish. In all their born days they hadn't heard that the Strypa ever gave forth fish which wore phylacteries, and even the outstanding fish-eaters of Buczacz said that never in their lives had they seen a fish crowned with a phylactery.[29]

These lines clarify a central stage in the course of the plot, where the artist separates the man from the fish and combines them. Only art can combine these incommensurable beings and create a grotesque unity between man and animal, where the man lacks what the fish has and the fish has what the man lacks:

When he stretched forth his hand to paint, the figure of the fish turned into that of Reb Fishl, and the figure of Reb Fishl turned into that of the fish, and he painted a picture of Reb Fishl on the fish's skin. The ways of artists are strange, for when the spirit throbs within them, their individuality is wiped out, and they are driven to act as commanded by the spirit, which acts by the command of the God of the spirit of all flesh. And how is it that Reb Fishl was changed into the figure of a fish? It was because he was a lover of fish. [30]

This blurring of distinctions is not only an act of art. In his forms the artist brings what is implied by the fictional reality to a final inner conclusion; reality proves, on the level of oxymoron, that the artist's perception is correct.

The artist in "Pisces" perceives correctly because the two figures try to blur themselves. The aspiration and desire for life, expressed in the lust to overeat, leads to death. Thus, in dialectical fashion, the desire for life contains within it a loss of identity, which resembles a loss of autonomy — being swallowed up in the great tomb of oblivion. He who swallows, the text teaches us, also is swallowed. Both the fish and the protagonist lose their identities because they are intermingled and swallowed up in each other. Fishl Karp resembles the fish, even in his name. On the other hand, the fish acts like a man, thinks like a man, and his actions are like those of flesh and blood. We have the king of the gluttonous fish versus the king of the gluttons. The only one who can rescue them from being swallowed up and forgotten is the artist, graced with the talent to perpetuate both of them and also something beyond them (as we shall see later in the discussion of Betsalel Moshe).

Only art can counter the forces of swallowing because art eternalizes itself and turns itself into an object. The significance of this is that symbols that transcend any individualization, despite their particularity as unique symbols, are endowed with a figure that transcends the individual subject.

"Pisces" is a grotesque story about the loss of identity, and its form is unique. One could say that the story resembles a traditional homiletical speech because it tells the story about Rabbi Fishl who is caught like a fish in the snare of his instincts, which causes him to disappear in the same way that he wanted to make the fish disappear in his guts. This is actually a bizarre inversion of the story of Jonah, which is mentioned in "Pisces." The devourer of the fish is devoured in the belly of the fish, which is an extension of the earth as the Great Mother. The one who is swallowed because of his swallowings meets his death.

The story conveys much of Agnon's deep existential pessimism, through which he sees the course of mortal life as one swallowing after another, until the swallower is himself devoured in the great maw of existence—the grave. What remains after a man's death is the artistic symbol—a sign that something like him once was. One can also view the story as a transition from the metaphorical to the literal: Fishl, who is like a fish by virtue of his gluttony, gradually becomes a fish himself. Conversely, as the plot progresses, descriptions repeatedly pass from the literal level to the world of symbols. For example, those who were like fish become a symbol of the great devouring fish in the artist's painting of Pisces.

On the one hand, we have Fishl Karp, the greatest glutton of Buczacz, who contends that the world was created only for eating: "When he saw a fat chicken, a luscious piece of meat, a fruit worthy of a benediction, or a vegetable that would supplement a meal nicely, he would take it so that no one else would beat him to it."[31] On the other hand, we have the king of the fishes, who treats all creatures as though they were born merely to serve and nourish him: "In mighty waters did he swim, before him trembled every scale and fin. Here a fish he ate, and there a crab or squid. Here he'd celebrate, and there feast well he did. Here he set out on his trails, with blood his fins dyed red. There in blood he dipped his scales, crushing a noble's head, . . ."[32]

It is noteworthy that in the previous passage, Agnon moves from balanced prose to overbalanced prose to rhyme. In Agnon's works, rhymed prose is a mark of the grotesque, and he makes use of it in the grotesque passages of both *Only Yesterday* and "Pisces." An excess of symmetry that lays bare its own emptiness is one of the traits of the traditional Arabic and Hebrew literary form called *magama,* which is based on artificial, rhymed connections. This stylistic technique is in keeping with the content of Agnon's "Pisces." Thus, in Agnon's works mechanical doggerel frequently is a stylistic sign that points to the appearance of the unexplained or the irrational. The outsized proportions of the fish and its role as the id are intensified by exaggerated rhyming.

The two creatures in the story are metaphors of "fishness"; they symbolize beings that have nothing in the world but their mouths. In their world, the id and formlessness rule; and the formlessness becomes ever more so as it swallows additional forms. Both beings are driven by irrational, organic forces, which finally dominate them. The id is controlled by anarchical forces that deprive man of his individuality and bring him nearer to a world where all bodies are equal. When the two beings are combined, eating becomes a process of entanglement and death. As long as the fish—the alter ego —is separate from the ego—Fishl Karp—the ego can continue to exist. When the fish is swallowed—and it must be emphasized that the swallowing is merely apparent for the fish is not physically eaten—the swallowed takes over the swallower, and the consciousness that separates man from beast and man from id sinks into the maze of the id. The heightening of the synonymity between the two figures until they become one causes a loss of differentiation and a return to the primordial, prelinguistic realm, where there is no differentiation between synonyms.

The paradox, of course, is that the author manages to make his audience fond of the grotesque power of his two protagonists, who break down the boundaries of human limitations. The vital power of the grotesque and the enormous appetites of the powers expressed in it fascinate the addressee. It casts a spell over him because the limited and routine human dimensions of life have been shattered. The addressee feels as though all of the reins have been cast off for a moment and that all of the boundaries have been rubbed out. The experience of law-lessness and abandon also causes the entanglement and the dreadful awakening, for breaking through boundaries is the breaking of human possibilities. The grotesque shattering contains death within it because the grotesque figure trans-gresses the boundary of what is permissible to a human being and what makes him human—that which distinguishes the human being from a beast and that which is permitted to him according to his proportions and abilities. Whoever swallows more than lies within the human ability to swallow ends by having his own gullet swallow him.[33]

The process of swallowing and being swallowed changes from symbol to reality only to become a symbol again in the drawing by the third protagonist, the artist who paints the two grotesque figures as the constellation of Pisces. The art-ist's Pisces is a symbol of man's eternal gluttony—gluttony unto death.

This is the grotesque intermingling: a man is like a fish, and a fish is like a man. The combination of the two creates a grotesque effect that is both humorous and frightening be-cause the addressees realize that the combination is not an artificial or imaginary one but instead represents a human truth—one that is both frightening and attractive.

The one who is capable of creating the combination and remaining alive—in contrast to the objects of the combina-tion, who die when they are grafted together—is the artist, Betsalel Moshe. (This is not the first time Agnon used the symbolic name of one of the archetypes of Jewish art, Betsalel ben Hur, the builder of the tabernacle.) In a great many respects, the character Betsalel is the double of the author of "Pisces," who identifies himself with the author who writes a history of his hometown, Buczacz.[34]

Just as Betsalel Moshe combines the two grotesque elements in his painting, so does Shmuel Yosef in his story. Betsalel Moshe is the one who discovers that the phylactery missing from Fishl Karp's head is found with the fish, although he doesn't know that the ones not found with the fish are indeed found with Fishl:

Betsalel Moshe said to the fish, "If a cat, which isn't even a kosher animal, merited a single tefillin, you, who are kosher for the sabbath dinner, and perhaps the soul of a righteous man has been reborn in you, are so much the more worthy of tefillin. But what can I do? Your Creator didn't make you with a head suitable for tefillin. For your head is narrow and long and resembles a duck's head. At any rate I'll bind the tefillin to you with its straps, and if you aren't distracted from the tefillin, you will be dressed in splendor.[35]

From the moment that Betsalel Moshe binds the phylactery on the fish's head (like one of the secular intellectuals of the time who did so to a cat), he brings about a final and extreme summation of the principal processes that this grotesque story creates: the process of the breakdown of the boundaries between the profane and the secular and between what can be described as religion and life—the difference between a bag for phylacteries and a bag of food, between a fish and a phylactery. What went awry in life as a result of the frightful appetites of human creatures went awry for the artist by the power of his art. The confusion of areas is a sin; the confusion of boundaries through a metaphorical stratagem in art is a good deed. There is no art without breaking down the boundaries that separate identities, for that is the secret of the metaphor, just as life itself never tries to break down boundaries and make homonyms into synonyms. Moreover, art is capable of presenting the human symbol before protagonists who have spoiled existence.

The artist overcomes a grotesque suicide through the power of his art: "Were it not for the paintings he paints, he would consider himself no better than a beast whose only thought is for eating and drinking."[36] Fishl's repeated encounter with the fish and with the phylactery that has been profaned[37] shows him that because he broke through human borders, his own life has broken down. Following that discovery Fishl suffers a stroke; henceforth, he declines into death. Therefore, the plot demonstrates that it is impossible to live with an awareness of the breakdown of boundaries and that, in fact, it is impossible to live with the breakdown itself. The individual merely can imagine such a breakdown, as does art.

The function of the grotesque artist is to lay bare the grotesque identity, to shake up the elements that took part in the process, and to shock the viewers through its artistic re-creation. The function of grotesque art is to reveal the destroyed world because the world cannot subsist with its tensions. Only the artist, who enjoys the portrayal of these tensions, is capable of coping with them and remaining safe.

When the artist wishes to draw a form he removes his eyes from all else in the world except what he wants to draw. Immediately everything but that form departs. Since it regards itself as unique, it stretches and expands, filling the entire world. That is what happened to the fish. When Moshe made up his mind to draw it, it started to enlarge itself, as though to fill the world. Betsalel Moshe was gripped by cold shivers, his heart began quivering, and his fingers started trembling, like artists who tremble with the torments of desire because they want to recount the deeds of the Holy One blessed be He, each in his own way, the writer with his pen and the artist with his brush.[38]

The passage cited refers to a passage from Genesis, *Rabbah* 46a: "I am the one who said to my world and to the heavens 'enough' and to the earth, 'enough.' For if I hadn't said 'enough' to them to this day they would keep expanding and expanding." It also reminds the reader of the following passage from the Babylonian Talmud, *Brakhot* 10a: "Come and see how the abilities of the Holy One blessed be He are not the same as those of flesh and blood. Flesh and blood can paint a picture on a wall, but they cannot endow it with spirit and soul and innards and guts, but the Holy One blessed be He is not like that. He draws a form within a form and endows it with spirit and soul. . . . For what else is meant by 'there is no rock [in Hebrew, *tsur*] like our Lord'? There is no *tsur* like our Lord, there is no painter [in Hebrew, *tsayyar*, ostensibly from the same root, *ts-u-r*] like our Lord."

These homilies are implicit in Agnon's text, which relates to them in parodic fashion. I present them because the author uses them with regard to the hubris of the artist, who, with his grotesque brush, is capable of bringing together what cannot be contained in reality. Like the Lord of the Universe, the artist creates a grotesque existence, where the enormous attractive power of grotesque vitality and its inner dialectic—

which destines both fish and man for slaughter—are inter-mingled.

The artist, like the whore who ate and wiped her mouth, is capable of describing horror without bearing responsibility for its truth. As in other works, such as *A Guest for the Night,* the artist is shown here in an ironic light. The artist is none other than that small, orphaned boy who has nothing in the world except the power of his brush.

In "Pisces," Agnon's revolutionary traditionalism reaches one of its peaks. The revolutionary here is the opposite pole of the erudite religious scholar. The earthy figure and the mate-rial of the story produce a carnival-like revolution, which, as Agnon sensed very well, contains an inner contradiction. Here, we find the man of tradition lurking behind the revo-lutionary. He discovered that revolution against tradition and its vessels and customs, such as the holiday dinner, phylacter-ies, and prayers, is liable to bring about the destruction and downfall of the revolutionary tradition and of the entire way of life. This is a revolution that, in dialectical fashion, con-tains its own destruction. Agnon described the process and hinted at the dreadful forces that are liberated by the process and are liable to bring destruction. After the destruction, only a splendid, aesthetic condition will exist.

"Pisces" is one of Agnon's final poetic expressions and one of his last self-reflective confessions. In it, he hints at the "moral" responsibility of the ironic reproducer of the gro-tesque. The grotesque is not merely the objective correlative of a "revolutionary" reality; the creator of this model probably has brought the grotesque into existence. (The creator has,

like Betsalel Moshe, put the phylactery on the fish's head.)
Art is not only a reflection of models. It also produces them,
and the artist who has depicted models of total anarchy—that
is, those that cause human self-destruction—ought to be
guilt ridden. The implied author maintains that, although
the tradition has been desecrated and debased by powerful
symbols of materialism (which the implied author, with his
ambivalent attitude toward the two main characters, Fishl and
the fish, somehow also admires), the "revolutionary" artist
(the author?) is guilty of creating the models and symbols that
desecrate and degrade the tradition.

"Pisces" combines realistic and fantastic elements, using
the features of the traditional style. The combination of a
grotesque plot and an intertextual parody is an outstanding
demonstration of the originality shown by Agnon in several of
his novellas.

The examination of these two novellas, "Betrothed" and
"Pisces," reveals some of the most original artistic aspects of
Agnon's work. In fact, Agnon never wrote conventional novellas. Most of Agnon's novellas lack a normal dramatic character, and they also fail to develop a quick dramatic plot
leading to a climax and catastrophe. Most employ literary
stratagems that give them a modern character.

Agnon might be termed a progenitor of the modern novella.
His contribution goes far beyond the borders of Hebrew or
Jewish culture. Moreover, the modernism of his novellas increased over the years. Just as his later novels are what I call
decoherent and symbolic novels, so too did his novellas and
short stories become symbolic and decoherent. Symbolic factors and grotesque elements that are expressed in the combi-

nation and splitting of motifs are found in the two novellas just discussed, but they are used increasingly in his later novellas. Two examples of the augmentation of these elements to the greatest extent possible are found in "Until Now" (in Hebrew, "Ad Hena") and "Edo and Enam."

In "Until Now" and in "Edo and Enam," Agnon used opposite techniques. "Until Now" is a decoherent novella based on aimless travels, and the intratextual connections are not tight. "Edo and Enam" has a dramatic structure—the narrator is witness to the emergence of a romantic triangle that involves Gamzu, Gemula, and Ganit—the (linear) climax of which is two disasters: the husband discovers his wife with her lover, and the lover and his beloved die a tragic death. The characters are projections of the author's ego (as symbolized by the use of the Hebrew letters *'ayin* and *gimel,* which are the first letters of Agnon's name in Hebrew). Among the figures and the situations are connections established through the use of analogies, synonyms, and antonyms (for example, Gemula and the moon; the moon in the postcard sent by the Greifenbachs; the moon in the narrator-witness's dreams). The novella's structure is wrenched apart by thematic parallels (for example, the world of Gamzu and Gemula and that of Amrami and Edna) but mainly through Agnon's use of intertextual connections with Jewish tradition, such as midrash, books of spells, and the *Zohar;* and with semihistorical literature, such as the tales of travels to Kurdistan.[39]

Only in "The Disappeared" did Agnon return, in quite an original way, to the dramatic tradition of stories about kidnappings (like Yehuda Steinberg's "In Those Days"). The novella develops linearly from a kidnapping, through the victim's apparent return, to the hero's seduction by a gentile woman, to the climax toward the end — the hero's death.

Agnon's achievements in the area of the novella are impressive because within a relatively short format he managed to present extremely complex significances. Agnon was not merely a traditional revolutionary nor a revolutionary traditionalist in the themes he presented in these novellas; but also, as in the novels, he was a revolutionary who changed the form of the novella and gave the traditional framework new internal forms.

The Short Stories

The Fantastic Folk Tale.   A thorough study of even one story belonging to each of Agnon's genres is beyond the scope of this study; thus, I have chosen to analyze five so-called poles from the entire work, beginning with the short folk story "Three Sisters."

"Three Sisters" was first published in 1937 and is typical of Agnon's fantastic tales. It is outstanding in its brevity and tight structure. Its source is a ballad of social commentary that reached Agnon from English literature through Isaac Leib Peretz's Yiddish translation.[40] What characterizes "Three Sisters" is the extreme modification of the motif, the social message of which has been raised to balladic-mythical significance.

Three Sisters
(TO B. KATZENELSON, GREETINGS)

Three sisters lived in a gloomy house, sewing linens for others from morning light to midnight, from the end of Sabbath to Sabbath eve never moved from their fingers either scissors or needle, and the sigh never ceased from their heart, not on hot days nor rainy ones. But blessing came none from their work. And what dry bread they found was never enough to sate their hunger.

Once they were occupied making a fine dress for a rich bride. When they finished their labor, they remembered their sorrow, that they had nothing but the skin on their flesh, and that too was growing old and weak.

Their hearts filled with sorrow.

One sighed and said, "All our days we sit wearying ourselves for others, nor have we even a scrap of cloth to make ourselves shrouds."

The second one said, "Sister, don't invite misfortune."

She too sighed till she shed a tear.

The third wanted to say something too. As she started to talk, a blood vessel burst in her mouth and splattered, soiling the dress.

When she brought the dress to the bride, the rich man came out of his salon. He saw the stain. He scolded the seamstress and dispatched her with obloquy. And needless to say, he did not pay her.

Alas, if the second had spit blood, and the third had wept, we could have washed the dress with her tears, and the rich man would not have become angry. But not everything is done in timely fashion. Even if everything were done in timely fashion, that is, if the third one had wept after the second spat blood, there would still be no true consolation here.[41]

The stylistic fabric of this story in Hebrew is quite rhythmical, bringing out the balance both within and between the sentences. The author heightened the emotional effect by sonorous means and through the use of rhetorical strategies, such as the anaphora ("from . . . from") and antitheses in the sentence structure ("morning . . . midnight"; "hot . . . rainy"), and also in the strategy of gradual intensification (skin "growing old and weak"). The story would merely be pathetic if its content were not based on a series of ironic antitheses.

The legendary elements of the story are conspicuous, for none of the figures is characterized. They are formulaic characters—as the number three is itself formulaic—acting in an eternal time (for example, dawn to midnight; from the end of the sabbath to the eve of the following sabbath; and rain and shine). The eternal act of sewing connects these sisters to the three sisters of Greek mythology who knit the threads of destiny.

The story is based on a tale of social protest about three sisters in their poverty, a rich bride, and a cruel rich man who does not pay the sisters' wages. However, Agnon broadened the scope of the tale. In the dialogue, which pierces through the eternal time frame, each of the sisters laments her bitter fate—one in words, one in tears, and one in blood. Yet sighs do not change fate; indeed, they make it worse. The order of the world does not depend on the social situation but on chance or on a blind force, which also brings suffering to humanity. The decree does not strike only the poor and destitute but penetrates the depths of the human situation. At the end, in ironic fashion the narrator responds to his "story" with aphorisms taken from Ecclesiastes 3:11—the sense of which are reversed. A change in the events would not change the situation, which is fundamentally bad. The ballad —the high point of which is the burst blood vessel and the culmination of which is the meeting with the rich man—is thoroughly and ironically epitomized in the remarks of the narrator. Thus, here is a structure based on folkloric components—contrasts between light and dark, the dialogue, the depiction of time, and the characters who are emblematic of the fates. Yet the content is modern, describing the human condition.

This particular story is not exceptional. When compared to other folk tales, both long and short, told by Agnon (for example, "Agunot: A Tale," "The Tale of the Scribe," "The Dance of Death," "The Dead Girl," and "The Tale of Rabbi Gadiel, the Infant"), it shows the author's tendency toward formulaic characterization and tight, dramatic plots advancing toward a climax that is a crisis—or a decree of fate—that is close to the world of imagination, myth, and universal significance. What is lacking in detailed visual description is made up by rhythms, intertextual mythical references from various cultures, and rhetorical intensification. Most of these texts are intense and tightly wrought. Their components do not simply interrupt the act of reading or break the linear continuity; rather, they deepen them.

The story is based on the parodic deautomatization of the folk tale. Peretz's version of this story is already an ironic retelling of the story about the three sisters waiting for a groom. Agnon made use of this motif and gave it a positive folk conclusion with "the rooster—ex machina" in *The Bridal Canopy* but not in "Three Sisters," in which he placed greater emphasis on the ironic aspect of the situation, denying any chance for the fortunate conclusion commonly found in folk tales about poor young girls. The source of evil is not the social struggle but rather the human condition. Man is thrown into a world where arbitrary powers rule without mercy. In this story, through the use of a traditional literary device— that is, the standard structure of a folk legend—Agnon described an absurd existential situation. Parody is one of the typical devices used by the revolutionary in his war against the tradition or in his attempt to reveal its vacuousness.

The Realistic Story. One would expect Agnon's realistic stories to be the opposite of his folk tales. In contrast to a plot and characters that lack specificity—the purpose of which is to make an emotional and ideological point—here is a plot derived from reality and peopled with well-depicted characters, all of which represent a full realization of literary structures. Agnon's first stories in the Land of Israel, such as "The Hill of Sand," were written in this fashion, as were later ones, such as "Metamorphosis," "The Doctor's Divorce," "Fernheim," and "Between Two Cities."

"Ovadia the Cripple" (1921), which tells the story of an errant maidservant betrothed to a miserable cripple, borders on naturalism. After a flirtation with the son of her employers, the maidservant sleeps with another servant and becomes pregnant. When her crippled fiancé returns from the hospital, he finds her with a bastard in her arms.[42]

The crippled fiancé is a pathetic figure taken from melodramas and is reminiscent of Victor Hugo's Quasimodo or Mendele Mokher Seforim's Fishke the Lame. Knut Hamsun also wrote a story about an innocent cripple, Minutte, in *Mysteries*. The mistreatment of Minutte recalls the sadistic tormenting of Agnon's Ovadia in the dance hall.[43] The wayward servant girl is also a rather familiar melodramatic figure (see Gerhard Hauptman's *Rose Bernd* [1903] and Peretz Hirschbein's *Miriam* [1905]). The relationships among the oppressed and miserable were a favorite topic in naturalistic literature. By exploiting this topic, naturalistic literature appealed to the basic instincts of its readership. The danger in depicting such characters is excessive sentimentality; and, in fact, the richness of the material can be its own undoing.

The problem confronted by authors who use such material, which can border on cliché, is how to give the details new meaning, how to motivate the plot, and how to specify its message. Agnon solved these problems through structure. The story takes place first in the consciousness of the hero, Ovadia the Cripple, and then in the dance hall, where Ovadia finds Shayne-Seril dancing and where he is tormented by the young men. Afterward, the paths of the two characters diverge. Ovadia goes to the hospital, and Shayne-Seril returns to her master's home. In the end, the author brings them back together. The hero leaves the hospital and finds that his betrothed has taken another lover.

A conspicuous line in the plot is the effort to forge a hidden link of cause and effect between Ovadia's deeds in the hospital and those of Shayne-Seril in her master's house. The fact that Ovadia does not leave the hospital somewhat determines the girl's fate, just as Shayne-Seril directly causes Ovadia's two failures. Thus, the relationship between the cripple and the sensual girl is based on mutual culpability; social circumstances and the characters' personalities are the root of the evil. The sages said, "Everything is predictable, and the choice is in our hands."[44] But here everything is predictable, and people have very little freedom of choice. The fateful bond between the pair is presented ironically, both in the protagonists' thoughts and in the connections among the chapters. The hidden text, which expands the significance of the story, is revealed mainly in structural ways, such as links and gaps among the components of the story and the explanation of the heroes' fate.

One does not customarily look for a hidden text with multiple meanings in a naturalistic story. However, it is not Agnon's wont to go completely without hidden meanings. The story also implies intertextual connections that expand its significance; however, this expansion is not allegorical. The male protagonists, Ovadia and Reuven, allude only indirectly to biblical figures, although the story has affinities with the portion of the Bible beginning with "Vayishlah."[45] The Book of Ovadia, for whom Agnon's character is named, is read in the synagogue on the sabbath when that portion of the Bible is read.[46] Indeed, upon examining the text from Genesis, one finds many indirect parallels with "Ovadia the Cripple." Just as the patriarch Jacob was maimed in the thigh by the angel, so, too, is Ovadia a cripple. In Genesis, Reuben violates his father's marriage bed and sleeps with Bilhah;[47] similarly, Reuven, the redhead in Agnon's story, violates Ovadia's marriage bed. The hidden parallels between Ovadia and the patriarch Jacob and between the biblical Reuben and Reuven in the story have yet another aspect, suggested by the passage from the prophet Ovadia—which deals with the bitter war between Israel and Edom, the descendants of Esau. If the people of Israel are the seed of Jacob (or Ovadia), then redheaded people are the descendants of Esau. Jacob epitomizes the spirit; and Esau, the one who is enslaved to his instincts, epitomizes flesh and blood.

Agnon does not intend the connection to the tradition to indicate that the characters should not be taken as they are. On the contrary, the story's protagonists are just what they appear to be. However, the instinctual struggle waged in the story is enhanced by the biblical connotations, which are partially parodic and partially archetypal. Those connotations do not (to use the elder Israeli critic Dov Sadan's phrase) create "a story within the story." Rather than make the story of Ovadia more profound, the biblical comparison mocks the hidden archetype—that is, Jacob, the "plain man dwelling in tents."[48] The two forces, flesh and spirit—the hands of Esau and the voice of Jacob—are presented here in an ironic, sarcastic light—the latter in its hopeless impotence and the former in all its naked coarseness. The references do not intensify and expand but rather limit and dwarf the stature of the protagonists. That is to say, the structure and the texture (the hidden text) are meant to alter and deepen the naturalistic materials.

Moreover, toward the end the author brings the story to a climax, giving it a new and broader meaning. The tale does not merely recount the story of a couple that has been over-whelmed and crushed by eros and thanatos, as well as by the hypocrisy of bourgeois society, but goes beyond the exposure of the victims. Here is the final passage of the story:

Ovadia's mouth was open, his tongue like an immovable rock, and the sweets in his hand kept melting and melting. The baby suck-led with pleasure at his mother's breast, with a still small voice. Ovadia took the candies with his right hand and the crutch with his left. The baby stretched and removed one hand from the teat, and Shayne-Sirel's anger was still not appeased. Ovadia feared to give her the candies and bent down and laid them on the infant's palm.[49]

The reader might have expected that Ovadia would turn on his heels and leave the mother and her child to their sighs. But Ovadia does not. He feels that Shayne-Seril is not guilty. Apparently, in such affairs there are neither sinners nor guilty parties but merely creatures in need of mercy. The story is cruel and naturalistic and is cleared of all sentimentality by the author's sarcasm, but it concludes with a catharsis of human compassion. Different faces are brought to light. Agnon does not convey compassion via the shortcut of sentimentality but rather by following the path of woe.

"Ovadia the Cripple" is an example of Agnon's delicate handling of coarse naturalistic material, just as "Three Sisters" is an example of his ability to craft an entire world within a balladlike dewdrop without portraying actual human situations. The two stories illustrate the concept of fate from different points of view. The characters in the balladlike story accept and submit to fate, while the characters in the naturalistic story find a humane way of overcoming it. In the folk tale, depiction is formal and restricted; hence, the function of the intratextual features is expanded. In the realistic story, the description is detailed and extensive, thus limiting the function of those features; and allegorization is prevented despite them.

"Ovadia the Cripple" may also be seen from another viewpoint. Agnon writes ostensibly as a believer to a readership of believers, as a typical bourgeois to a bourgeois audience.

According to customary laws, Shayne-Seril's baby was born out of wedlock; thus, judged by the standards of the Jewish bourgeoisie he is a social outcast from every point of view.

However, Agnon turns the moral tables here. Toward the end of the story he creates an effect of moral deautomatization, which is also an effect of literary deautomatization. The child, according to this view, need not be ostracized and cast out because Ovadia, although he is not the biological father, gives the child the candies—thus, accepting moral responsibility. This is not in keeping with the naturalistic school's material world of flesh and blood, although the protagonists are portrayed throughout most of the story according to that world's basic assumptions.

The naturalistic story receives a moral and spiritual dimension from the world of grace. In contrast to the bourgeois morality based on genetic rules and regulations, a humanistic ethos is portrayed, based on relationships of grace, mercy, and responsibility—all of which contrast with traditional bourgeois values. Agnon once again shows himself to be a traditional revolutionary both in form and in content.

The Abstract Story: The Humorous Feuilleton.   The comic perspective is central in Agnon's work. He exploited every possible variety of comedy—from social satire, in "Of Our Young People and Our Elders," to farce, in "With the Death of the Saint" and "The Frogs." Agnon even employed Rabelaisian grotesquery in "Pisces" and "At Hemdat's." Most of the comic stories tend to hyperbole, thus intensifying the sense of realism, although a few are stripped bare.

One example of stark, comical abstraction is the feuilleton

"On Taxes" (1950), included in *The Book of the State*. It is an abstract story without reference to place or time, to real characters, or to human situations. Furthermore, the protagonist is not an individual but rather a collectivity—that is, the state. The fictional situation with all its ramifications provokes laughter because it evokes official bureaucracies everywhere. It is taken as a comic hyperbole, a mechanism for its own sake beyond any actual need or purpose. In the story an imaginary state is about to go bankrupt, which leads to a strike threat by the officials. From the very first the bureaucracy is characterized as a superfluous body, creating work where there was none but to no purpose: "The grumblers quipped and mocked, saying, 'What work will the bureaucrats stop doing? Perhaps they'll stop their idleness and thumbtwiddling.' "[50]

Meaningless activities are reiterated in various contexts. Committees are constantly being formed, each merely a comic synonym of its predecessor. Agnon's technique is to amass details that do not advance the plot, showing that every action is merely repetition and that the entire plot is superfluous:

They formed a new committee. Since the active intellect is active equally in every person, that committee proposed what the first committees had proposed, aside from the bill for expenses, which was slightly different from the bills of the first committees, since in the meanwhile the cost of living had risen by several points.[51]

The coincidental and arbitrary turning point occurs when salvation comes to the state in the form of the cane, upon which taxes had not yet been imposed. The cane deflects the course of events, giving the plot a goal. In the author's words:

"However the state was fortunate. Even in a trivial matter, its luck held. It happened that a certain elderly member of the House of Lippery-waggers forgot his cane."[52]

That turning point provokes a chain reaction: taxation of canes, discussions of the form of taxation, a black market in canes, legislation obliging people to carry canes, the importing of wood from abroad, the burning of wood, the transfer of the ashes from the site of the fire to the sea, and finally the importing of finished canes—a precipitous decline in which each event pulls down its fellow. Since the actions do no one any good, the author intervenes to repair a fault but cannot do so. His attempt comes to little more than adding fault upon fault, a comic snowball showing with increasing clarity that action does not improve matters but simply drives them round and round to no purpose, until the cycle itself attains a value of its own.

Since everything done in the state is foolishness, only that which is not done is intelligent. The state is itself evil. The author is weary of an other-oriented society whose only force is verbal, taking its own social organization as a value in itself. The story does not relate to people; it is not people who pervert the world. The root of evil does not lie in the Weichsls and Deichsls or Mundspiegels who populate "Of Our Young People and Our Elders" but rather in the House of Lippery-waggers, the tax bureaucracy, and the state itself. Moreover, the bureaucrats, so long as they are not connected with the bureaucracy, are like anyone else—trivial people who would not harm a fly, collectors of jokes and scissors who serve in high positions. However, as soon as they put on their official hats, they are liable to do damage:

So the Treasurer sat there with the members of the Committee with a cordial expression and a smile on his face, not passing over a single prominent figure in the state without telling a joke about him, one of those jokes that people amuse themselves by telling. He said, "Most likely these will commemorate our colleagues rather than their actions, even though their actions are one long joke." He kept talking that way until the members of the Committee recalled why they had come. They raised their voices and spoke to him. Immediately his bright countenance altered, his lips twisted, his nose swelled, his ear-lobes turned black, and he looked entirely like a state official. If we didn't know him, we could not discern that he was capable of understanding a joke.[53]

Here, the comic element is impersonal. The fictional world is detached from actual social materials and is presented as a bare skeleton. It is funny because the schematization of phenomena exposes their vacuity better than would a concrete description. The abstract scheme removes the coincidental, human, and individual element from the world, and everything is frozen. The world is driven like a mechanism without direction, a comic wheel revolving upon itself without significance. The reader is left without air to breathe. Even the narrator, who appears as an objective chronicler called "the author of *The Book of the State,*" has no human reality.

Agnon's comic point of view is, to a large extent, anarchical. He does not advocate social reform or changes in the system; rather, the entire state mechanism seems fundamentally ridiculous to him. The story might be aimed at the political establishment of the State of Israel, which had just been born and already had managed to erect its own bureaucracy. (This story was printed in *Haaretz* in 1950!) However, it applies to any bureaucratic system in any place at any time. Agnon saw bureaucracy as a mechanism that feeds on itself and expands at the citizen's expense without any regard for common sense. This is an anarchical work written in a classical style.

Even when writing a satirical piece with comic abstraction of social reality, Agnon remained faithful to himself. Here, too, he played the role of a revolutionary who, using irony tinged with sharp sarcasm, destroys the most sanctified establishment in any society—the bureaucracy, which feeds upon itself, and the people's representatives, who make the parliament (which Agnon called "the house of lippery") into an institution that acts in its own behalf and supports itself with meaningless jabber and pointless laws.

This sort of work has various artistic limitations. Agnon's tendency toward an abstract worldview and toward situations merely hinted at is evident in his earliest writings. It is a style that appears in various proportions in different works. The better the equilibrium between the concrete and the abstract, or the specific and the universal, the more significant is the work. Agnon's abstract writing, in its many forms, is limited to a single meaning. This is because its components are not sufficiently concretized but rather are presented as abstractions or as a series of allegorical keys; thus, the situations are not open to more than one interpretation. The paradox is, of course, that the abstract texts are much more closed and unequivocal than are the concrete and ostensibly realistic ones. These techniques, which were supposed to reflect the modern formal revolution explicitly, are not always as open-ended and multivalent as Agnon's more conservative, traditional techniques.

In Agnon's traditional techniques, the modern "revolution" is implicit and alluded to in intertextual parodies and in minuscule stylistic and compositional shifts and deviations from traditional literary conventions. If any sin may be laid at the door of Agnon's work, it is the sin of abstraction. He exerted a negative influence on younger writers primarily because they seized upon the abstract and unequivocal aspects of his work.

The Abstract, or Nonrealistic, Story. The tendency toward abstraction is found mainly in the so-called modern stories that Agnon began publishing in the early 1930s, which ultimately were collected in *The Book of Deeds.* That book was Agnon's attempt to satisfy modern man's need to express a new realm of experience.[54] Such an expression might simply have been a vital need for Agnon himself and represented a fulfillment of tendencies that had existed within him almost from the first (see, for example, "Agunot: A Tale"). In any case, I do not consider *The Book of Deeds* to be the finest of his works, although its influence on younger writers has been greater than the influence of his realistic fiction.

I will take the example of "Quitclaim" (in Hebrew, "Hefker"), published in *Haaretz* in 1945, which follows the pattern typical of *The Book of Deeds.*[55] Generally, the narrator is the hero. The pattern is a kind of journey ending in a dead end or in an unexpected reversal; and, since all the stories appear in a single collection, each sheds light on the others.

At first we seem to be reading a story about a man who has made an appointment to meet a friend in a café. He lingers for a long time and later tries to go home. Since he seems to have missed the last bus, he goes by foot, enters a cul-de-sac, and becomes entangled with an eccentric character who apparently summons him to judgment. Finally, for no reason at all and with no explanation, he appears before a strange judge. The judge does not judge him, and he sets out once again. On his way, he notes another group of Jews who apparently also are waiting for their trial. The overt text is neither plausible nor logical; the circumstances are extremely surprising and bizarre. The story has no meaning unless the reader attempts to descend to its deepest depths and rescue the latent text.

A detailed analysis shows the story's message to be that the lower and upper worlds, which are not depicted in the overt text, are controlled by powers that do not permit a person to choose his own path. The protagonist vacillates from crisis to crisis and is forced to seek his way, but the inner obstacles are beyond his strength. Not only can he find no shelter in his own home, he also cannot resolve whether he has behaved properly.

That meaning is implicit in the name of the story, "Quit-claim," which suggests a world where the law has been abnegated, without judge or judgment. It is a world in which the holy and the profane and laughter and dread are intermingled. The plot is not bound by realistic cause and effect but is instead held together by bits and snippets having the same cohesive power or meaning—that is, a unified atmosphere. The inner journey of "that man" passes through various emotional stations and reaches the destination intended from the start.

I will now analyze in detail one of those stations along the way to show how the general meaning of the story crystallizes within the reader. Here is a central passage in which the protagonist stands before the mysterious judge to pay the forfeit for a sin he has not committed:

He asked me nothing but sat before his desk and took up pen and ink and paper and started writing. In the room it was quiet and the smell of kerosene wafted up from the heater. Only the sound of the pen scratching the paper was heard. If the pen does not break and the paper does not tear, he will never stop his writing. I stood in my place and thought to myself, hasn't the middle of his mustache turned white in the meanwhile? The middle of his mustache had not turned white, but its two ends were befouled.[56]

This text is interesting because of the relationship between the overt text and a latent one. Earlier in the story, Agnon used expressions in reference to the judge that recall attributes of the Creator found in "The Song of Honor," a kabbalistic hymn incorporated in the sabbath liturgy.

"Quitclaim"	"The Song of Honor"
I saw before me a man, neither young nor aged.	And Thou art held to be aged and youthful.
Gray was sown on it at both its ends.	The hair of Thy head is gray and black.

224

And in the middle of the black
     mustache . . .

| He stood and donned a miter | He donned the miter of re- |
| with several ends.[57] | demption. |

Such a comparison seems to indicate that God is the hidden hero, latent in the figure of the judge. The figure in the overt text might also be a parody of the latent figure, by means of which the oxymorons attributed to the Creator are illuminated from a new point of view. Traditionally, the oxymoron is a way of expressing the ineffable greatness of God. This story, however, reveals a contradictory aspect of the oxymoron— that is, the eternal ambivalence of the highest judge, who lacks unequivocal answers to man's questions. In the description of the God-judge, the grotesqueness, characteristic of the previous passages, reaches a peak. The God-judge, a central figure in the story, throws the narrator-hero's world into such confusion that he is unable to reach any decisions.

When the narrator stands there like a pupil before his master or a sinner before his judge, the authority figure can be perceived as either comic or threatening. The ambiguity rests on the relationship between the overt text and the hidden one, a reciprocity that exists throughout and determines the special character of these stories.

What is the typical method of Agnon's abstract stories? As noted, the structure is based on the plot of a journey. The hero wanders through space. However, that space is not concrete but is rather the metaphorical embodiment of the soul or of a metarealistic world. Hence, the journey is not situated in historical or chronological time; it is the time of the soul, in which anterior and posterior are merely various stages in the hero's development.[58] Such a method is closely related to expressionistic techniques, in which reality does not exist in itself; there are merely expressions of the fragmented ego or the ego's outcry.

The plot of the story knows neither causality nor probability but rather elliptical connections, which are both intratextual and intertextual. The materials that permit the discovery of the connections among the various links are given as the latent content of the overt text, and they are revealed to the interpreter as he or she fills the gaps through semantic, rhetorical, and structural analyses.

I have noted already that the overt text may be a parodic substitute for the subject hinted at by the latent text (the judge, the Lord of the Universe). The contrast sometimes reaches grotesque dimensions, as, for example, when the feeling of dread seems justified in the latent text but is comical and unfounded in the overt text. The relationship between what is implied in the two levels of expression is typical of the grotesque in these texts.

The latent text emerges for the reader both through a metaphorical understanding of the physical settings (for example, the cul-de-sac appearing in this story) and also through the accretion or extension of motifs as later ones shed light on those that came earlier. Thus, for example, the handkerchief (in the sense of a scarf or a shawl) appears in "Quitclaim" as the garment in which the narrator-protagonist wraps himself, not wanting any connection with the world about him.

All of these factors indicate that the world depicted is not anchored in reality but rather in a realm including far more than what the narrator-hero, who presents the story to the reader, is capable of interpreting for himself. The world of the story is a kind of psychological pattern. It could be interpreted as a repressed reality (in psychoanalytic terms), or as a metareality (following various metaphysical systems), or as a world of archetypes (according to Jung). In any case, the determining factor is the material representing multisemantic relationships between the latent subject and the overt one.

Naturally, one must realize that in fiction of this sort characterization declines in importance, and the protagonists cease being portrayed as unique individuals. As in folk tales, the character in the abstract story has a largely formal function. Even when the author gives names to his characters, they do not exist in their own right but must be taken as anonymous embodiments of emotional and ideational elements of the psyche. Their appellations are likely to be allegorical, hinting at the latent text—the broad cultural connotation. But in such a case, one must understand the character from various points of view—that is, according to the meaning implicit or implied by the character's name (for example, Yekutiel = God shall acquit me and Ne'eman = faithful; both of these are epithets of Moses in midrashic literature, and they are used in Agnon's "A Whole Loaf") or through the cultural links derived from the epithets (such as in "The Song of Honor").

Although the story is told by a narrator-hero, a consciousness with a psychological structure, he functions within the story without comprehending his context. In his journeys, the narrator-hero encounters various characters that seem to be superfluous to the logic of the plot. Through the use of chance appearances, the "I" encounters projections of himself, which become aspects of the structure of the relationship between him and the emotional factors that comprise the work's internal structure. The parallel between microcosm and macrocosm gives these emotional factors metarealistic significance; as a result, the interpretation of the story is transferred from the psychological level to an abstract level and thus to metaphysical concepts and values.

Since Agnon's fiction of this type attempts to present the realm in which problems exist rather than the realm in which they are solved, the parodic technique of multiple meanings is an appropriate one. Agnon portrays an ambiguous world that is filled with anonymous heroes and settings and is studded with epigrams and generalizations. The symbolic coloration of the elements leads us to interpret them as though the author sought to identify the Everyman in his story with every person outside of the story, and that the author attempted to provide a complete exposition of what is known as the human condition. That is to say, he presents his own inability and the inability of Everyman to give unequivocal ratification to the content of the work or to any values as a general truth. Human alienation, the solitude of his generation, the opacity of reality, and the impassivity of the powers that be are the subjects of the story.

If this assumption is correct then the form of the story fits its subjects, and the latter are suited to the form. This story is the most extreme instance of the embodiment of the modern worldview in Agnon's oeuvre. Here, Agnon also used intertextual techniques related to the cultural tradition. The intertextuality is generally parodic in effect; it is extreme and, in most cases, leads to grotesque results. The messages of these texts are ambivalent. However, it is not the kind of ambivalence that portrays something and its opposite at the same time but an ambivalence that disorients the addressee. Despite the traditional style and the intertextual connection to a latent traditional text, the story exposes the social and moral anarchy of modern man.

Agnon was quite conscious of the "writerly" effect of these stories. The dreamlike codification demanded an "analytical" decodifier. The signifiers in these texts do not have determinable signifieds but are quite multivalent and have, of course, no definitive referent. Moreover, they do not have any informant-analysand in presentia who could provide the reader with further information by bringing up "unique" connotations and associations in reference to specific signifieds—by excluding irrelevant information and including relevant data. The result is that the analyst-addressee (the reader) has to fill the "empty" semantic units, using paradigms and semantic connotations alluded to in the text or drawn from the addressee's own life experience. In addition, the addressee must fill in missing links and gaps, sometimes using analytical (that is, Freudian) techniques.

The addressee must "rewrite" the text to the best of his or her abilities in the areas of explication, elucidation, and interpretation. In a sense, the text "wants" to be and actually becomes a "writerly" text. As a result of this demand upon the addressee, the circle of potential readers is diminished. The author expects his readership to be composed of analytical readers who act as critics or of critics who act as analytical readers.

Nonetheless, this type of story does not represent Agnon at his greatest. His powers are most impressive in stories where reality is mingled with what is beyond, in the private and collective spheres, as in the novellas or in the short stories, such as "Three Sisters" and "Ovadia the Cripple"—one of which is built mainly upon sonorous, rhythmic, and stylistic effects; whereas the other is based on scenes and concrete situations. The best of Agnon's nonrealistic stories are those with an element of the concrete, such as "The Overcoat," "Edo and Enam," and "From Lodging to Lodging."

Between Abstract and Concrete: Stories Conveying a Philosophy of History. Several of Agnon's stories can be interpreted in many ways and operate simultaneously on several levels of meaning; these include "The Overcoat," "From Lodging to Lodging," "Edo and Enam," and "Forevermore," stories that are both existential and sociohistorical. Of course, the main meaning is existential, and the historical stratum is not a chronicle but rather the penetration to the roots of a situation through mythical writing.[59] The mythic character of these stories, particularly "Edo and Enam" and "Forevermore," tilts them toward a bond with traditional texts, which convey themes bearing on a philosophy of history.

"The Covering of Blood," included in the posthumously published *Within the Wall* (1975), constitutes the final link in that chain of stories. The existential level is less pronounced in "The Covering of Blood" than in the earlier stories, and the emphasis is placed on the historical stratum. This long short story may be regarded as a social survey of the history of the Jewish people in past generations. It is a general summa-

230

tion by the author, who looks at the past and anticipates the future. The traditional revolution reached its peak in these stories. In them, Agnon concretized the social and historical significance of the revolution that contained its own end within it. The revolution destroyed the tradition and, in the process, sowed the seeds of its own destruction.

The narrator-witness is confronted with the life stories of the three protagonists: Hillel, Adolf, and the old American. The three men are uprooted from Europe; two end up in the Land of Israel and one in America. They are not victims of the Holocaust; however, they are victims of the Jewish history that is epitomized by the Holocaust.

Hillel, an ordained rabbi, never is appointed to a rabbinical post because of baseless hatred within Jewish society, and even the post of ritual slaughterer is given to him as a favor rather than by right. Jewish society rejects him because it no longer believes in the values of the Torah and prefers material values. When he is exiled to the United States, his leg is amputated because Gittele-Frumtshis, the owner of the slaughterhouse, demands that he work day and night—not even releasing him to break his fast after the seventeenth of *tammuz*. Hillel is the victim of Jewish society in two versions of its exile, the European and the American (the latter is a kind of exacerbation of the former).

Adolf, a sergeant in the First World War, saves Hillel from death but is a victim of events between the two wars. He eats with Gentiles and lives with their women; assimilation makes him need their favors. He drifts from place to place and meets with destruction everywhere, until he emigrates to the Land of Israel. There, too, he is a beggar.

231

The old American reaches the New World as a child. He serves as a cantor's assistant until he marries a wealthy woman. Then he goes through a miniature holocaust: his daughter commits suicide after being deserted by the gentile singer who has gotten her pregnant, and his son is murdered by his friends after joining a band of thieves. The old man is bereft and solitary, undone by the assimilation of the second generation in the new place of exile.

The Holocaust is in the background, melding the three into a single figure that represents different aspects of the surviving remnant. The main character, Hillel, is a kind of Job whom the Lord does not bless in his later years. Both of Hillel's wives die because of the war, as do all of his children. He never has any possessions. In his confessions to the narrator-witness, there is a touch of a reproach directed on high. By choosing the name Hillel, Agnon asserted a connection between his character and the historical personage: the ancient rabbi who founded a school called the House of Hillel and who tempered the letter of the law with mercy. It was a later sage by the same name, Hillel, who said: "The Jews have no Messiah because they already devoured him in the days of Hezekiya."[60] The reproaches of Hillel the sage, like those of Hillel in the story, are directed chiefly against the Jews who gobbled up their Messiah, both in earlier times (represented by the quarrel between the Hassidim and the Mitnagdim) and in the time of the State of Israel. National redemption brought no change. Rather than redemption replacing exile, exile usurped the place of redemption. The ordained rabbi became a slaughterer, and the slaughterer became a beggar. Hillel is now without the House of Hillel.

In the course of the story, Hillel mediates between the two other characters: Adolf, who saved Hillel from death in the First World War, and the old American, who saves him from starvation after his leg is cut off on the seventeenth of *tammuz* in Gittele-Frumtshis's slaughterhouse.

The irony, or rather the grotesquery, of history is shown mainly in Gittele-Frumtshis's slaughterhouse, where Hillel says the benediction over the slaughtering and is covered with blood. The implicit parallel in the written language is the legend about the prophet Zechariah, who was slaughtered by the Jews and whose blood bubbled up and could not be covered until Nevuzaradan came and slaughtered ninety-four thousand residents of Jerusalem on the blood of the prophet.[61] That event took place on the seventeenth of *tammuz* (an unlucky day in the personal life of Agnon's Hillel). According to tradition, that is the day when the first tablets were broken, when the walls of Jerusalem were broken through, and when an idol was placed in the Temple. Such linguistic and cultural allusions also point to Bialik's poem "On the Slaughterer." Perhaps one is justified in viewing the hundreds of chickens that are slaughtered while multitudes of Jews were being murdered overseas as part of the ceremony of repentance. (The owner of the slaughterhouse sends Hillel eighteen dollars as compensation for his leg.) The parallel creates an unusual link between reward and punishment. Hillel's "blood" will not be atoned for until the Jews are slaughtered. Gittele-Frumtshis operates an assembly line of slaughter; she presses for increased productivity, her heart bent on gain. Jews eager for money lost sight of what was happening across the ocean. The dreadful "hand in hand" (the subtitle of the story) shows that the

Jews are bound up with each other, creating a strange and grotesque kind of logic—a justification of fate, which is not sufficiently justified. It is almost possible to say that the technique of analogy ("hand in hand") is no longer a literary stratagem here but has become the ironic and grotesque subject of the story.

Analogy is an important device in most of Agnon's writings and serves various functions in his works. For example, in *A Guest for the Night*, he uses analogy to depict the disintegration of society despite the common fate of the individuals within it. In "The Covering of Blood," ironic analogy is an expression of Agnon's ironic view of history. The parallels among various phenomena that affect the social group shed ironic light both on the group itself and on the ironic author—the hidden entity, the master of history who creates phenomena so different and yet so similar. The writer's revolutionary irony is directed against both the Master of the Universe and the chosen people, whom He chose above all other nations.

Another ambiguous parallel, as though blaming the Jews themselves for the Holocaust, is the name Adolf given to the Jewish sergeant:

Hard days came to him. He had no choice but to beg from door to door. At any rate he praised himself for not doing what Hitler did and standing at the doorways of convents for the bowl of sauce they handed him.[62]

Adolf is a fornicator. A number of gentile women give birth to his progeny, and he suspects that the destroyers of the Jewish community are descended from him. Adolf confesses to Hillel, who describes the state of affairs to the narrator-witness:

> I found him very depressed. I asked him what had happened to him, and he told me he had dreamt that a certain heathen of Hitler's party had struck a Jew and killed him cruelly, and that Jew was his nephew, and the heathen was the son of the lady who had had him by Adolf. In the daytime as well he sees all kinds of visions, and most of them are related to the results of that sin.[63]

It is as if the victim created his murderer. But the ambivalent relationship to basic situations is created not only through the context of the names but principally by a parodic view of extraliterary situations, which are shown in a new light in the text. For example, the heroes frequently are caught in predicaments with no way out, and only saviors from the outside can rescue them from starvation and death. Their rescue offers neither consolation nor salvation. Rather than bringing redemption to the rescued, it brings profit to the rescuers, as when the slaughterer saves Hillel from starvation in order to exploit him (to keep a place open for his grandson) and when Gittele-Frumtshis behaves similarly. The story becomes a parody of the Jewish efforts at rescue between the two world wars. Even basic Zionist values, such as the ingathering of the exiles, are seen in a new light. The two immigrants—the survivors—do not journey to the Land of Israel of their own free will. Adolf is brought to Palestine by mistake. He is asked to serve as a translator for a circus, although he knows no Hebrew; he wanders about the country as a beggar without finding a place for himself. Hillel is sent to the Land of Israel at the expense of a rich American, but the ingathering of exiles does not bring unity. Here, art—as parody always has—distorts extraliterary motifs. As the reader compares fiction to reality, the meanings of the motifs are altered.

What is achieved through the intra- and intertextual connections, by means of the parodic use of extraliterary states of affairs, also is achieved through several fundamental symbols of the story: the severed leg, the hurdy-gurdy, the monkey, the parrot, and the dollars. Hillel's leg was not cut off when he was a child; a prince's coach did nearly run him over; and he was saved by a poor Jewish porter. His leg was not severed when he was buried in a landslide during the First World War; then, Adolf, another poor Jew, saved him. Only after ending up in Gittele-Frumtshis's slaughterhouse is his leg cut off because of her lust for wealth. All of the tension between rescue and rescue for the purpose of profit is exposed by the fate of Hillel's leg. The leg's value decreases progressively in the Land of Israel: an automobile destroys the rubber leg, and a wooden one takes its place (the gift of the Fair Measures Brotherhood); and holes turn up in the leg because a mad Hassid has done something with it. As the value of the leg decreases, so, too, does the value of Hillel's dollars. The state takes the dollars intended for the survivors of the Holocaust and derives profit from them.

Another central symbol is the hurdy-gurdy. Adolf receives the instrument from a beggar in Europe. He wanders through Austria with it and then brings it to the Land of Israel. The hurdy-gurdy plays the song of the sons of Korah (a rebel who opposed Moses) at the gates of the underworld ("Moses is one and his Torah is one"),[64] but the song no longer expresses actual values. There is only the hidden echo of a not-so-splendid past. What remains is the hurdy-gurdy as a symbol of wanderings, to which the "Gypsy" monkey and the parrots are joined. The wandering Jews, Adolf and Hillel, have inherited a Gypsy legacy of aimless roaming.

In contrast to Agnon's decoherent stories, "The Covering of Blood" is not broken off but actually comes to a conclusion. The end attempts to predict the future of the native Israeli generation, as though returning to the question posed in *A Guest for the Night*.[65]

The heroes of "The Covering of Blood" are alone. The American branch of survivors has no posterity. The children commit suicide or are murdered because they have assimilated. Yet Hillel is not alone in the way that Adolf, whose illegitimate sons are the murderers and destroyers, is. The only son and inheritor is Adolf's nephew:

I do not recall whether I mentioned Adolf's sister's son. Adolf told me he was the Adolf from a certain city, all of whose Jewish inhabitants were killed by Hitler, to the last man, and of those who went to the Land of Israel, some died of hunger during the First World War and others were killed by the Arabs' shells during the conquest of the land. Adolf had one sister whose second marriage was to a Hebrew teacher, and she had a son by him. The boy's father, his sister's husband, that is, died, leaving her nothing. She raised the son in poverty, by dint of hard work, and every penny she saved she spent on his education. When he got older he joined the youth movement, and in the end he settled in the Land of Israel and promised his mother he would bring her. He arrived in the Land of Israel close to the time of the war between the Jews and the Arabs. He took part in the war, was wounded, and recovered. After the war he went to a kibbutz and became a tractor driver. One day the Syrians crossed the border, seized him, and took him prisoner. Since that time no one has heard anything of him.[66]

According to Agnon, because the Jews of the Land of Israel did not change, even in their own country, their fate is liable to be like that of the Diaspora Jews. Regarding both the children of the American father and those of Hillel, we could say in the most general fashion that the fathers ate sour grapes, and the children's teeth are set on edge. But in the case of Adolf's nephew, we are stunned. There is no proportion between the sour grapes and the setting on edge of teeth. The narrator is himself astonished at that strange fate, just as he wonders over and over again whether there is any connection regarding reward and punishment between the behavior of an individual and the fate of the nation.[67]

The fate of Adolf's nephew, the last remnant of a destroyed family, remains obscure. Hillel is waiting for the young man, who might not be alive. If he is alive, his life might not be worth living, considering the inheritance left for him by his Uncle Adolf—that is, things from the Diaspora and symbols of Gypsy life: the hurdy-gurdy, the monkey, and the parrot. That, of course, is a harsh vision. It is a prophecy of agonies that do not purify; it is exile with no redemption.

The only light in that darkness is Benyamin, an American boy whose soul yearns for Torah and who has settled in the Land of Israel to study with Hillel. Perhaps that is the final life raft: the Torah, which is independent of place or time and exists beyond the dialectic of exile and redemption and holocaust and rebirth.

In this story, abstraction and concrete illustration are inter-mingled. Each episode—Hillel during the war, Hillel in the slaughterhouse, Adolf in the Land of Israel—is detailed and stands by itself. However, the connections among the episodes and the paradigmatic, or intertextual, links with various cultural materials give the story its meaning as a statement of a philosophy of history. The technique of the multifaceted parallels is an adequate correlative for the subject: what happened to the Jews, "hand in hand," in different historical settings. We have here an actualization of history that has become fantastic, or else a grotesque illumination of real situations that seem to compete with each other in their deformation.

This long short story more or less sums up the thematics of the traditional revolution: On the one hand, it describes the dead end in which the Zionist revolution culminated after inheriting the inner crises of the traditional society—as shown by the life and wanderings of Hillel and Adolf. However, on the other hand, the story shows clearly that, according to Agnon, the Zionist revolution did not bring a balm to cure the protracted ills of the Jewish people. In the Land of Israel —where the revolution took place, where everyone believed that "all hopes would be fulfilled" (to quote a famous song of the Second Aliya), and where the "Divine Presence would also dwell"—the revolution did not bring the longed for results. This story seems to show that the solution to the inner paradoxes of the revolution that destroyed the tradition might be a strange return to the *roots of the Jewish tradition*—before it was established in any traditional or secular institutions. That return, which could be a way out of the morass, is embodied in the figure of the young American Jew who comes to the Land of Israel to combine the study of Torah and working the land. The Torah, in its purity, might be one way out of the situation with no way out.

The narrative situation in "The Covering of Blood" resembles the situation in A Guest for the Night, and I believe that the analogy was a conscious one. Here again, the narrator-author is an addressee-witness to Hillel's story or confession. In turn, Hillel is the addressee and witness of Adolf's story. These are two modern interpretations of the myth of Job—recollections of the suffering of two individuals who happen to be victims of the last fifty years of Jewish history. Like Job, they have lost their loved ones and their possessions. The two storytellers are victims of the collective history of their community. The addressee is similar to the "guest" in A Guest for the Night—that is, an aesthetic involved/noninvolved spectator. His guilt is the "implied" blame of Job's companions, who bear witness and listen to Job's complaints but who were mere bystanders, seeing Job's afflictions and doing nothing but misunderstanding and misinterpreting them intellectually.

The implied author's goal and message is the transference of the implicit guilt feelings of the narrator as addressee to the implied readers. In the act of reading, the readers become witnesses and spectators for the primary and secondary narrators of the story. The implied authors demand that the readers take responsibility upon themselves for the miseries inflicted upon their brethren. The readers also belong to the social circle (Jews in America and Israel) that, in the literary model, was at least partly responsible for the suffering of the victims and the survivors. Moreover, I believe that Agnon indicates that any survivor must accept some responsibility for the miracle of survival while his or her group was victimized. This is the meaning of the stories of Hillel and Adolf, and this is their significance for the narrator, for their addressees, and for the narrator's addressees as well.

Based on the inner logic of the plot, "The Covering of Blood" is also one of Agnon's most ambiguous and grotesque stories. For example, Adolf, the pursued, is given the first name of Hitler—the arch pursuer. Between the two a bizarre synonymity is created. The story also ends in deep despair, with a strange prophecy for the future of the Jewish state— the children of which are liable to inherit the Gypsy heritage. However, with the motif of Benyamin, Agnon concludes one of his last stories—apparently written in the 1960s—in a manner similar to the author of Ecclesiastes, the most pessimistic of the twenty-four books of the Hebrew Bible. There, it is written:

The end of the matter, all having been heard: fear God, and keep His commandments; for this is the whole man. For God shall bring every work into the judgment concerning every hidden thing, whether it be good or whether it be evil.[68]

CHAPTER 6

SUMMARY: THEMATICS AND INFLUENCE

Thematics

NO SUBJECT was alien to Agnon. Various readers and critics have attempted to exhaust and formulate the central problem of his writings. Agnon described the history of the Jewish people in the modern period with most of its tensions. He stood at the crossroads between faith and heresy, between tradition and crisis, between exile and redemption, and between the community of pious believers and the new secular community—which cannot have faith in the tradition, though several of Agnon's heroes yearn for it as for a lost paradise. Agnon's heroes do not fit into the new Zionist reality, which is being constructed before their eyes. They are torn between their bond with their people and their wish to cut the "umbilical cord."

Some of these problems already had perturbed Berdy-

czewski, and some of them led to the depiction of the deracinated characters of Brenner's generation (which was also
Agnon's). Agnon's particular contribution is his dual point
of view, so typical of him and of him alone. He looks at both
Buczacz and Jerusalem—symbols of tradition—from the
viewpoint of a man who has gone through the melting pot
of Jaffa—a symbol of the new society—returning to them
in his yearnings and visions. Both are shown in an ironic
light and also, in moments of grace, in a positive light, with
the author reconciled to the weaknesses of both worlds (as in
A Guest for the Night). The positive light always reveals a
fundamental deficiency that afflicts the society of Agnon's
generation, striking out at every norm with its antinorm.

Agnon raised the problems of the religious scholar and the
artist in an alien, twilight world in "Edo and Enam," "Forevermore," and *Shira.* In "Until Now," he tried to understand the position of a man in a society that has lost its way
in the war. In "Metamorphosis" and "The Doctor's Divorce,"
he penetrated the world of lovers deprived of the power of
their love by social conventions inimical to interpersonal relationships. He presented humble people far away from the
centers of power—Rabbi Alter, Toni Hartmann, Tehilla, and
Dan Hofmann—in contrast to characters who lose their
identity through minding other people's business—Deichsl
and Weichsl, Spaltleder, and Professor Bachlam.

Agnon's writing excels in presenting the absolute contrast
between the inner and authentic and the outer and false—
that is, the contrast underlying the patterns and distinguishing among the characters within the literary structure. Here,
too, he exposed the gap that opened up in a social system

that usurped the "monarchy" from Torah scholars and gave it to extroverted ignoramuses. In contrast to others of his generation, Agnon never sang a song of praise to ignorance.

Another contrast, no less important, is between the grotesque, pleasure-loving, Rabelaisian figure—rooted in Reb Yudel of *The Bridal Canopy* and reaching peak expression in Fishl Karp of "Pisces"—and the miserable victim of circumstances, the pathetic figure worthy of mercy and love—Hemdat, in "The Hill of Sand," and Yitzhak Kumer, in *Only Yesterday*—who bows weakly to fate, represented by unrequited love and death. These contrasts, as well as the contrast between the hedonistic, renascence figure and the ascetic religious scholar, coexist in Agnon's works. The renascence monster breaks down all the conventions, and the scholar is a victim worthy of elegies, such as Ginat, Adiel Amzeh, and the heroes of *The Book of Deeds*.

From the social point of view, there is one major topic to be emphasized, which is formulated in a question that went beyond the interests of most of the writers of the Second Aliya, though it was used in a popular pioneering song, "Would the Divine Presence Reside Here?" In "Agunot: A Tale," the first story written by Agnon in the Land of Israel, from the contrast between the midrashic epigraph and the story itself, it appears that the Divine Presence is sometimes found in the Diaspora rather than in the Land of Israel, which is destined for dreadful disharmony and, therefore, will be deserted by its heroes. The question is reiterated in many of Agnon's works about the Land of Israel, such as *Only Yesterday,* "Tehilla," "The Priest of Truth," "Under the Tree," "Edo and Enam," *Within the Wall,* and "The Covering of

Blood." Is it possible to build a positive Jewish existence in the Land of Israel, achieving redemption of the soul and not merely physical redemption? The answer remains open, and in various stories the answer is interpreted in different ways. In any event, it is a question that disturbed Agnon throughout his life, and he was also not one to take the Zionist norm at face value.

One may sum up the overall message of Agnon's works with the oxymoron the "traditional revolutionary." This is a line that passes through both the subjects and the forms of Agnon's oeuvre like a silk thread. The traditional side predominates in the style of his works—that is, in their deep intertextual connections with the Jewish tradition and in the Greek classical point of departure of their poetics, in which inner feelings are shown rather than described. Agnon employed the literary devices of *naive* authors (in Schiller's sense of the word) to deal with a sentimental thematics.

The naive poetics of the microtext ostensibly opposes the modern and sentimental poetics revealed in the composition of the narrative structures. Schiller used the term *sentimental* to describe literature that, in contrast to naive works, does not convey an acceptance of reality as it is but is instead characterized by the use of satire, elegy, and utopias to cope with an undesirable reality.

At the beginning of his career, Agnon based the composition of his narrative structures on a parodic relationship to traditional Jewish culture, which was the common ground connecting the writer and those who were likely to read his works. The parodic relationship to cultural traditions is found in such early works as "Agunot: A Tale" and "And the Crooked

Shall Be Made Straight"; and it increases in strength over the years, reaching its peak expression in *The Book of Deeds* and in the metahistoric works, such as "Edo and Enam," "Forevermore," and "The Covering of Blood."

In the composition of the plots of Agnon's novels and in many of his novellas and short stories, various elements are intermingled. Most of the works are based ostensibly on traditional genres and include the elements contained within these genres. However, the genres do not appear in their pure form. *The Bridal Canopy* is not purely picaresque. Instead, it is a novel in which banquet stories delay the action that the picaresque travel tale advances, and the two are intermingled. In addition to these two elements, there is the motif of the double, producing a new pattern that recasts the tradition and the various conventions of the genre.

Similarly, *A Simple Story* is not merely a social novel. Profound romantic elements in this work fracture the boundaries of the genre. By the same token, *Shira* is neither a novel of aging, nor a university novel, nor a novel about a relationship with a femme fatale. It is both more and less than all of these elements. *A Guest for the Night* is not merely a travel novel; nor is it a nostalgic work about a protagonist who returns to his old home. *A Guest for the Night* expands the analogic devices infinitely, producing a new pattern that describes how impersonal fate takes over the lives of many individuals—thus giving the artist a feeling of guilt, for he is self-conscious and self-reflective, observing history from an aesthetic, uninvolved vantage point. Similarly, *Only Yesterday* is not a historical chronicle of the Second Aliya; nor is it a decidedly modern metapsychological novel, where a dog plays the role of the protagonist's alter ego. It is both simultaneously.

In Mr. Lublin's Store parallels the stories in *The Book of Deeds,* which were written in a metarealistic literary technique, as were "Edo and Enam" and "Forevermore." From the generic point of view, Agnon expanded the stories and the descriptions of the settings, making them into a genre that must stand by itself.

Most of the works have catastrophic conclusions, ending with the downfall of the protagonist. The implied author often places a naive plot in the background behind a modern, sentimental plot. Toward the end of a story, the naive plot is brought to the foreground.[1] Such a conclusion can be interpreted as an attempt on the part of the author to find a balance between the tradition and the revolution that leads to catastrophe. Reb Yudel Hasid might have reached a dead end in his efforts to marry off his daughters and to combine "flour" with Torah — that is, matter and spirit. He certainly would have failed if it weren't for a miraculous external force that hints that faith can overcome the economic and cultural norms of Jewish society. When a traditional force intervenes in the figure of the psychologist, Dr. Langsam, Hirshl returns to his family and overcomes the romantic dreams that would have broken through the bourgeois framework. The guest is saved from the collective fate of his hometown because as an individual, he has the power of escaping. In contrast to Yitzhak Kumer, who fails in his life tasks in *Only Yesterday,* a marginal minority do realize the ideals of the Second Aliya. They establish their utopian dream on their holding, the dream that had been Yitzhak's when he came to the land to build and to be rebuilt by it. Like Hirshl, Professor Herbst in *Shira* returns to his family after trying to flee from it and trying to escape the academic labor that had become oppressive to him.

The return to the tradition, or to roots, frequently is described ironically. For example, Susanna's victory in "Betrothed" or the victories of the bourgeois families in other novels do not arouse the implied author's admiration; nor does he guide the reader to take a positive attitude to these phenomena. *In Mr. Lublin's Store* and "Until Now" express the rule of anarchy in the world. In the latter, the decoherent pattern reaches its peak, being an adequate expression of that anarchy.

Agnon developed from a revolutionary author, struggling against the tradition and praising the revolution, to an author who described in innovative literary forms the revolution that took place. He revealed through his texts that the result of the new revolutionary reality was not a new order but rather a decoherent anarchy, which places humanity in a grotesque condition—that is, a condition of total disorientation. In creating a new configuration of literary genres, conventions, and forms, Agnon made a huge contribution to world literature that goes far beyond the national or religious boundaries of his origins. He also wrote of the inner struggle of a man who is bound by his figurative umbilical cord to the tradition but acknowledges the revolutionary power of modern life.

The conclusion I have reached through this discussion is that Agnon was, above all, a modern writer. Even his stories that seem "readerly" are basically "writerly" and are open to diverse and contradictory interpretations. Moreover, Agnon's implicitly modern novels and stories, those with an ostensibly realistic foreground, sometimes are much more multivalent and complex than are his explicitly modernistic stories where modern techniques are foregrounded.

Just as Agnon's writing from a formal point of view extends beyond the boundaries of his cultural circle—as an original contribution to the development of modern fiction—so, too, his writings go beyond the historical, ethnic, and national frameworks of their content. His writings constitute an original contribution in describing the confrontation between a man well versed in a tradition and a social reality that no longer permits him to return to innocent faith because, as an ingenuous man who wishes to believe (like the boy in *A Guest for the Night*), he lacks arms upon which he can place the phylacteries that symbolize his faith.

As with every great body of work, the readers of each generation will regard themselves as the first to read the writings and will discover in them new layers of meaning. Agnon remains central in the history of Hebrew literature. All rivers lead to him, and most of the new streams flow out of him.

Influence

Agnon's oeuvre represents a crossroads in the history of Hebrew fiction. His writings are an important link in the history of traditional Jewish literature and of European literature. He drew from every source and altered everything he absorbed, producing his own original work. Surprisingly, his influence on the generation following him was limited. The writers of the modern school between the two world wars, which included the authors Hayim Hazaz (1898–1973), Simon Halkin (1898–1987), and David Vogel (1891–1944), followed either foreign sources or Uri Nisan Gnessin (1835–1917) and Gershom Shofman (1880–1971), and only occasionally Mendele Mokher Seforim (1835–1917).[2] Agnon's influence on the later literature of the land is marginal, and one finds it only in stylistic imitation. Signs of his influence can be found in the works of Yitzhak Shenhar (1902–57), Yehoshua Bar-Yosef (b. 1912), and Yehudah Yaari (1900–1982), all of whom make use of Agnon's stylistic patterns and subjects as epigones. A direct and visible influence is found in the stories of Dov Sadan (b. 1902).

The writers of the so-called native generation, who entered the literary scene during the 1940s, did not have a taste for such writing. They kept their distance from Agnon both thematically and structurally. The writer whose works are the most stylized, S. Yishar (Smilanski) (b. 1916), is closer in style to Gnessin than to Agnon. Aharon Meged (b. 1920) is the only author who tried, with limited success, to imitate Agnon's (and Kafka's) surrealistic techniques (see *Fortunes of a Fool* and *The Escape*).[3]

Interest in Agnon's works was revived among the grandchildren—the generation of the State of Israel—who began their literary careers in the 1950s. In the dialectic of Hebrew literature, which oscillates between direct representation of reality and its distortion, Agnon was viewed by members of that generation as the forefather of nonrealistic creativity. Of course, that does not mean that Agnon lacked a taste for realism. On the contrary, his stylized realistic works are sometimes his best. However, when the younger writers sought to break free from the realism of the first Israeli-born, or native, generation (Yizhar, Shamir, Meged, and so on), they grasped the trunk of that mighty tree, using their literary grandfather to outdo their fathers and elder brothers.

Agnon is what the formalists call a *grandfather*—that is, the figure who permits the grandchildren to rebel against their parents. The literary process is one of rebellion against fathers. It is an oedipal struggle against the assurances and certainties of the Zionist revolution and against the Jewish religious tradition at the same time. Agnon permits young people to doubt the conventions of their fathers and older brothers and to view both yesterday and the day before in an ambivalent light. With his help, they succeed in changing their works from being answers to questions asked by previous generations into question marks that challenge future generations.

These writers used Agnon to struggle with the tradition and with the conventions that their immediate predecessor had tried to shed. Henceforth, however, they would have to struggle with their chosen source of influence, trying to pave a way for themselves—with the ever-present danger that the cornerstone they grasped could prove to be a stumbling block because of the enormous power of its influence.[4]

That creative tension can be found in the works of various writers, each of whom created an Agnon in his own image. Thus, for example, the structure of Yehuda Amichai's (b.

1924) novel *Not of This Time and Not of This Place*[5] is similar to the structure of *A Guest for the Night*. The style and atmosphere of Agnon's works left their mark on David Schachar's (b. 1926) Jerusalem stories and on Pinchas Sadeh's (b. 1929) religious subject matter, such as in *Life as a Parable*[6]—nor is Sadeh's style all that far from Agnon's. *The Book of Deeds* deeply influenced the stories of Abraham Yehoshua (b. 1936) and Yitzhak Orpaz (b. 1923). Aharon Appelfeld's (b. 1932) later work is influenced by Agnon's style and is close to Agnon's works in many of its subjects. Agnon's influence was a blessing because it helped the younger writers throw off the bonds of the here and now. However, his influence was also a curse because they imitated the abstract shell (as did Orpaz and Yehoshua in their early works) without penetrating its depths.

The struggle with this great author brought about a renewed confrontation between the writers of the generation of the State of Israel and the rich cultural realm that Agnon represents. Their struggle is in contrast to the attitudes of the writers of the 1930s and 1940s, who avoided Agnon's works.

Agnon's direct influence on individual writers is less important than is the general impact of his work. Without question he is the greatest Hebrew fiction writer of this century. Moreover, since biblical times no one has used the Hebrew language more effectively to depict the interplay of individual existences and the history of the nation.

NOTES

For complete publication data for works by Shmuel Yosef Agnon
cited in the Notes, see the Select Bibliography.

Chapter 1

1. Shmuel Yosef Agnon, *Meatzmi el Atzmi* (From myself to myself), 71.
2. Ethics of the Fathers 5:22.
3. See Shmuel Yosef Agnon, *A Guest for the Night,* trans. Misha Louvish, 447–49.
4. Yosef Haver [Yosef Hayim Brenner], "From Literature and the Press in the Land of Israel: Critical Remarks on the Fourth Issue of *Ha-Omer*" (in Hebrew), *Ha-Po'el ha-Tsair* 2, no. 13 (1909): 7–9.
5. Agnon, *Meatzmi el Aztmi,* 29.
6. Shmuel Yosef Agnon, "Yosef Hayim Brenner, in Life and in Death," *Molad* 156 (June 1961): 271–90.
7. Gershon Shaked and Refael Weiser, eds., *Shmuel Yosef Agnon: Studies and Documents* (in Hebrew) (Jerusalem: Mosad Bialik, 1978), 41 (hereafter cited as *Studies and Documents*).
8. *Studies and Documents,* 47.
9. Ibid., 54.

10. Agnon, *Meatzmi el Atzmi,* 140.

11. See also Agnon's remarks about Aharonovitz in articles collected in *Meatzmi el Atzmi,* 164–92. Agnon's admiration for Katzenelson was reciprocated. The following letter demonstrates the relationship of the labor leader and ideologue to the writer. It was written after the publication of *A Guest for the Night,* to which Katzenelson refers:

   Last night I dreamed about you. During our conversation I asked you whether you'd received my letter. You answered that if one doesn't write, one doesn't receive. I tried warmly to persuade you that I'd written to you just a few days ago. In my dream I followed up my thoughts with words. Upon awakening, I found you were in the right. . . . I admit to you, my friend, some of the chapters were like a present-day Book of Job for me, and the entire book is full of mercy and love of the Jewish people, and their sorrow grieves me. (Katzenelson to Agnon, 21 November 1940, Agnon Archives, 5.2204, National Library, Hebrew University, Jerusalem)

12. Arnold Band, *Nostalgia and Nightmare: A Study in the Fiction of Shmuel Yosef Agnon* (Berkeley and Los Angeles: University of California Press, 1968), 16–20. In general, the titles of Agnon's works and the spellings of characters' names appear here as in Band's work. I also followed in Band's footsteps in the biographical descriptions.

13. Shmuel Yosef Agnon, "Be'era shel Miryam" (Miryam's well), *Ha-Po'el ha-Tsair* 14 (1909): 7.

14. Meir Wilkansky, *Biymej Ha-Aliya* (In the days of the ascent) (Tel Aviv: Omanut, 1935). This collection of stories is based on an earlier one. See Meir Wilkansky, *Sippurim meHayey Ha-Aretz* (Stories from the life in the land) (New York: Kadimah, 1918).

15. Yosef Hayim Brenner, *Shechol ve Kishalon* (Breakdown and bereavement) (New York: Stybel, 1920). See also Yosef Hayim Brenner, *Breakdown and Bereavement,* trans. Hillel Halkin (Ithaca: Cornell University Press, 1971).

16. Aharon Reuveni, *Ha-Oniyot Ha-Akhronot* (The last ships) (Warsaw: Stybel, 1923).

17. Moshe Smilanski, *Hadassa, haSiloah* 24, 25 (January–June 1911; July–December 1911).

18. Shmuel Yosef Agnon, *Temol Shilshom* (Only yesterday), 7. This is a description of the young Agnon in Jaffa, using his story "Leilot" (Nights) *Al Kapot haManul,* the first version of which appeared in *Benatayim* (1913). See also Alan Mintz, "Agnon in Jaffa: The Myth of the Artist as a Young Man," *Prooftexts* 1 (1981): 62–83.

19. Shmuel Yosef Agnon, "Ha-Galila" (To the Galilee), in *Pitkhei Devarim*, 197–209.

20. Ibid., 204.

21. Agnon, *Temol Shilshom*, 607.

22. Shmuel Yosef Agnon, *Shira* (in Hebrew), 489.

23. See *Buczacz Memorial Volume*, Hebrew edition ed. Yisrael Cohen (Tel Aviv: Am-Oved, 1956).

24. Shmuel Yosef Agnon, "Ir Hametim" (The city of the dead).

25. The first publication of Agnon's "Vehaya he'Akov Lemishor" (And the crooked shall be made straight) was in *Ha-Po'el ha-Tsair* (January–May 1912).

26. Agnon, "And the Crooked Shall Be Made Straight," in *Elu veElu*, 57.

27. See Baruch Kurzweil, *Essays on Shmuel Yosef Agnon's Fiction* (in Hebrew) (Jerusalem: Schocken, 1962), 50–68. In his book Kurzweil discussed *A Guest for the Night* and other works by Agnon that address the collapse of the *shtetl*. Cf. Miriam Mindle W. Roshwald, "The *Shtetl* in the Works of Karl Emil Franzos, Sholom Aleichem, and Shmuel Yosef Agnon" (Ph.D. diss., University of Minnesota, 1972).

28. Shmuel Yosef Agnon, *A Guest for the Night*, trans. Misha Louvish, 2.

29. Buber wrote: "Agnon is one of those few who have holy authority regarding Jewish life. That authority is neither dry nor sentimental, it is white hot and solid. That's how Agnon is. Holy authority: I don't refer to that false authority which touches on pride and on falsification, but on true authority; quiet, modest, and trustworthy. That's how Agnon is. He is called upon to be the recorder and chronicler of Jewish life; that life which today is dying out, but also to other life, which is coming into being and still unknown. A Galician, and Palestinian, a Hassid and a pioneer, he still bears in his faithful heart the essence of two worlds, balanced by that holy authority" (Martin Buber, "Ueber Agnon," in *Treue (Eine Juedische Sammelschrift)*, ed. Leo Harmann [Berlin: Juedischer Verlag, 1916], 59).

Cf. Gershom Scholem "Agnon's German Sojourn" (in Hebrew), remarks delivered at the president's residence, in *Devarim BeGo, Explications and Implications, Writings on the Tradition and the Rebirth* (Tel Aviv: Am-Oved, 1975), 463–66.

30. Shmuel Yosef Agnon, "Sod Ketivat Sipurei Maasiyot" (The secret of writing fables). "Hush Hareakh" (The sense of smell), in *Elu veElu* (Jerusalem: Schocken, 1953), 297–98. See also the translation by

Louise Ben-Yaakov, in Gershon Shaked, "Midrash and Narrative: Agnon's 'Agunot,' " in *Midrash and Literature,* ed. Geoffrey H. Hartman and Sanford Budick (New Haven: Yale University Press, 1986).

31. Shmuel Yosef Agnon, "Agunot: A Tale," in *Twenty-one Stories,* trans. Baruch Hochman, 41.

32. Various interpretations of "Agunot: A Tale" have been written, based on real or imagined sources. Some are similar to my remarks; others are quite different. See Band, *Nostalgia and Nightmare,* 57–63; Hillel Barzel, "Shmuel Yosef Agnon at Seventy-five: 'Agunot: A Tale,' the First Story" (in Hebrew), *Haboker* 26 (July 1963); Arnah Golan, " 'Agunot: A Tale' and the Second Aliya" (in Hebrew), *Moznayim* 32, no. 3 (January 1971): 215–33 (an example of excessive use of sources); Yitzhak Bakon, "On 'Agunot: A Tale,' by Shmuel Yosef Agnon" (in Hebrew), *Moznayim* 46, no. 3 (1978): 167–79 passim; and Shaked, "Midrash and Narrative," 285–303.

33. Agnon, "Agunot," in *Twenty-one Stories,* 30.

34. Ibid., 31.

35. Song of Songs 4:1, 5:7, 5:6, 5:8.

36. Agnon, "Agunot," 31, 35.

37. Midrash on the Song of Songs 4:1.

38. Ibid., 5:8.

39. Rabbi Elijah Son of Solomon Ha-Cohen Haittamari, *Shevet Musar* 35, 274–75.

40. Regarding the symbol of the garment, see *Sefer Hahinukh* 28; *Zohar,* part 2, 210a–b; 11, 101a. See also Rabbi Nissim of Kairouan, *Hibbur Yafe Meyeshua.* Cf. Gershom Scholem, "The Garment of the Soul and the Rabbinical Robe" (in Hebrew), *Tarbitz* 24 (1956): 290–306.

   Regarding the "thread of mercy," see the Babylonian Talmud tractates *Hagiga* 12b; *Tamid* 28a; and *Megila* 13a. See also the *Zohar,* part 1, 826:11 and 56b–57a; and the Hebrew translation and interpretation of the *Zohar* passages in Jehudah Ashlag, *Hasullam* (commentary to the *Zohar*), vols. 1–22, 1945–58.

41. The Kurdish sources of "Edo and Enam" are the *Itinerary of Benjamin (of Tudela),* ed. and trans. M. N. Adler (London: Henry Frowde and Oxford University Press, 1907), 46–47, 50–51, 60–62; and *The Book of the "Travels of Yisrael" by Yisrael ben Yosef Benjamin* (in Hebrew), trans. David Gordon (Z. H. Petzal, 1859), 24, 25, 29, 33, 40, 99, 126–32. See also Erich Brauer, *History of the Jews of Kurdistan*

(in Hebrew) (Jerusalem: Hamakhon Harzisraeli Le-Folklor, 1948), 41, 90, 139–40.

The sources are from Shlomo Zucker, "Sources for the Molding of Space and Characters in 'Edo and Enam' by Shmuel Yosef Agnon" (in Hebrew), *Studies in Hebrew Literature* 3 (1983): 28–66.

42. *Zohar Hadash, Shir Ha-Shirim* (New Zohar, Song of Songs) (Livorno, 1866), 89b (*Avir Tahor,* pure air); 2 *Zohar,* f.1 (recto and verso) (*Segulot,* qualities).

43. Agnon, *Temol Shilshom,* 473–74.

44. Agnon, "Mazal Dagim" (Pisces), in *Ir Umeloah* (A city and the fullness thereof), 613–14.

45. See Fritz Mordechay Kaufmann, "Der Erzaehler S. J. Agnon," in *Vier Essais ueber ostjuedische Dichtung und Kultur* (Berlin: Welt Verlag, 1919), 21–31. Kaufmann discusses the German translation of "And the Crooked Shall Be Made Straight" (translated by Max Strauss in 1918), viewing it as a contribution to a positive evaluation of the Jewish culture of eastern Europe.

46. The reciprocal relationship between Jewish esoteric literature, halakhic writing, and the works of Agnon has been studied in detail by many scholars. See, for example, Gershom Scholem, "The Sources of 'Gadiel, the Wonder Child' in Kabbalistic Literature" (in Hebrew), in *LeAgnon Shai: Devarim al HaSofer veSippurav,* ed. Dov Sadan and Ephraim Elimelech Urbach (Jerusalem: HaSokhnut haYehudit, 1959), 289–305 (hereafter cited as *LeAgnon Shai*). In it, Scholem pointed out the sources of "The Tale of Rabbi Gadiel, the Infant" in Jewish esoteric literature. See also Meshulam Tochner, *The Meaning of Agnon* (in Hebrew) (Ramat Gan: Massada, 1968), 106–22. Tochner sought the connections between esoteric literature and "Edo and Enam," noting the connection of that story with the midrash.

See also Ephraim Elimelech Urbach, "Sources and Interpretation" (in Hebrew), in *LeAgnon Shai,* 9–25. Urbach points out the halakhic aspects of the story "Two Great Scholars Who Were in Our Town." See also Shmuel Werses, "Quotations in Their Speakers' Names" (in Hebrew), in *Sippur veShorsho* (Ramat Gan: Massada, 1971), 183–200. Werses discusses the method of quotation also used by Agnon in *The Bridal Canopy.* The question of the relationship to the sources in these works has been discussed by Meir Bosak and Yosef Dan.

See also Gershon Shaked, *The Narrative Art of Shmuel Yosef Agnon* (in Hebrew) (Tel Aviv: Siphriat Poalim, 1973); Kurzweil, *Essays,* 86–94, 141–60; and Abraham Holtz, "The Triple Profanation: Remarks on 'Another Talit' " (in Hebrew), *Hasifrut* 3 (1971–72): 518–32. Holtz notes the use of references to Jewish culture in the stories, in which the implicit takes precedence over what is explicit (in *The Book of Deeds,* for example).

Hillel Weiss investigated the sources of several of the posthumously published stories in "An Interpretation of Agnon's 'Covering of Blood' " (in Hebrew), *Bikoret Ufarshanut* 9–10 (October 1976): 117–59. See also Hillel Barzel, *"Shira* and 'Forevermore' " (in Hebrew), *Bikoret Ufarshanut* 4–5 (March 1974): 11–23; and Arna Golan, " 'Agunot: A Tale' and the Second Aliya" (in Hebrew), *Moznayim* 32, no. 3 (January 1971): 215–23. Golan uses the sources in an attempt to allegorize various works. Many other scholars have done the same, both in the field of literature and in other areas of Jewish studies.

47. Rabbi Abraham Bar Hiya Hanassi, *Megilat Hamegale,* ed. Adolf Posnanski (Berlin: Mekizey Nirdamim, 1924).

48. Shmuel Yosef Agnon, ed., *Yamim Noraim* (Days of awe) (Berlin: Schocken, 1938).

49. Shmuel Yosef Agnon, ed., *Sefer, Sofer, veSippur* (Book, scribe, and tale) (Jerusalem: Schocken, 1938).

50. Shmuel Yosef Agnon, ed., *Sifreihem shel Tsadikim* (The books of the righteous) (Jerusalem: Schocken, 1961).

51. Shmuel Yosef Agnon, ed., *Atem Reitem* (You have seen) (Jerusalem: Schocken, 1959).

52. Moshe Kanpfer, "Between Buczacz and Jerusalem" (first published in Polish in 1930), Hebrew trans. Dov Sadan, *Davar* (literary suppl.), vol. 4, 25 July 1958.

53. Shmuel Yosef Czaczkes, "Fragments," *Ramat haMitspeh* 1 (1907): 16.

54. See Gavriel Tsuran, "The Hand of Nature Is upon Us: Agnon's Method in Translating 'Dust' by Bjornson" (in Hebrew), in *Studies and Documents,* 57–94. Bjornson's *Stoev* was published in Norwegian in 1882. It was first published in German in 1900, and authorized publication took place in 1911 (the Elias edition). It was translated into Yiddish in 1909 by Avraham Frumkin (apparently, from the German). Agnon seems to have translated from the Yiddish, although he might have had the Elias edition of the German translation; see

Tsuran, "The Hand of Nature," 60. Agnon's translation appeared in *Japhet* (1913).

55. Agnon considered Flaubert to be important, and in this letter to Lachover, dated 1 May 1913, he wrote: "Sir, I have read Flaubert's *Salammbo*. How good it would be to bring it into our tent. But Frishman is the one who should do it" (*Yediot Genazim* 4 [1970]: 586).

56. Malachi Beit-Arieh, ed., *Selected Letters of Shmuel Yosef Agnon to Salman Schocken* (in Hebrew), in *Studies and Documents*, 99–100. In his letters, Agnon writes of his interest in ballads and mentions those of Fontane. In a letter of 1916, he mentions the "mother" of German neoromanticism, Ricarda Huch; and in a letter dated 16 May 1918, he mentions *The Arabian Nights*. Thus, the sources that influenced him were rich and varied.

57. Knut Hamsun, *Mysterien,* Uebers. von Norwegisch, Maria von Borch (Munich: Albert Langen Verlag, 1904), 2 Auflage. The main character of the novel is Nagel, who arrives in a small town and falls in love with Dagny Kielland. As a result, another man, named Karlsen, kills himself. Dagny is herself engaged to a lieutenant. At a party, the young men "baptize" Minutte and cause a kind of fracture of his neck (see pages 221–23). The way in which he is treated is quite similar to the way that Ovadia the Cripple's so-called friends treat him. The cripple gradually becomes a faithful friend of the main character. Minutte is himself in love with a wretched girl named Martha. The complexity of this plot is quite distant from Agnon. On this subject, Yair Mazor has recently published a number of articles. See Yair Mazor, "The World of Fantasy and the Secret of Influence (Introductory Remarks to a Comparative Study of the Fiction of Hamsun and Agnon)," *Moznayim* 55, nos. 4–5 (September–October 1982): 22–27.

See also Yehezkel Mark, "The Influence of European Writers on the Hebrew Writer S. Y. Agnon," 151–99 (Ph.D. diss., Potchefstroom University, South Africa, 1974); and Warren Bargad, "Agnon and German Neoromanticism," *Prooftexts* 1 (1981): 96–98.

58. Agnon, *Meatzmi el Atzmi,* 245.

59. Hillel Barzel, in *Between Agnon and Kafka* (in Hebrew) (Ramat Gan: Bar Uryan, Bar-Ilan University, 1972), indicates in his introduction

that he is aware of the problem and also points out Agnon's reservations regarding the efforts to match him up with Kafka. However, Barzel goes on to make a number of comparisons based on the premise that the two authors have certain concerns and techniques in common and that it is useful to bring out the similarities and differences between them. See also Band, *Nostalgia and Nightmare*, 27, 187, 199.

60. Agnon, *Meatzmi el Aztmi,* 245.

Chapter 2

1. "Iber hebreishe dikhter, A. Mordechai Tsvi Maane," *Der Yiddishe Weker* (Stanislav) 2, nos. 27, 28, 29 (May–June 1906).

2. Arnold Band, *Nostalgia and Nightmare: A Study in the Fiction of Shmuel Yosef Agnon* (Berkeley and Los Angeles: University of California Press, 1968), 54–92.

3. Shmuel Yosef Agnon, *Meatzmi el Atzmi* (From myself to myself), 74.

4. Agnon Archives. Israel National Library. MS. 756:1, f.1.

5. Agnon, *Meaztmi el Atzmi,* 57.

6. See Erich Auerbach, *Mimesis* (Berne, Switzerland: A. Francke, 1946), 7–30.

7. Shmuel Yosef Agnon, "The Tale of the Scribe," in *Twenty-one Stories,* 20.

8. Arnold Band, "Agnon Before He Was Agnon" (in Hebrew), *Molad* 21 (January–April 1963): 54–63, 175–76. Cf. Band's study in English, *Nostalgia and Nightmare,* 29–53. See also Dov Sadan, "The First Year," in *On Shmuel Yosef Agnon* (in Hebrew) (Tel Aviv: Ha-Kibbutz Hameuchad, 1959), 125–38.

9. "Toytentants" apparently was written in 1908 and published in the *Yudisher Folkskalender* in 1911.

10. A description of Agnon's life in Germany can be found in the editor's introduction to Agnon's letters to Salman Schocken, in *Haaretz,* 26 July 1963. See Gershom Scholem, "Chapters on Shmuel Yosef Agnon, Notes and Reflections" (in Hebrew, in honor of Agnon's sixtieth birthday), in *Devarim BeGo, Explications and Implications: Writings on the Tradition and the Rebirth* (Tel Aviv: Am-Oved, 1975), 463–65 (first published in *Haaretz,* 31 August 1948). See also idem, "Agnon's

German Sojourn, Remarks Made at a Ceremony in the President's Residence," ibid., 466, 471. "Die Erzaehlung vom Toraschreiber" (The tale of the scribe), Uebers. Max Strauss, *Der Jude* 2 (1917–18): 253–64.

11. On the atmosphere among the writers in Bad Homburg, see Frida Kahn, *Generation in Turmoil* (Great Neck, N.Y.: Chanell Press, 1960), 107–9.

12. See their correspondence in Malachi Beit-Arieh, ed., "A Bundle of Letters to Salman Schocken," *Haaretz,* 26 July 1963. See also Malachi Beit-Arieh, ed., "Selection of Letters from Shmuel Yosef Agnon to Salman Schocken," in *Shmuel Yosef Agnon: Studies and Documents* (in Hebrew), ed. Gershon Shaked and Refael Weiser (Jerusalem: Mosad Bialik, 1978), 97–117 (hereafter cited as *Studies and Documents*).

13. Shmuel Yosef Agnon, "Seelenverbannung, Uebers. Ernst Mueller," *Die Welt* (Berlin), 4 March 1910, 189ff.

14. Shmuel Yosef Agnon, "Ha Pincha Hashvura" (The broken plate), *Hamitspeh* 3, no. 49 (1906).

15. Cf. "Ven Hayml—ingel fun a yor dreytsen mit royte bekalekh, mit tsvey sheyne shwartse gekrayzelete peahkelikh—iz aheym gekumen fraytog-tsunakht, ahaym fun der shul, tsu zeyn muter di almone iz er gevezen shtark fertraft, un zeyn moyakh iz geven fernemen mit fil makheshoves, un fantasiez hobn arum getanst in zeyn kleyn kepil" [Yiddish transliteration]. From Shmuel Yosef Agnon, "Der Tsebrokhene Teler," *Der Yiddisher Weker* 38, 10 August 1908.

16. Shmuel Yosef Agnon, "Halomo shel Yacob Nahum" (Yakov-Nahum's dream), 8.

17. Shmuel Yosef Agnon, "Yatom ve Almanah" (Orphan and widow), in *Elu veElu,* 165.

18. Agnon, "Halomo shel Yacob Nahum," 8.

19. Without going into detail, Arnold Band already had noted these stylistic and structural processes. See Arnold Band, "From Folk Tale to Myth: Germany and Jerusalem (1912–1929)," in Band, *Nostalgia and Nightmare,* 93–125.

20. Agnon, "Halomo shel Yacob Nahum," 10.

21. Agnon, "Yatom ve Almanah," 165.

22. Exod. 16:21, in reference to gathering manna in the desert.

23. Agnon used the Hebrew word *rakhuvit,* a word that is found in

Tosefta, Truma 13 and in the Jerusalem Talmud, tractate *Peah* 7:4. Abba Ben-David views the suffix *-it* as a classic example of rabbinical Hebrew.

24. "Coarse bread" in Hebrew is *pat kebar,* which also is found in rabbinical literature.

25. Agnon used the Hebrew *peleg,* a word that is discussed in the Babylonian Talmud, *Brakhot* 4a.

26. Agnon, "Yatom ve Almanah," in *Elu veElu,* 169. (This version is slightly different from the one published in *Rimon.*)

27. See Don Yosef ben Yehie, *The Chain of Kabbala* (in Hebrew) (Venice, 1576), 56b–57a.

28. Agnon, "Yatom ve Almanah," 169.

29. *Sefer Hassidim,* ed. Jehuda Wistinetzki and Jacob Freiman (reprint, Frankfurt am Main: Wahrman, 1924), sig. 281. On the function of *Sefer Hassidim* in this and other stories by Agnon, see Aryeh Wineman, *Aggadah and Art: Studies in the Writings of Agnon* (in Hebrew) (Jerusalem: Rubin Mass, 1982), 11–14.

30. Micha Yosef Berdyczewski, "Crooked and Straight" (in Hebrew) *Hatekufa* 5 (1920): 484–85.

31. Yeruham Fishel Lachover, " 'And the Crooked Shall Be Made Straight' " (in Hebrew), *HaTsefira* (Warsaw), 16 August 1912.

32. Ibid.

33. "Discussion of Recent Books, 'And the Crooked Shall Be Made Straight,' " *Hamitspeh* 9 (October 1912).

However the story is ointment with a fly in it. In form it is a pietistic tale for the extremely religious such as are found in the introductions to old books, but its conclusion is unworthy of any pious person such as Menashe Hayim or any author who uses this language and style. Imagine a righteous, innocent man knowing that, while he is alive, and his wife is a married woman, he sees her living with another man and giving birth to his son, and he hides his face in the ground and keeps silence, taking his secret to the grave, and thus causing the proliferation of illegitimate children among the Jews: no God-fearing man would behave that way. (5)

This anonymous critic understood the story better than Lachover, but his halakhic criteria does not permit him to perceive the beauty of the thematic contradiction, by means of which the author broke down the conventions of his generation.

34. Jacob Fichman, "Bibliographical Notes *Ha-Omer*" (in Hebrew), *Haolam* (Vilna) (December 1908): 10.
35. Yosef Haver [Yosef Hayim Brenner], "From Literature and the Press of the Land" (in Hebrew), *Ha-Po'el ha-Tsair* 2 (May 1909): 7.
36. Ibid.
37. Because of their importance, I will quote Brenner's remarks in full:

> And did we not read the work by Shmuel Yosef Agnon in *Ha-Omer*, the truest, most powerfully original piece, even though the Eretz Israel element, in the technical sense of that term, does not occupy such an important place, and its content is the mystical bond between souls who love each other and are bound to each other, an eternal, psychological, theme taken from real life? The story, called "Agunot: A Tale," and I doubt whether many of our readers know this, is not the sort of thing one can knock out every New Moon! In the vision, the poetic vision, it recalls the more poetical of Rabbi Nachman's stories, or the best of the fables of Micha Yosef Berdyczewski (like "The Legend of the Dead Woman" and others). However, to our taste, it surpasses the former by its marvelous language and its artistic form, like the ark built by Ben-Uri (one of the abandoned souls in this awesome story), and it is closer to us than the fables of Berdyczewski in that in this story taken from life there are no miracles or supernatural events, but everything is simple and fine, making a powerful and indelible impression and providing mighty aesthetic pleasure. And was not this masterpiece of our literature, a masterpiece in every sense, brought to us by the third issue of *Ha-Omer?* (Yosef Haver [Yosef Hayim Brenner], "From Literature," 7)

38. Yosef Hayim Brenner, "From My Notebook" (in Hebrew), *Revivim* 3–4 (Jerusalem) (1913): 159–60. What is marvelous and surprising about Brenner's remarks is the way he rejects the comparison between Agnon and Knut Hamsun. He sees the connection with Hamsun in the "great and immediate estrangement," but he emphasizes that Agnon's works do not have "Hamsun's smell of meadows and woods and paradise" and that "he is ultimately and primarily, a scribe, that is, part of the Hebrew culture of the dusty house of study, and not born in the trails and lands of the homeland, where the Norwegian's heroes roamed." Brenner noted at that early date, 1913, the strange and marvelous mixture of cultures that takes place in Agnon's works. As a critic, he was ahead of his time in his insights.
39. Shmuel Streit, "A Few Words about Shmuel Yosef Agnon" (in Hebrew), reader's letter to *Revivim* 3–4 (Jerusalem) (1913): 40.

40. Aharon Abraham Kabak, "Zephyrs" (in Hebrew), *Ha-Po'el ha-Tsair* 6 (March 1914): 9.

41. Eliezer Meir Lipschuetz, *Shmuel Yosef Agnon* (in Hebrew) (Berlin: private publication, 1926), 24.

42. Ibid., 25.

43. David Aryeh Friedman, "Shmuel Yosef Agnon" (in Hebrew), *Hashiloah* 42 (1924): 80–86. Reprint, in *Studies in Prose* (Tel Aviv: Makhbarot LeSifrut, 1966), 161–71, esp. 163.

44. See Aryeh Leib Mintz, "Shmuel Yosef Agnon and His *Bridal Canopy*" (in Hebrew), *Beitar* 2 (1934): 245–62.

   Apparently at every moment Mr. Agnon writes under the influence of that moment, and influence, as is well known, continually changes, so that there are many surprising features in his stories in this respect, and it is impossible to discern their absolute character: ultimately, what is he, a realist or a romantic? However we do see one thing: when he is realistic, he descends down to the mud, and when he is romantic—he rises to "signs and wonders." In general Mr. Agnon likes extremes. (249)

45. For example, see Bentsion Benshalom, *"The Bridal Canopy:* A New Work of Agnon's" (in Hebrew), *Moznayim* 4, no. 23 (November 1932): 6–9; *Moznayim* 4, no. 25 (December 1932): 9–12. See also Mintz, "Agnon and His *Bridal Canopy,*" chap. 2, n. 44. For the beginnings of criticism of Agnon's works, see Judith Halevi-Zwick, *Agnon—His Early Critics (1909–1931)* (in Hebrew) (Haifa: Haifa University Press, 1984).

46. Sadan published his essays quite early. Two of his first were: Dov Sadan, "Human Perplexity and Its Metamorphoses" (in Hebrew), *Davar* (suppl.), 25 May 1934. See also idem, *"A Simple Story (Beyond Simplicity)"* (in Hebrew), *Davar,* 8 November 1935. Both essays are included in the collection of Sadan's essays. See Dov Sadan, *On Shmuel Yosef Agnon* (in Hebrew) (Tel Aviv: Hakibbutz Hameuchad, 1959), 28–31, 32–35.

47. Gustav Krojanker, "The Central Problem in the Works of Agnon" (in Hebrew), *Moznayim* 7, no. 5 (1938): 611–19. Cf. idem, "The Great Epic (on *The Bridal Canopy*)" (in Hebrew), *Haaretz,* 12 August 1938.

48. The first articles are on *Elu veElu, Haaretz,* 30 January 1942; and "Shmuel Yosef Agnon's 'A Whole Loaf,' " *Gazit* 4, nos. 7–12 (Jan-

uary–June 1942): 145–47 (all in Hebrew). Kurzweil diverted attention from the classical stories to those in *The Book of Deeds,* which express that inner split better than in other works.

49. The following words of Tochner sum up the matter well: "Is he opening or closing an era?" and "He is likely to be more influential, as he becomes better known, because his work is an expression of immanent Judaism, with the historical tradition of its sacred literature, in contrast with all the streams of the secular spirit." See Meshulam Tochner, *The Meaning of Agnon* (in Hebrew) (Ramat Gan: Massada, 1968), 231.

50. See Band, *Nostalgia and Nightmare.* Another book in English is Baruch Hochman's *The Fiction of S. Y. Agnon* (Ithaca: Cornell University Press, 1970), which notes Agnon's humanistic weaknesses. It appears to me that Hochman tends to avoid the contradiction by concentrating on a one-sided emphasis on the modern aspects of Agnon's works.

51. David Canaani, "The Hidden and the Revealed in Agnon's Works" (in Hebrew), *Luah Haaretz* (1948–49): 164–90.

52. Gavriel Moked, *The Praises of Adiel Amzeh* (in Hebrew) (Tel Aviv: Hamahadir, 1957). See also idem, "Agnon as a Modern Author" (in Hebrew), *Yediot Ahronot,* 13 April 1962; idem, "Agnon as an Existential Writer" (in Hebrew), *Yediot Ahronot,* 19 April 1963; and idem, "Agnon and the Literature of Our Time" (in Hebrew), *Molad* 16, no. 120 (July 1958): 411–16.

53. Barzel published articles on that topic in the early 1950s. See Hillel Barzel, " 'Edo and Enam' by Shmuel Yosef Agnon" (in Hebrew), *Ashmoret* 36 (October 1950). See especially idem, *Between Agnon and Kafka: A Comparative Study* (in Hebrew) (Ramat Gan: Bar Uryan, Bar-Ilan University, 1972).

54. Shlomo Tsemakh, "Graven Images and Idols," in *Shtei Mezuzot* (two doorposts) (in Hebrew) (Ramat Gan: Massada, 1965), 134. This was first printed in *Davar* (1958–59).

55. See Dan Miron, "Reflections on Agnon Criticism" (in Hebrew), *Haaretz,* 13 September 1963. Miron lists what is demanded of criticism and has not yet been supplied: the essence of the style, description of the physical world, Agnon's humor, the allegorical moment, stages in development, and the artistic context. Some of his demands have been satisfied since the writing of that article.

56. Recently, the study of Agnon's sources has developed considerably.

Active in that area have been Dov Sadan, Gershom Scholem, Ephraim Elimelech Urbach, Shmuel Werses, Yitshak Bakon, Abraham Holtz, Yehezkel Mark, Moshe Y. Hertsl, Hillel Weiss, Arna Golan, Hayim Nagid, Yosef Dan, David Tamar, Aryeh Wineman, and others.

Agnon's language has been studied recently by Jacob Mantsur, Aharon Bar-Adon, and Edna Afek (following in the footsteps of Hayim Rabin, Israel Iser Seidman, and Hanoch Yalon). The history of the texts has been studied by Judith Halevi-Zwick, Shlomo Zucker, Sara Hager, Gideon Katzenelson, Jacob Bahat, and many others.

57. The trail in the study of Agnon's art of fiction was blazed by Ludwig Strauss, Lea Goldberg, and Jacob Bahat; and, following in their footsteps, I published a study on that subject. See Gershon Shaked, *The Narrative Art of Shmuel Yosef Agnon* (Tel Aviv: Siphriat Poalim, 1973). My first article in this area was "Structural Problems in the Work of Agnon" (in Hebrew), in *LeAgnon Shai: Devarim al HaSofer veSippurav,* ed. Dov Sadan and Ephraim Elimelech Urbach (Jerusalem: HaSokhnut haYehudit, 1959).

Shmuel Yeshayahu Penueli, Adi Tsemach, and David Tsimmerman have taken a psychoanalytic tack. Recently, studies of that type by Devora Schreibaum, Yael Feldman, David Aberbach, Abraham B. Yehoshua, and Nitza Ben-Dov have appeared. Yoav Elstein, Dina Stern, and Hayim Nagid have studied Agnon from the point of view of myth. Neomi Tamir, Yoseph Even, Dov Landau, Harry Golomb, Alan Mintz, Yair Mazor, Esther Fuchs, Malka Shaked, William Cutter, and many others have described the work with methods allied to the New Criticism or to structuralism. I could present a list of methods applied (such as the structuralist study by Abraham Shaanan); but, in the long run, for the history of Agnon's reception, the interpretive results are more important than are the systems themselves.

Chapter 3

1. Abraham Jacob Brawer, "On the Need for Historical and Geographical Reference for Agnon's Works" (in Hebrew), in *Yovel Shai,* ed. Baruch Kurzweil (Ramat Gan: Bar-Ilan University, 1958), 36.
2. Eliezer Meir Lipschuetz, *Shmuel Yosef Agnon* (in Hebrew) (Berlin:

private publication, 1926), 34–35. Lipschuetz argues that the chief source of Agnon's language is *Hemdat Yamim,* a link that has not yet been sufficiently explored.

3. The question of allusion and quotation has concerned many scholars, some of whom have been mentioned in other contexts. Two prominent examples are the articles by Shmuel Werses, *"In the Heart of Seas* by Shmuel Yosef Agnon: The Sources of the Story and the Methods of Their Use" (in Hebrew), *Hasifrut* 2 (1969–70): 310–32; and Israel Iser Seidman, "A Sketch of Agnon's Style" (in Hebrew), in *Yovel Shai,* 49–59.

4. Jacob Bahat, "S. Y. Agnon—The Sentimental Dreamer," in *Shmuel Yosef Agnon and Hayim Hazaz, Readings* (in Hebrew) (Haifa: Yovel Publishing House, 1962), 133–74.

5. A prominent example is wordplay with three letters forming different roots. The following words from "Ad Hena" (Until now) are examples: *bakar* (beef), *rekev* (rot), *krav* (battle), *bareket* (emerald), *marbek* (a place name), *kever* (grave), *karav* (he neared). See Shmuel Yosef Agnon, "Ad Hena," 27. Cf. Edna Afek, *Arrays of Words* (Tel Aviv: Dekel Academic Publications, 1979). See also Hayim Rabin, "Linguistic Remarks about the Problem of Translating Agnon into a Foreign Language" (in Hebrew), in *Yovel Shai,* 13–25.

6. Benjamin De Vries, "Conversive *Vaw*" (in Hebrew), in *LeAgnon Shai: Devarim al HaSofer veSippurav,* ed. Dov Sadan and Ephraim Elimelech Urbach (Jerusalem: HaSokhnut haYehudit, 1959), 281–88.

7. Boaz Shachewiz, "The Timing of Syntactic Signs" (in Hebrew), in *LeAgnon Shai,* 281–88. Jacob Mantsur expanded on that statistical study and compared the versions in *A Study of Agnon's Language* (in Hebrew) (Tel Aviv: Dvir, 1968), 37–53. Mantsur's conclusion is as follows: "Around 1931–33 he [Agnon] removed many punctuation marks from his writing," and "later, from *Only Yesterday* on (1946), the author frequently used the comma, mainly in place of the colon." Finally, "today writers tend to use punctuation mainly based on principles of syntax: since they structure a sentence in a certain way, they must use appropriate punctuation, willy nilly.

8. Shmuel Yosef Agnon, "Leilot" (Nights) *Al Kapot haManul*, 391.

9. Shmuel Yosef Agnon, *Temol Shilshom* (Only yesterday), 289.

10. See Bilhah Ben-Eliyahu, "The Function of Documentary Materials in

the Elucidation of the Second Immigration in Agnon's Novel *Only Yesterday*" (in Hebrew), *Iton* 77 9 (July–August 1985): 26–27, 66–67.

11. See Jeffrey R. Smitten and Ann Daghistany, eds., *Spatial Form in Narrative* (Ithaca: Cornell University Press, 1981).

12. The technique of analogy has been noted in Shakespeare by scholars such as Francis Ferguson, in *The Idea of the Theater* (Garden City, N.Y.: Doubleday, 1953), 115–28. It is easy to describe its role in the works of Dostoyevsky (for example, Raskolnikov-Svidrigalov in *Crime and Punishment*, Ivan-Smerdyakov in *The Brothers Karamazov*, and others).

13. Shmuel Yosef Agnon, "Vehaya he'Akov Lemishor" (And the crooked shall be made straight), in *Elu veElu*, 108. See also Jacob Katz, "Agnon and Religious Perplexity" (in Hebrew), in *LeAgnon Shai*, 163–77.

14. Agnon, "Vehaya he'Akov Lemishor," 73–74.

15. Ibid., 74.

16. Ibid., 76–79.

17. Baruch Kurzweil, *Essays on the Stories of Shmuel Yosef Agnon* (in Hebrew), *Haaretz*, 8 February 1946, pp. 50–54.

18. Agnon, "Vehaya he'Akov Lemishor," 293.

19. See Baruch Kurzweil, "On Balak, the Fictional Dog in Agnon's *Only Yesterday*," in *Essays on Shmuel Yosef Agnon's Fiction* (in Hebrew) (Jerusalem: Schocken, 1962), 104–15; Meshulam Tochner, "On *Only Yesterday*" (in Hebrew), *Gazit* 10, no. 89 (April–May 1948): 6–10; Eliezer Schweid, "The Stray Dog—and Man" (in Hebrew), *Molad* 16, no. 120 (July 1958): 381–88; and Jacob Katz, "Agnon and Religious Perplexity" (in Hebrew), in *LeAgnon Shai*, 163–77.

20. *Mishnat ha-Zohar* (in Hebrew), ed. Yeshaya Tishby (Jerusalem: Mosad Bialik, 1961), 627–28. See also the translation by Louise Ben-Yaakov in Gershon Shaked, "Midrash and Narrative: Agnon's 'Agunot,' " in *Midrash and Literature,* ed. Geoffrey H. Hartman and Sanford Burdick (New Haven: Yale University Press, 1986).

21. Ibid., in the commentary to this passage, 627.

22. Ibid., in the commentary to this passage, 628.

23. Ibid., introduction to the chapter "Personal Life," 607–8.

24. "Tractate on Punishment in the Grave" (in Hebrew), in *Beit ha-Midrash*, vol. 1, ed. Adolph Jellinek. Reprint. (Jerusalem: Bamberger

and Wahrmann, 1938), 150–52. See also *Midrash Yona,* ibid., 96–105.

25. Lipschuetz, *Shmuel Yosef Agnon,* 11.

26. Shmuel Yosef Agnon, *Al Kapot haManul* (The handles of the lock), 314.

27. Shmuel Yosef Agnon, "Edo and Enam," in *Two Tales,* trans. Walter Lever, 166.

28. Shmuel Yosef Agnon, *Ir Umeloah* (A city and the fullness thereof), 620.

29. Agnon, *Al Kapot haManul,* 286.

30. Shmuel Yosef Agnon, "Ad Hena" (Until now), 88.

31. Shmuel Yosef Agnon, *Bahanuto shel Mar Lublin* (In Mr. Lublin's store), 169.

32. Agnon, "Ad Hena," 329–30.

33. Agnon, *Al Kapot haManul,* 470–71.

34. Gen. 5:24.

Chapter 4

1. "A Sabbath Song."

2. Shmuel Yosef Agnon, *The Bridal Canopy,* trans. Israel Meir Lask, 2.

3. See Arnold Band, *Nostalgia and Nightmare: A Study in the Fiction of Shmuel Yosef Agnon* (Berkeley and Los Angeles: University of California Press, 1968), 181–82. See also Shmuel Werses, "On the Structure of *The Bridal Canopy*" (in Hebrew), in *Sippur veShorsho* (The story and its roots) (Ramat Gan: Massada, 1971), 27–49.

   A new approach to the structure and the thematics of the novel based on a comparative study between its sources, a Yiddish chapbook entitled *Nissim V'Niflaot* that contains four short hagiographic stories about the Apter Rav and the "artistic" novel by Agnon, is by Abraham Holtz, *The Tale of Reb Yudel Hasid* (in Hebrew) (New York: Jewish Theological Seminary, 1986).

4. Agnon, *The Bridal Canopy,* trans. Israel Meir Lask, 369.

5. Cf. Gustav Krojanker, "The Central Problem in the Works of Agnon" (in Hebrew), *Moznayim* 7, no. 5 (September 1938): 611–19. Band, in *Nostalgia and Nightmare,* 184, points out that this story is a modern effort at mythic creation.

6. Cf. The Ethics of the Fathers 4:1.

7. Dov Sadan, *On Shmuel Yosef Agnon* (in Hebrew) (Tel Aviv: Hakibbutz Hameuchad, 1959), 32–35.

8. Baruch Kurzweil, *Essays on Shmuel Yosef Agnon's Fiction* (in Hebrew) (Jerusalem: Schocken, 1962), 40–41. See also some recent interpretations, such as the following psychoanalytic ones: Abraham B. Yehoshua, "The 'Solution' in *A Simple Story*" (in Hebrew), *Maariv*, 23 May 1980; idem, "Madness and Recovery" (in Hebrew), *Maariv*, 30 May 1980; and David Aberbach, *At the Handles of the Lock* (London: Oxford University Press, 1984), 126–27, 147–48. In addition, a deconstructivist point of departure is expressed in the interpretation in Malka Shaked, "Was Hirshl Insane? A Pluralistic View of Agnon's 'Sippur Pashut' [A simple story]," *Hasifrut* 32 (July 1983): 132–47.

9. Shmuel Yosef Agnon, *A Simple Story,* trans. Hillel Halkin, 198ff. The soldier is a parallel figure with a metaphorical function in relation to the protagonist.

10. Agnon, *A Simple Story,* 81.

11. Ibid.

12. Ibid., 115.

13. Ibid., 93.

14. Ibid., 113.

15. Ibid., 164.

16. Shmuel Yosef Agnon, *A Guest for the Night,* trans. Misha Louvish, 383.

17. Ibid., 205.

18. Cf. Kurzweil, *Essays,* 197–227, and the extensive discussion of the subject in my book. See Gershon Shaked, *The Narrative Art of Shmuel Yosef Agnon* (Tel Aviv: Siphriat Poalim, 1973), 228–78. Numerous essays have been written on this novel from various points of view. One of the most recent attempts is complementary to some of Kurzweil's assumptions — from the psychoanalytic point of view. See Yael Sagiv Feldman, "Between a Key and a Lock: A Rereading of Agnon's Key Irony in *Ore'ah nata lalun* [A guest for the night]" (in Hebrew), *Hasifrut* 32 (July 1983); and idem, "The Latent and the Manifest: Freudianism in *A Guest for the Night,*" *Prooftexts* 7 (January 1987): 29–39.

19. See Sara Hager, *"Only Yesterday:* The Emergence of Its Structure and Its Unity" (in Hebrew), in *Shmuel Yosef Agnon: Studies and Documents*

(in Hebrew), ed. Gershon Shaked and Refael Weiser (Jerusalem: Mosad Bialik, 1978), 154–84.

20. Shmuel Yosef Agnon, *Temol Shilshom* (Only yesterday), 7.
21. Ibid., 607.
22. Ibid., 606.
23. Ibid. Translation of this quote from the Hebrew is by Jeffrey M. Green.
24. Cf. Arnold Band, "Crime and Punishment in *Only Yesterday*" (in Hebrew), *Molad* 1, no. 24 (May–June 1967): 75–81.
25. Parts of *Shira* were first published in *Luah haaretz* 8 (1948).
26. Shmuel Yosef Agnon, *Shira* (in Hebrew), 488.
27. Ibid., 522.
28. Ibid., 348.
29. Ibid., 44, 491, 532, 534, 536.
30. Ibid., 532.
31. Ibid., 80.
32. Ibid., 527–31.
33. Ibid., 409, 424.
34. Ibid., 165.
35. Ibid., 458–59.
36. For an interesting psychoanalytic interpretation of the character of Shira and the relationship between her and Elisabeth, see Robert Alter, "Agnon's Last Word," *Commentary* 51 (June 1971): 74–81.

    Baruch Hochman's account claims that *Shira* is a failure because the author was unable to separate his own personality from that of his hero, Herbst. Thus, Shira (according to Hochman, this is negative) becomes an internalized psychological process without her own personality. See Baruch Hochman, "Agnon's Radical Incoherence" (in Hebrew), *Jerusalem Post*, 22 October 1971.

    Hillel Barzel leans toward a symbolic interpretation of the novel. He interprets *Shira* as an anagram for Rabbi Shmuel Yosef Halevi. See Hillel Barzel, *Agnon's Love Stories* (in Hebrew) (Ramat Gan: Bar-Ilan University, 1975), 138–39. To my mind, Barzel's argument seems exaggerated.
37. Shmuel Yosef Agnon, *Bahanuto shel Mar Lublin* (In Mr. Lublin's store), 32.
38. Ibid., 172.
39. Ibid., 162.

40. Ibid., 150–52.
41. Ibid., 60; cf. ibid., 77, 106, 125.
42. Ibid., 91.
43. Ibid., 100, 150.
44. Ibid., 143–44. Cf. Hillel Barzel, "From the *Book of Customs* to *In Mr. Lublin's Store*" (in Hebrew), *Yediot Ahronot,* 8 November 1974. Barzel tries to find a meaningful connection between the theater and this book, but he seems to me to go too far.
45. Gershom Schocken, "Taking Leave of Ashkenaz, Taking Leave of Old Europe—On *In Mr. Lublin's Store*" (in Hebrew), in Baruch Kurzweil, *Essays on Agnon's Fiction* (enl. ed.) (Jerusalem: Schocken, 1976), 444–45. According to Schocken, the dream is meant to emphasize the cordial and friendly atmosphere. It testifies to the integration of German Jews within German society. Lublin is the last representative of those German Jews who had been involved in the social life of their country for generations. The novel brings out the historical connection between Jews and Germans and also indicates the parting of the ways. Schocken's interpretation also seems stilted and far-fetched to me, and it does not follow from the entire structure. See also Dan Miron, "German Jews in Agnon's Work," *Leo Baeck Institute Yearbook* 23 (1978): 265–80.

Chapter 5

1. Dan Miron, "Domesticating a Foreign Genre: Agnon's Transaction with the Novel," *Prooftexts* 7 (January 1987): 1–27.
2. Ahad Ha'am was the pen name of Asher Ginzberg, who was born in 1856 in the Ukraine and died in 1927 in Tel Aviv. Ginzberg was a Jewish essayist and philosopher and was the founder of the idea of spiritual Zionism. Moshe Leib Lilienblum (1843–1910) was a Jewish essayist in Russia who advocated religious reform. After the pogroms in southern Russia, he became a protagonist of Zionism. Abraham Menahem Mendel Ussishkin was born in Russia in 1863 and died in Jerusalem in 1941. He was one of the founders of the Zionist movement in Russia, and in Israel he was a Zionist leader. As chairman of

the Jewish National Fund, he was responsible for purchasing large tracts of land in Palestine.

3. Song of Songs 5:2.

4. Cf. various interpretations, such as Dov Sadan, "The Legend of the Seven and the Seven" (in Hebrew), in *On Shmuel Yosef Agnon* (Tel Aviv: Hakibbutz Hameuchad, 1959), 74–88; Arnold Band, *Nostalgia and Nightmare: A Study of the Fiction of Shmuel Yosef Agnon* (Berkeley and Los Angeles: University of California Press, 1968), 367–82; Abraham Kariv, "Betrothed: Why and for Whom?" (in Hebrew), *Molad* 4 (May–June 1971): 102–9; Neomi Tamir, "Betrothed—Four that Are One" (in Hebrew), *Hasifrut* 3 (September 1972): 497–506; and especially Robert Alter, "Agnon's Mediterranean Fable," in *Defenses of Imagination* (Philadelphia: Jewish Publication Society, 1972), 187–88. See also David Aberbach, *At the Handles of the Lock* (London: Oxford University Press, 1984), 92–94.

5. Shmuel Yosef Agnon, "Betrothed," in *Two Tales by S. Y. Agnon,* trans. Walter Lever, 136.

6. Ibid., 89–90.

7. Ibid., 113.

8. Hayim Nahman Bialik, "Take Me under Your Wing." This poem was published in Hebrew in 1905. This English translation is by Ruth Nevo, in C. N. Bialik, *Selected Poems* (bilingual ed.) (Tel Aviv: Dvir and Jerusalem Post, 1981), 56–57.

9. Agnon, "Betrothed," 17, 19.

10. G. Wilson Knight, "The Embassy of Death, an Essay on Hamlet," in *The Wheel of Fire (Interpretations of Shakespearian Tragedy)* (1930; reprint, London: Methuen, 1964), 17–46.

11. Agnon, "Betrothed," 57.

12. Ibid., 91–92.

13. Cf. ibid., 50–51.

14. Ibid., 94–95.

15. Ibid., 133.

16. In that sense, Jacob Rechnitz is similar to Alex Portnoy, who is impotent in Israel because there, as elsewhere (though the reaction is opposite), he is under the influence of the Great Mother. See Phillip Roth, *Portnoy's Complaint* (New York: Random House, 1969).

17. Shmuel Yosef Agnon, "Mazal Dagim" (Pisces), in *Ir Umeloah* (A city

and the fullness thereof), 602. Some of the traditional sources for this story and their meanings in the new context were brought to my attention by Refael Weiser, curator of the Agnon Archives.

18. Cf. ibid., 620.

19. Cf. ibid., 611.

20. Cf. ibid., 616–17.

21. Cf. ibid., 610–13.

22. Ibid., 611.

23. There are many tall tales of Rabba Bar-Bar-Hana. See Bab. Tal., *Ketubot* 11b; Bab. Tal., *Yoma* 39b; Bab. Tal., *Gittin* 4a; Bab. Tal., *Baba Batra* 73–74. Fishl is an avatar of Aryeh Ba'al Guf (Man-Mountain Aryeh) in "Aryeh Ba'al Guf" and the cook in "Shor Avus Ve'aruhat Yarak" (The stalled ox and the meal of greens), stories by Bialik. See H. N. Bialik, "Aryeh Ba'al Guf," in *Collected Works* (Jerusalem: Dvir, 1947), 97–111. This story was first published in *Hashiloah* 5 (January–June 1899).

24. Agnon, "Mazal Dagim," 602.

25. Ibid.

26. Ibid., 611.

27. Ibid., 631.

28. The problem of identity and being devoured, which is central to this story, has particular importance in Agnon's work in general—both on the artistic level and on the thematic level. This subject appears again in works such as "And the Crooked Shall Be Made Straight," "The Overcoat," "At Hemdat's," and "The Lady and the Peddler."

29. Agnon, "Mazal Dagim," 629.

30. Ibid., 624.

31. Ibid., 603.

32. Ibid., 611.

33. See Mikhail Bakhtin, *Rabelais and His World* (Cambridge: M.I.T. Press, 1968), 6–30, 76ff. Another view of the grotesque in "Pisces," especially the relationship between realism and the fantastic, can be found in Esther Fuchs, *Art and Ingenuousness: On Shmuel Yosef Agnon's Irony* (in Hebrew) (Tel Aviv: Makhon Katz, Tel Aviv University, 1985), 145–46.

See also Shmuel Werses, "Between Man and Animal," in *From Mendele to Hazaz* (Jerusalem: Magnes Press, Hebrew University, 1987), 263–73. Werses compares Agnon's "Pisces" with animal stories of one of the major allegorical writers of Hebrew enlightenment literature, Yitzhak Erter (1791–1851) and describes Agnon's accomplishments in the art of the grotesque.

34. Agnon's hints at self-reference—as the figure of the narrator or the writer, or the protagonist as a writer or an artist—is one of the central subjects of his writing. He began with this theme with Ben-Uri in "Agunot: A Tale," raised interesting and complex aspects of it in the figure of the scribe in "The Tale of the Scribe" and also in the narrator-protagonist of *A Guest for the Night.* He generally tended to show the artist in an ironic light.

35. Agnon, "Mazal Dagim," 621.

36. Ibid., 619.

37. Ibid., 628.

38. Ibid., 620.

39. Meshulam Tochner, "The Meaning of 'Edo and Enam,' " in *The Meaning of Agnon* (in Hebrew) (Ramat Gan: Massada, 1968), 106–22. See also Shlomo Zucker, "Sources of the Molding of Space and Characters in 'Edo and Enam' by Shmuel Yosef Agnon," in *Jerusalem Studies in Hebrew Literature,* vol. 3 (in Hebrew) (Jerusalem: Hebrew University, 1983), 28–66.

40. The reference is to "The Song of the Shirt" by Thomas Hood (1799–1845), translated by Morris Yintshevski and printed in *Polysh Yidl* in 1884. Following in Hood's footsteps, Isaac Leib Peretz published his own poem, called "Three Dressmakers." See Nahman Meyzel, *The Works of Isaac Leib Peretz* (in Hebrew, translated from Yiddish) (Merhavia: Siphriat Poalim, 1960), 298–300.

41. Shmuel Yosef Agnon, "Shalosh Akhayot" (Three sisters), in *Elu veElu,* 196–97.

42. This is close to what the Germans call *Trivialliteratur,* or popular fiction. A prime example of scholarship in this field is Hans-Joerg Neuschaefer, "Erotische Wunschwelt und buergerliche Familienmoral," in *Populaerromane im 19. Jahrhundert* (Munich: Wilhem Fink Verlag, 1976), 55–102.

43. See n. 42.

44. Avot 3:19.

45. Gen. 32:4.

46. See Shmuel Yosef Agnon, *Al Kapot haManul* (The handles of the lock), 414.

47. Gen. 35:22.

48. Gen. 25:27.

49. Agnon, *Al Kapot haManul,* 428.

50. Shmuel Yosef Agnon, "Al Hamissim" (On taxes), in *Samuch venir'e* (Nearby and seen), 274. The name of the series of stories is "The Book of the State," but at least some of the stories were published years before the establishment of the State of Israel. One of those early stories, "Orange Peel: A Fantasy," was translated by Elias M. Epstein and published in the *Palestine Review* (Jerusalem, 1939–40): 393–94.

51. Agnon, "Al Hamissim," 277.

52. Ibid., 280.

53. Ibid., 278.

54. On the issue of the relationship between the works of Agnon and Kafka, see Hillel Barzel, *Between Agnon and Kafka* (Ramat Gan: Bar Uryan, Bar-Ilan University, 1972).

55. On *The Book of Deeds,* see Baruch Kurzweil, *Essays on Shmuel Yosef Agnon's Fiction* (in Hebrew) (Jerusalem: Schocken, 1962), 74–85.

56. Shmuel Yosef Agnon, "Hefker" (Quitclaim), in *Samuch venir'e,* 194.

57. Ibid., 193–94.

58. Natan Rotenstreich, "The Experience of Time in *The Book of Deeds*" (in Hebrew), in *LeAgnon Shai: Devarim al HaSofer veSippurav,* ed. Dov Sadan and Ephraim Elimelech Urbach (Jerusalem: HaSokhnut ha-Yehudit, 1959), 265–79.

59. On this topic, see Adi Tsemach, "On the Philosophy of History in Two of Agnon's Late Stories: 'Edo and Enam' and 'Forevermore' " (in Hebrew), *Hasifrut* 1–2 (Summer 1968): 378–85.

60. *Sanhedrin* 99a. See Hillel Weiss, "Interpretation of 'The Covering of Blood' by Shmuel Yosef Agnon" (in Hebrew), *Bikoret Ufarshanut* 9–10 (October 1976): 120. As to the Holocaust implications of this long short story (or novella), see Sidra Dekoven-Esrahi, "Agnon before and After," *Prooftexts* 2 (January 1982): 78–94.

61. *Gittin* 57; *Sanhedrin* 96.

62. Shmuel Yosef Agnon, "Kisui Hadam" (The covering of blood), in *Lefanim min Hahoma* (Within the wall), 82.

63. Ibid., 96.

64. See Num. 16.

65. There are obvious links between "Kisui Hadam" (The covering of

blood) and *A Guest for the Night*. See Agnon, *Lefanim min Hahoma*, 35.

66. Agnon, "Kisui Hadam," 95.
67. Ibid., 97–101.
68. Eccles. 12:13–14.

Chapter 6

1. Gershon Shaked, "By a Miracle: Agnon's Literary Representation of Social Drama," in *The Shadows Within* (Philadelphia: Jewish Publication Society, 1987), 133–44. For a quite interesting formulation of Agnon's religious conflict, see Murray Roston, "The Agnon Paradox," in *Explorations,* ed. Murray Mindlin with Chaim Bermant (Chicago: Quadrangle Books, 1968), 38–44.
2. Halkin and Vogel followed in the footsteps of Shofman; Hazaz was influenced by Mendele Mokher Seforim.
3. Aharon Meged, *Fortunes of a Fool,* trans. Aubry Hodes (London: V. Gollancz, 1962); idem, *The Escape* (Tel Aviv: Hakibbutz Hameuchad, 1962).
4. Gershon Shaked, "Kafka, Jewish Heritage, and Hebrew Literature," in *The Shadows Within,* 16–20.
5. Yehuda Amichai, *Not of This Time and Not of This Place,* trans. Shlomo Katz (New York: Harper & Row, 1968).
6. Pinchas Sadeh, *Life as a Parable,* trans. Richard Flantz (London: A. Blond, 1966).

SELECT BIBLIOGRAPHY

Listed here are the writings that have been used in the preparation of this book. This bibliography is not a complete record of all the works and sources I have consulted. The best available bibliography in English for the works by and related to Shmuel Yosef Agnon can be found in Arnold Band's *Nostalgia and Nightmare: A Study in the Fiction of Shmuel Yosef Agnon.* Berkeley and Los Angeles: University of California Press, 1968.

Texts in Hebrew

Agnon, Shmuel Yosef. "Ad Hena" (Until now). Jerusalem: Schocken, 1953.
———. "Al Kapot haManul" (The handles of the lock). Jerusalem: Schocken, 1953.
———. *Atem Reitem* (You have seen). Jerusalem: Schocken, 1959.
———. *Bahanuto shel Mar Lublin* (In Mr. Lublin's store). Jerusalem: Schocken, 1974.
———. "Be'era shel Miryam" (Miryam's well). *Ha-Po'el ha-Tsair* 14–18 (1909).
———. *Elu veElu* (These and those). Jerusalem: Schocken, 1953.

Agnon, Shmuel Yosef. "Halomo shel Yacob Nahum" (Yakov-Nahum's dream). *Yezreel* (Jaffa, 1913): 8–16.

———. "Ir Hametim" (The city of the dead). *Haet* (Lemberg) 19 (March 1907).

———. *Ir Umeloah* (A city and the fullness thereof). Jerusalem: Schocken, 1973.

———. *Lefanim min Hahoma* (Within the wall). Jerusalem: Schocken, 1975.

———. *Meatzmi el Atzmi* (From myself to myself). Jerusalem: Schocken, 1976.

———. *Pitkhei Devarim* (Opening remarks). Jerusalem: Schocken, 1977.

———. *Samuch venir'e* (Nearby and seen). 1950. Reprint. Jerusalem: Schocken, 1953.

———. *Sefer, Sofer, veSippur* (Book, scribe, tale). Jerusalem: Schocken, 1938.

———. *Shira*. Jerusalem: Schocken, 1971.

———. *Sifreihem shel Tsadikim* (The books of the righteous). Jerusalem: Schocken, 1961.

———. *Temol Shilshom* (Only yesterday). Jerusalem: Schocken, 1945.

———. "Vehaya he'Akov Lemishor" (And the crooked shall be made straight). *Ha-Po'el ha-Tsair* 7 (January 1912): 11–13; 8 (January 1912): 9–12; 9–10 (February 1912): 16–20; 12 (March 1912): 12–13; 13 (March 1912): 11–12; 14–15 (May 1912): 16–17; 16 (May 1912): 12–13.

———. *Yamim Noraim* (Days of awe). Berlin: Schocken, 1938.

Czaczkes, Shmuel Yosef. "Iber Hebreishe Dikhter: A. Mordechai Tsvi Maane" (About Hebrew poets). *Der Yiddishe Weker* (Stanislav) 2, nos. 27–29 (May–June 1906).

———. "Ha Pincha Hashvura" (The broken plate). *Hamitspeh* 3, no. 49 (December 1906).

Reuveni, Aharon. *Ha-Oniyot Ha-Akhronot* (The last ships). Warsaw: Stybel, 32.

Smilanski, Moshe. "Hadassa." *Ha Shiloah* 24 (January–June 1911); 25 (July–December 1911).

Wilkansky, Meir. *Biymej Ha-Aliya* (In the days of the ascent). Tel Aviv: Omanut, 1935. This was based on *Sippurim Mehayej Ha-Aretz* (Stories from the life in the land). New York: Kadimah, 1918.

SELECT BIBLIOGRAPHY

Texts in English and German

Agnon, Shmuel Yosef. *A Guest for the Night*. Translated by Misha Louvish. New York: Schocken, 1968.

————. *A Simple Story*. Translated by Hillel Halkin. New York: Schocken, 1985.

————. *The Bridal Canopy*. Translated by Israel Meir Lask. 1937. New York: Schocken, 1968.

————. "Die Erzahlung vom Toraschreiber" (The tale of the scribe). Translated by Max Strauss. *Der Jude* (Berlin and Vienna) 2 (1917–18).

————. "The Secret of Writing Fables." In *Elu veElu* (These and those), 297–98. Jerusalem: Schocken, 1953. Translated by Louise Ben-Yaakov in Gershon Shaked, "Midrash and Narrative: Agnon's 'Agunot,' " in *Midrash and Literature*, edited by Geoffrey H. Hartman and Sanford Burdick.

————. "Seelenverbannung" (Agunot: A tale). Translated by Ernst Mueller. *Die Welt* (Berlin) (March 1910): 189ff.

————. *Twenty-one Stories*. New York: Jewish Publication Society of America, 1970.

————. *Two Tales by S. Y. Agnon*. Translated by Walter Lever. New York: Schocken, 1966.

Brenner, Yosef Hayim. *Breakdown and Bereavement*. Translated by Hillel Halkin. Ithaca: Cornell University Press, 1971.

Hamsun, Knut. *Mysterien*. 2d ed. Translated into German from Norwegian by Maria von Borch. Munich: Albert Langen, 1904.

Criticism in Hebrew
(Most Titles Appear in English Translation)

Afek, Edna. *Arrays of Words*. Tel Aviv: Academic Publications, 1979.

"And the Crooked Shall Be Made Straight." *Hamitspeh* (Cracow) 9 (October 1912): 5.

Bahat, Jacob. *Shmuel Yosef Agnon and Hayim Hazaz, Readings*. Haifa: Yovel Publishing House, 1962.

Bakon, Yitzhak. "On 'Agunot: A Tale,' by Shmuel Yosef Agnon." *Moznayim* 46 (February 1978): 215–33.

Band, Arnold. "Agnon before He Was Agnon." *Molad* 21 (January–April 1963): 54–63.

———. "Crime and Punishment in *Only Yesterday*." *Molad* 1 (May–June 1967): 75–82.

Barzel, Hillel. *Agnon's Love Stories*. Ramat Gan: Bar-Ilan University, 1975.

———. *Between Agnon and Kafka: A Comparative Study*. Ramat Gan: Bar Uryan, Bar-Ilan University, 1972.

———. "From the *Book of Customs* to *In Mr. Lublin's Store*." *Yediot Ahronot*, 8 November 1974.

Ben-Eliyahu, Bilhah. "The Function of Documentary Materials in the Elucidation of the Second Immigration in Agnon's Novel *Only Yesterday*." *Iton* 77 9 (July–August 1985): 26–27, 66–67.

Benshalom, Bentsion. "*The Bridal Canopy*: A New Work of Agnon's." *Moznayim* 4, no. 23 (November 1932): 6–9; 4, no. 25 (December 1932): 9–12.

Berdyczewski, Micha Yosef. "Crooked and Straight." *Hatekufa* 5 (1920): 484–85.

Brenner, Yosef Hayim [Yosef Haver, pseud.]. "From Literature and the Press in the Land of Israel: Critical Remarks on the Fourth Issue of *Ha-Omer*." *Ha-Po'el ha-Tsair* 2, no. 13 (1909): 7–9.

———. "From My Notebook." *Revivim* 3–4 (1913): 159–60.

Canaani, David. "The Hidden and the Revealed in Agnon's Works." *Luah Haaretz* (1948–49): 164–90.

Cohen, Yisrael, ed. *Buczacz Memorial Volume*. Tel Aviv: Am-Oved, 1956.

Feldman, Yael Sagiv. "Between a Key and a Lock: A Rereading of Agnon's Key Irony in *Ore'ah nata lalun* [A guest for the night]." *Hasifrut* 32 (July 1983): 148–54.

Fichman, Jacob. "Bibliographical Notes: *Ha-Omer*." *Haolam* (Vilna) 3 (December 1908): 10.

Friedman, David Aryeh. *Studies in Prose*. Tel Aviv: Makhbarot Lesifrut, 1966.

Fuchs, Esther. *Art and Ingenuousness: On Shmuel Yosef Agnon's Irony*. Tel Aviv: Makhon Katz, Tel Aviv University, 1985.

Golan, Arna. " 'Agunot: A Tale' and the Second Aliya." *Moznayim* 32 (January 1971): 215–23.

Halevi-Zwick, Judith. *Agnon—His Early Critics (1909–1931)*. Haifa: Haifa University Press, 1984.

Holtz, Abraham. *The Tale of Reb Yudel Hasid*. New York: Jewish Theological Society Seminary, 1986.

———. "The Triple Profanation: Remarks on 'Another Talith.' " *Hasifrut* 3 (1971–72): 528–32.

Kabak, Aharon Abraham. "Zephyrs." *Ha-Po'el ha-Tsair* 6 (March 1914): 9.

Kanfer, Moshe. "Between Buczacz and Jerusalem." Translated into Hebrew by Dov Sadan. *Davar* (literary suppl.), 25 July 1958. This was first published in Polish in 1930.

Kariv, Abraham. " 'Betrothed': Why and for Whom?" *Molad* 4 (May–June 1971): 102–9.

Krojanker, Gustav. "The Central Problem in the Works of Agnon." *Moznayim* 7 (September 1938): 611–19.

———. "The Great Epic (on *The Bridal Canopy*)." *Haaretz*, 12 August 1938.

Kurzweil, Baruch. *Essays on Shmuel Yosef Agnon's Fiction*. Jerusalem: Schocken, 1962. Enl. ed., 1976.

———, ed. *Yovel Shai*. Ramat Gan: Bar-Ilan University, 1958.

Lachover, Yeruham Fishel. " 'And the Crooked Shall Be Made Straight.' " *Hatsefira* (Warsaw) 38 (August 1912).

Lipschuetz, Eliezer Meir. *Shmuel Yosef Agnon*. Berlin: private publication, 1926.

Mantsur, Jacob. *A Study of Agnon's Language*. Tel Aviv: Dvir, 1968.

Mazor, Yair. "The World of Fantasy and the Secret of Influence." *Moznayim* 55 (September–October 1982): 22–27.

Meyzel, Nahman. *The Works of Isaac Leib Peretz*. Merhavia: Siphriat Poalim, 1960.

Mintz, Aryeh Leib. "Shmuel Yosef Agnon and His *Bridal Canopy*." *Beitar* 2 (1934): 245–62.

Moked, Gavriel. "Agnon and the Literature of Our Time." *Molad* 16 (July 1958): 411–16.

———. *The Praise of Adiel Amze*. Tel Aviv: Hamahadir, 1957.

Sadan, Dov. *On Shmuel Yosef Agnon*. Tel Aviv: Hakibbutz Hameuchad, 1959.

Sadan, Dov, and Ephraim Elimelech Urbach, eds. *LeAgnon Shai: Devarim al HaSofer veSippurav*. Jerusalem: HaSokhnut haYehudit, 1959.

Schocken, Gershom. "Taking Leave of Ashkenaz, Taking Leave of Old Europe—On *In Mr. Lublin's Store*." In Kurzweil, *Essays on Shmuel Yosef Agnon's Fiction*.

Schweid, Eliezer. "The Stray Dog—and Man." *Molad* 16 (July 1958): 382–88.

Shaked, Gershon. *The Narrative Art of Shmuel Yosef Agnon*. Tel Aviv: Siphriat Poalim, 1973.

Shaked, Gershon, and Refael Weiser, eds. *Shmuel Yosef Agnon: Studies and Documents*. Jerusalem: Mosad Bialik, 1978.

Shaked, Malka. "Was Hirshl Insane? A Pluralistic View of Agnon's *Sippur Pashut* [A simple story]." *Hasifrut* 32 (July 1983): 132–47.

Scholem, Gershom. *Devarim BeGo, Explications and Implications: Writings on the Tradition and the Rebirth*. Tel Aviv: Am-Oved, 1975.

Streit, Shmuel. "A Few Words about Shmuel Yosef Agnon." *Revivim* (Jerusalem) 3–4 (1913): 40.

Tamir, Neomi. " 'Betrothed'—Four That Are One." *Hasifrut* 3 (September 1972): 497–506.

Tochner, Meshulam. *The Meaning of Agnon*. Ramat Gan: Massada, 1968.

Tsemach, Adi. "On the Philosophy of History in Two of Agnon's Late Stories, 'Edo and Enam' and 'Forevermore.' " *Hasifrut* 1–2 (Summer 1968): 378–85.

Tsemakh, Shlomo. *Shtei Mezuzot* (Two doorposts). Ramat Gan: Massada, 1965.

Weiss, Hillel. "An Interpretation of Agnon's 'Covering of Blood.' " *Bikoret Ufarshanut* 9–10 (October 1976): 117–59.

Werses, Shmuel. *From Mendele to Hazaz*. Jerusalem: Magnes Press, Hebrew University, 1987.

———. *Sippur veShorsho* (The story and its roots). Ramat Gan: Massada, 1971.

Wineman, Aryeh. *Aggada and Art: Studies in the Writings of Agnon*. Jerusalem: Rubin Mass, 1982.

Yehoshua, Abraham B. "Madness and Recovery." *Maariv*, 30 May 1980.

———. "The 'Solution' in *A Simple Story*." *Maariv*, 23 May 1980.

Zucker, Shlomo. "Sources for the Molding of Space and Character in 'Edo and Enam' by Shmuel Yosef Agnon." *Studies in Hebrew Literature* (Jerusalem) 3 (1983): 28–66.

Criticism in English and German

Aberbach, David. *At the Handles of the Lock.* London: Oxford University Press, 1984.

Alter, Robert. "Agnon's Last Word." *Commentary* 51 (June 1971): 74–81.

———. "Agnon's Mediterranean Fable." In *Defenses of Imagination,* 187–98. Philadelphia: Jewish Publication Society, 1972.

Band, Arnold. *Nostalgia and Nightmare: A Study in the Fiction of Shmuel Yosef Agnon.* Berkeley and Los Angeles: University of California Press, 1968.

Bargad, Warren. "Agnon and German Neoromanticism." *Prooftexts* 1 (1981): 96–97.

Ben-Dov, Nitza. "Dreams and Human Destiny in *Ad Hena.*" *Prooftexts* 7 (January 1987): 53–63.

Buber, Martin. "Ueber Agnon." In *Treue (Eine Juedische Sammelschrift),* edited by Leo Harmann. Berlin: Juedischer Verlag, 1916.

Esrahi-Dekoven, Sidra. "Agnon before and After." *Prooftexts* 2 (January 1982): 78–94.

Feldman, Yael S. "The Latent and the Manifest: Freudianism in *A Guest for the Night.*" *Prooftexts* 7 (January 1987): 29–39.

Fisch, Harold. *S. Y. Agnon.* New York: Frederick Ungar, 1975.

Hartman, Geoffrey H., and Sanford Burdick, eds. *Midrash and Literature.* New Haven: Yale University Press, 1986.

Hochman, Baruch. "Agnon's Radical Incoherence." *Jerusalem Post,* 22 October 1971.

———. *The Fiction of S. Y. Agnon.* Ithaca: Cornell University Press, 1970.

Hoffman-Golomb, Ann. "Housing the Past in Agnon's *A Guest for the Night.*" *Prooftexts* 2 (September 1982): 265–82.

Kahn, Frida. *Generation in Turmoil.* Great Neck, N.Y.: Chanell Press, 1960.

Kaufmann, Fritz Mordechai. "Der Erzahler S. J. Agnon." In *Vier Essais ueber ostjuedische Dichtung und Kultur,* 21–31. Berlin: Weltverlag, 1919.

Mark, Yehezkel. "The Influence of European Writers on the Hebrew Writer S. Y. Agnon." Ph.D. diss., Potchefstroom University, South Africa, 1974.

Mintz, Alan. "Agnon in Jaffa, the Myth of the Artist as a Young Man." *Prooftexts* 1 (1981): 62–83.

Miron, Dan. "Domesticating a Foreign Genre: Agnon's Transactions with the Novel." *Prooftexts* 7 (January 1987): 1–27.

———. "German Jews in Agnon's Work." *Leo Baeck Institute Yearbook* 23 (1978): 265–80.

Roshwald, Miriam Mindle W. "The *Shtetl* in the Works of Karl Emil Franzos, Sholom Aleichem, and Shmuel Josef Agnon." Ph.D. diss., University of Minnesota, 1972.

Roston, Murray. "The Agnon Paradox." In *Explorations,* edited by Murray Mindlin with Chaim Bermant, 38–44. Chicago: Quadrangle Books, 1968.

Shaked, Gershon. "By a Miracle, Agnon's Literary Representation of Social Drama." In *The Shadows Within,* 133–44. Philadelphia: Jewish Publication Society, 1988.

———. "Portrait of the Immigrant as a Young Neurotic." *Prooftexts* 7 (1987): 41–52.

INDEX

Most Hebrew titles of books and stories are given in English.
Boldface type indicates main discussions of titles.

INDEX

289

INDEX